Intellectual Property Law in Colombia

Intellectual Property Law in Colombia

Second Edition

Daniel Peña
Sarah Osma Peralta

This book was originally published as a monograph in the International Encyclopaedia of Laws/Intellectual Property Law.

Founding Editor: Roger Blanpain
General Editor: Frank Hendrickx
Volume Editor: Hendrik Vanhees

Wolters Kluwer

Published by:
Kluwer Law International B.V.
PO Box 316
2400 AH Alphen aan den Rijn
The Netherlands
E-mail: international-sales@wolterskluwer.com
Website: lrus.wolterskluwer.com

Sold and distributed in North, Central and South America by:
Wolters Kluwer Legal & Regulatory U.S.
7201 McKinney Circle
Frederick, MD 21704
United States of America
Email: customer.service@wolterskluwer.com

Sold and distributed in all other countries by:
Air Business Subscriptions
Rockwood House
Haywards Heath
West Sussex
RH16 3DH
United Kingdom
Email: international-customerservice@wolterskluwer.com

Printed on acid-free paper

ISBN 978-94-035-0302-8

e-Book: ISBN 978-94-035-0181-9
web-PDF: ISBN 978-94-035-0253-3

Printed in the United Kingdom.

The Authors

Daniel Peña – Founding partner of Peña Mancero Abogados since 2010. Previously, Partner at Cavelier Abogados (1999–2010) and Head of the Licensing and Information Technology Department. Mr Peña holds a law degree from Universidad Externado de Colombia, Colombia (1993); a diploma of specialized postgraduate studies (D.E.S.S.) in Intellectual Property, Industrial Agreements and New Technologies Law from Université Pierre Mendès, Grenoble, France (1994); and a Master of Laws (LLM) in Corporate and Commercial Law from University College London, UK (1999). Mr Peña also serves as a national and international arbitrator and professor of intellectual property and international e-commerce at his Colombian alma mater.

Sarah Osma Peralta, Miss Osma holds a law degree from Universidad Externado de Colombia, Bogotá (2013), Colombia; and a Master of Laws (LLM) in Law and Technology from Tilburg University, The Netherlands (2015). Currently Ms Osma is an associate at the Patents Department of a Colombian law firm and a lecturer of

The Authors

Internet Liabilities and Data Protection at Universidad Externado de Colombia, Colombia.

Table of Contents

List of Abbreviations

ACINPRO	Colombian Association of Interpreters and Phonogram Producers
CAN	Andean Community of Nations
DIAN	National Tax Bureau
GI	Geographical Indications
ICA	Colombian Institute of Agriculture and Livestock
INVIMA	National Institute for the Surveillance of Medicines and Foods
PCT	Patent Cooperation Treaty
PTA	Preferential Trade Agreement
SAYCO	Colombian Authors' and Composers' Association
TRIPS	Agreement of Trade-Related Aspects of Intellectual Property
UN	United Nations
UPOV	International Union for the Protection of New Varieties of Plants
WIPO	World Intellectual Property Organization
WTO	World Trade Organization

General Introduction

1 – 4

§1. Geography

1. Colombia is located in the north-western top of South America, bordering Panama, Venezuela, Brazil, Peru, and Ecuador. Its area is of 1,141,748 square kilometres, being the twenty-sixth largest country in the world and the fourth largest in South America (after Brazil, Argentina, and Peru). Colombia is the only South American country with coastlines in both Pacific Ocean and Atlantic Ocean (Caribbean Sea). It has 2,900 kilometres of coastline, of which 1,600 are in the Caribbean Sea and 1,300 in the Pacific Ocean. Furthermore, Colombia has several islands, some of which are San Andrés and Providencia, Gorgona, Gorgonilla, and Malpelo.

2. The Andes mountain range enters Colombian territory from the south and divides itself in three branches called *cordilleras*, separating four geographic regions of the country: (1) the Andean highlands, consisting of the three Andean ranges and intervening valley lowlands; (2) the Caribbean lowlands coastal region; (3) the Pacific lowlands coastal region, and; (4) the eastern region, the great plain that lies to the east of the Andes towards Venezuela.

3. Because of the country's close proximity to the Equatorial Line, there are no dramatic seasonal changes and the weather in every region remains stable all year long. The eastern lowlands and the Caribbean and Pacific coastal lowlands have tropical and equatorial climates with high temperatures, humidity throughout the year, and abundant precipitations. In the mountain regions, climate conditions are much cooler. The weather conditions depend on factors such as, altitude (elevation), topographic position, and prevailing winds, reason why, popular terminology recognizes distinct temperature zones (*pisos térmicos*): (1) the area under 900 metres in elevation is called the hot zone; (2) elevations between 900 and 1,980 metres are the temperate zone, and; (3) elevations from 1,980 metres to about 3,500 metres constitute the cold zone.

§2. Cultural Composition

4. Before the Spanish colonization of the region, the territory was the home of many different indigenous settlements. Due to its strategic location, Colombia has received several immigration waves. The immigrants were primarily Spanish colonists, but a small number of other Europeans immigrated during the Second World War and the Cold War (Dutch, German, French, Swiss, Belgian, Polish, Lithuanian, English, and Croatian). Other important immigrants come from other Latin-American nations and from Middle East countries, such as, Lebanon, Iran, Palestine, and Israel.

Moreover, Spanish colonists brought racial groups through slavery trade until the beginning of the nineteenth century. All this mixture has formed different racial groups, such as: (1) *Mestizos* – a white and Indian mix; (2) *Mulattoes* – a black and white mix, and finally; (3) *Zambos* – a black and Indian mix.

From 1918 to 2005, Colombia avoided the racial and colour classification altogether because the national census dropped reference to race. Nevertheless, in 2005 the latest census recognized the ethnic diversity present in the Colombian territory. According to the results, 1,378,884 of the inhabitants are indigenous (3.4% of Colombian population); 4,261,996 are Afro-Colombian (10.5% of Colombian population), and 4,832 are gypsies (0.01% of Colombian population). Finally, 34,955,512 people – the remaining 86.09% of the Colombian population – are the result of mixture of different races.

5. Moreover, according to the census of 2005, Colombia has 42,888,592 inhabitants.[1] Colombia is the third most populous country in Latin America. Approximately 78% of the country's population live in the Andean highlands; 17% live in the Caribbean lowlands; 3% live in the Pacific lowlands; and 2% live in the eastern plains. The Amazons region, covering a large part of the southern part of the country, has less than 1% of the population.

§3. Political System

6. Colombia is a state established under the rule of law and organized as a republic. It is a unified state, but grants certain autonomy to its territorial entities, given its decentralized form. According to the present constitution, promulgated in 1991, replacing the Centenarian Constitution of 1886, Colombia is a republic adopting the form of a presidential system, with a division of powers into the executive, the legislative, and judiciary.

7. The executive branch relates to the government-administrative structure. The president is elected together with the vice president by popular vote for a period of four years, with the possibility of a subsequent immediate re-election. He/she acts as head of government, head of state, and supreme administrative authority. The Council of Ministers is part of the executive branch as a cabinet of advisers to the President of Colombia. Currently, the Council is composed of: (1) Ministry of Justice and Law; (2) Ministry of Finance and Public Credit; (3) Ministry of Foreign Affairs; (4) Ministry of National Defence; (5) Ministry of Health and Social Protection; (6) Ministry of Agriculture and Rural Development; (7) Ministry of Trade, Industry, and Tourism; (8) Ministry of Education; (9) Ministry of Mines and Energy; (10) Ministry of Transport; (11) Ministry of Telecommunications; (12) Ministry of Environment and Development; and (13) Ministry of Culture. (14) Ministry of Interior; (15) Ministry of Labour; (16) Ministry of Interior.

8. The legislative branch consists of two bodies which form the Congress of Colombia: the Senate and the House of Representatives. Members of both houses are

1. *See* <http://www.dane.gov.co/index.php/estadisticas-por-tema/demografia-y-poblacion/censo-general-2005-1> (last visited 30 Nov. 2017).

elected by popular vote to serve four-year terms, with unlimited possibility of being re-elected.

9. The judiciary branch is conformed by the Constitutional Court, the Supreme Court of Justice, the Council of State, the Office of the Attorney General, the High Council for the Judiciary, and the civil, criminal, labour, administrative, and military judges. The Political Constitution of 1991 established the Constitutional Court as an independent entity that decides over actions of unconstitutionality against laws and decrees, and against judicial decisions related to fundamental human rights. The Supreme Court of Justice is the higher Court of ordinary jurisdiction. The Council of State is the highest Administrative Court, in charge of deciding judicial affairs involving the State.

10. Colombia is divided into thirty-two departments and 1,098 municipalities. Each department has a democratically elected governor and a departmental assembly, which take decisions and manage political affairs. At the municipal level, there is a democratically elected mayor and a municipal Council for such purposes. Furthermore, Colombia has a number of districts, which enjoy a special category, including Bogotá D.C., Barranquilla, Cartagena, and Santa Marta.

§4. Historical Background

11. In 1819, Colombia became an independent nation from the Spanish Crown after approximately 300 years of subordination. After its independence, Colombia was part of a greater country (*'La Gran Colombia'*) along with Venezuela, Panama, and Ecuador. In 1830, internal political and territorial divisions led to the separation of Venezuela and Ecuador. From 1830 to 1886, nine different governments followed. Almost each of those rewrote the constitution and gave different names to the country. Eventually, in 1886 the country adopted its present name, the Republic of Colombia (*República de Colombia*).

12. The Constitution of 1886 was in force for more than 100 years. It established a strong political centralization and an administrative decentralization. The powers of the presidents were increased and some fundamental rights were given special constitutional status.

13. In the early 1990s, several partisan disputes, the rise of guerrilla movements, and the increase of drug trafficking led to a national pact for a new constitution. By July of 1991, a new constitution was written, recognizing a pluri-ethnic, multicultural state, with extended rights for indigenous peoples and Afro-Colombians. The Constitution of 1991 is the current constitution in Colombia, although it has had some minor amendments during its first fifteen years. This supreme law establishes the fundamental principles of the Republic of Colombia and it creates an extensive bill of rights that inclines for the development and establishment of the rule of law.

14. From 1991, the latest governments have focused on obtaining peace and maintaining the public order given the persistent violence. The main goal of the latest governments has been the economic rise of Colombia in conformity with international standards, particularly in terms of investment protection, international trade, regulatory transparency, and democratic security.

§5. Colombia in the International Arena

15. Colombia is a member of numerous international and regional organizations. In this regard, Colombia is part of the United Nations (UN), the World Trade Organization (WTO), the International Monetary Fund, the World Bank, the International Labour Organization, the World Intellectual Property Organization (WIPO), the International Criminal Court, Inter-American Court of Human Rights, and other several organizations and treaties for the protection and promotion of economic, social, and political rights.

16. As to regional organizations, Colombia is a full member of the Andean Community of Nations (ACN) along with Ecuador, Bolivia, and Peru. Furthermore, Colombia is an associated member of Mercosur. It has also subscribed or is negotiating bilateral and pluri-lateral trade and/or investment agreements. Such agreements include free trade agreements, unilateral tariff preferences, and bilateral investment treaties with a wide portfolio of European, Latin American, and Asian countries, including the United States of America, México, Venezuela, Chile, Guatemala, Honduras, El Salvador, Spain, the European Free Trade Area (Norway, Liechtenstein, Switzerland, and Iceland), Canada, among others and it is currently in the process to become a member of the OECD and is expected to acquire the member status in 2018.

17. In terms of intellectual property, these memberships are very important since most of the regulation in the matter is dictated in the international arena. Accordingly, the role of enacting intellectual property legislation has been assigned to supranational and international entities, especially to the ACN and the WTO, to which we will refer subsequently.

18. As to the ACN, this regionalization process began in 1969 when representatives of Bolivia, Colombia, Chile, Ecuador, and Peru subscribed the 'Cartagena Agreement'. The object of this treaty was to promote a harmonious and equilibrated development among the Member Countries, and the acceleration of income-growth to improve the living standards of their populations.[2] Two principal regional institutions were created: the Commission, with political and regulatory power, and the Board, i.e., the technical-executive institution. The supervision of the compliance with the obligations derived from the treaty was granted to the Commission since the creation of the Andean Court of Justice came in 1979.[3] Nowadays, the Andean legal system contains provisions focused on the harmonization of integration policies, coordination of development processes, planning of industrial and liberation programmes, and most importantly, regulation of intellectual property.

19. Within the Andean Community, intellectual property is regulated by decisions of the Commission.[4] Pursuant to Article 3 of the Treaty Creating the Court of Justice of the Cartagena Agreement, these decisions 'shall be directly applicable in Member Countries', or, in other words, these regulations are applicable following a top-down

2. *See* G. Pico Mantilla, *Derecho Andino* (Quito-Ecuador, *Tribunal de Justicia del Acuerdo de Cartagena*, 1989), 17.
3. *Ibid.*, 18.
4. *See* Official website of the Andean Community of Nations, Structure of the Community, <http://www.comunidadandina.org/Seccion.aspx?tipo=SA> (last visited 30 Nov. 2017).

approach,[5] which, according to the Andean Court of Justice (the Andean Court), is a key concept in integration law. According to the Colombian Supreme Court, the Colombian State could validly yield its legislative competence on certain matters to supranational bodies whose mandates would derogate (according to Colombian law) the existing national law in the matter.[6] In that sense, several decisions of the ACN are the current regime in intellectual property. These decisions will be thoroughly addressed in each chapter as the need arises.

§6. Colombian Business Climate

20. Colombia is one of the most stable economies in Latin America. The Colombian economy was not as severely affected by the international financial crisis, as other countries; in 2009, the economy grew a modest 0.5%, which was a great achievement compared to other economies in the region whose numbers were negative.[7] In 2010, estimates showed that the Colombian economy grew 4.2%,[8] showing that the Colombian economy is on route to recovering its pre-crisis growth levels. However, due to the oil and gas global crisis that started in 2015, Colombian economy growth levels were reduced in 2017 to 1.6%, according to international risk assessment companies.[9]

21. Regarding foreign investment, it is allowed in almost any sector of the economy in Colombia and foreign investors may make portfolio investments or may make direct investments in Colombian based corporate entities.[10] In 2010 the country showed signs of recovery and received close to 10 billion dollars, placing Colombia as the fourth receptor of foreign investment in Latin America. Even though 2016 represented for Colombia and the Latin American region an economic slowdown, Colombia maintained its position as the fourth receptor of foreign investment.[11] According to the Economist magazine, these figures are expected to considerably improve after the signing of the peace process between the Colombian Government

5. This principle of immediate application was confirmed in the Decision 218 of 1987, which also stated that the Commission's decisions are of mandatory application since the date of their approval. In Colombia's case, the decisions are taken as a law and may be subject to further regulation by the administration, as happens with a regular law.
6. *See* Colombian Supreme Court, judgment of 1 Sep. 1988.
7. *See* <http://historico.presidencia.gov.co/sp/2010/marzo/25/pib.pdf> (last visited on 30 Nov. 2017).
8. *See* <http://www.larepublica.com.co/archivos/ECONOMIA/2011-01-27/planeacion-preve-que-pib-de-2010-solo-crecio-42_120261.php> (last visited on 30 Nov. 2017).
9. *See* https://www.larepublica.co/economia/standard-poors-bajo-el-pronostico-de-crecimiento-de-colombia-de-17-a-16-para-2017-2555026.
10. *See* J.M. Idrobo Cubides, *Principios Básicos de las Inversiones, Seis Países de América Latina* (First Edition, Bogota-Colombia, Legis, 2005), 57–58.
11. *See* <http://old.andi.com.co:8082/Documents/Documentos%202016/ANDI-Balance%20 2016-Perspectivas2017.pdf> (last visited on 30 Nov. 2017).

and the leaders of the Revolutionary Armed Forces of Colombia (FARC)[12] in 2017. Furthermore, this publication named Colombia 'Country of the Year' in 2016.[13]

22. Colombian legislation has established an articulated regulatory framework for business, which includes a competition regime, special import and export systems, specialized authorities for public utilities and major public services, a dynamic exchange regime, tax facilitation, and a growing infrastructure for trade. In this regard, there are import benefits available for the importation of capital assets into Colombia and export activities are also eligible for certain customs duties and tax benefits. Furthermore, income tax exemptions are available for certain activities, such as the editorial industry, the hotel industry, power generation industries, river transport companies, 'new products', software or pharmaceutical manufacturing companies, and seismic oilfield service companies.[14]

23. The main business centres are Bogotá, Medellín, Cali, Cartagena, and Barranquilla. In addition, Colombia has several ports on both oceans: Santa Marta, Barranquilla, Cartagena on the Atlantic Ocean, and Buenaventura on the Pacific Ocean.

---

12. *See* <http://old.andi.com.co:8082/Documents/Documentos%202016/ANDI-Balance%20 2016-Perspectivas2017.pdf> (last visited on 30 Nov. 2017).
13. *See* <http://www.economist.com/news/leaders/21712136-which-country-improved-most-2016-our-country-year> (last visited on 30 Nov. 2017).
14. *See* J.M. Idrobo Cubides, *Principios Básicos de las Inversiones, Seis Países de América Latina* (First Edition, Bogota-Colombia, Legis, 2005), 57.

Chapter 1. Copyright and Neighbouring Rights

§1. Sources and Legislation

24. Copyright protection in Colombia is a long-standing issue, going back to the Constitution of 1811, which established that inventors should be rewarded for their creations, and given exclusive property over them for a fixed period of time.[15] There were no explicit references to artistic and literary works in that constitution, but they were later included in Article 43.14 of the Constitution of 1858, which conferred on the president the ability to grant patents to protect literary creations. This same provision was copied in the Constitution of 1863 that also protected scientific and literary creations under the same provision. In turn, the Constitution of 1886 granted both figures protection but under different provisions. In that sense, Article 35 provided that literary and artistic property was a kind of 'transferable property, lasting the life span of the author, and 80 years more'. The current Constitution of 1991 returned to the tendency of encompassing all forms of intellectual property in the same article. In effect, Article 61 sets forth that 'the State will protect intellectual property for the time and by the formalities established in the law'.

25. Along with the constitutional protection, the Civil Code of 1873 also provides that 'the products of talent or inventive are property of their authors'.[16] In 1982, this protection was reinforced with the enactment of Law 23 which established a general and special framework for the protection of the 'right of author'[17] in Colombia. This statute, amended and supplemented by Law 44 of 1993 and still in force today, has to be read in harmony with the Universal Convention on Copyright of 1952, and the Rome Convention approved in Colombia by Law 48 of 1975; the Berne Convention for the Protection of Literary and Artistic Works[18] (the Berne Convention), approved by Law 33 of 1987; the TRIPS Agreement, approved by Law 170 of 1994; the WIPO treaties on copyright;[19] and Decision 351 of 1993 of the Andean Community (the Decision). This Decision is now the common Andean regime for copyright protection. In that sense, the same principles of immediate application of the Decision and of supremacy of the Andean dispositions explained in the introductory chapter are

15. *See* generally E. Rengifo García, *Propiedad Intelectual: El Moderno Derecho de Autor* (Bogotá, Universidad Externado de Colombia, 1996), 25.
16. *See* Art. 671 of the Civil Code.
17. This 'right of author' is a legacy of the French system, different from the Anglo-Saxon version of 'copyright'. The two systems are different in some aspects as will be portrayed in this part. In any case, and as the term copyright has more international recognition, we will continue to use it to refer to the Colombia system.
18. This Convention was first adopted in 1886 in Berne, Switzerland. It was later completed in Paris in 1896, revised in Berlin in 1908, completed in Berne in 1914, and revised in Rome, Brussels, Stockholm and Paris in 1928, 1948, 1967, and 1971, respectively.
19. These treaties are the Treaty on Interpretation and Execution of Phonograms approved by Law 545 of 1999 and the Copyright Treaty approved by Law 565 of 2000. *Convenio Antipiratería para Colombia, Derechos de Autor y Derechos Conexos en Colombia* (Bogotá, 2004), 16.

applicable here. However, it is important to clarify that, contrary to what happened with the patent and trademark regime,[20] Decision 351 did not affect the enforceability of domestic legislation in the matter. It only complemented the existing regime enacted by Law 23.

26. Apart from these norms, Colombia has a special criminal regime to penalize infractions against copyrights. Articles 270–272 of the Criminal Code (Law 599 of 2000) establish several infractions and the corresponding sanctions for violations to copyrights that range from infractions to moral rights of authors to economic rights. Actions are brought before the Office of the Prosecutor General, specifically before the National Unit in charge of Copyrights and Unlawful Access to or Supply of Telecommunication Services.

The aforementioned dispositions are the most important ones. However, there are others that are also relevant in the protection of copyrights in Colombia. They will be addressed in this chapter as they become relevant.

§2. Subject Matter of Protection

27. Copyright is the area of law that regulates the relationship of the author or artist with his/her work, and that of the work with society.[21] According to Article 2 of Law 23 of 1982, the subject matter of protection of copyrights is 'scientific, literary and artistic works, in which all the creations of the spirit in the scientific, literary and artistic field are included, regardless of the mode or form of expression and its destination'. This is consistent with Article 4 of Decision 351 whereby it grants protection over 'all literary, artistic and scientific works that may be reproduced or disclosed by any known or future means'. Those means are later described in said article as follows:

(a) works expressed in writing, that is, books, pamphlets and any other kind of work expressed in letters, signs or conventional marks;
(b) lectures, addresses, sermons, and other works of the same nature;
(c) musical compositions with or without words;
(d) dramatic and dramatic-musical works;
(e) choreographic and mimed works;
(f) cinematographic works and other audiovisual works expressed by any process;
(g) works of fine art, including drawings, paintings, sculptures, engravings, and lithographs;
(h) works of architecture; creations in the art sector relating to construction of infrastructure works;
(i) photographic works and works expressed by processes analogous to photography;
(j) works of applied art;
(k) illustrations, maps, sketches, plans, diagrams, and three-dimensional works relating to geography, topography, architecture or science;

20. *See* Chs 2 and 4.
21. *See* Legal Opinion (*Concepto*) of the National Direction of Copyright on the Generalities of Copyright of 13 Aug. 2003.

(l) computer programs;
(m) anthologies or compilations of assorted works and also databases, which, by the selection and arrangement of their contents, constitute personal creations.

28. It is important to clarify that, as provided for in Article 6 of the Decision, the subject matter of protection is independent from the ownership of the material medium in which the work is embodied. This means that the protection will be over the work itself, but that if a copy of such work is made, that specific medium containing the copy can belong to someone different than the author.

29. Along those lines, copyright protection cannot be over ideas even though they are the very source of the creation. Article 7 of the Decision provides that only the form in which the ideas of the author are described, explained, illustrated or incorporated in the works shall be protected. Neither the ideas contained in literary and artistic works, nor the ideological or technical content of scientific works, nor the industrial or commercial exploitation thereof shall be eligible for protection.

The rationale behind this prohibition, also contained in Article 6 of Law 23, is that copyrights seek to establish a balance between the particular interest of the authors and the public interest of the society concerning free access to knowledge and culture, which in the end is the development driving force of nations.[22]

Nonetheless, this balance between particular and public interest does not mean that the legal nature of copyrights is public. On the contrary, given that they regulate the relationship of the author with his/her intellectual creation,[23] they confer authors certain exclusive rights regarding the enjoyment and public display of their works in such a way that they can decide the way in which their work will be used.[24] These exclusive rights will be explained in detail in Section 5.

I. Special Categories of Works

A. Computer Software

30. Article 3.13 of the Decision defines computer software as the expression in words, codes, plans or any other form of a set of instructions which, on being incorporated in automated reading apparatus, is capable of causing a computer, an electronic or similar device capable of processing information, to execute a particular task or produce a particular result. The concept of software comprises the computer program, program description, and auxiliary material. The creation process of software is recorded in a written document, which in the end is a literary work, suitable of receiving copyright protection.[25]

22. *See As Colombia Ltda. v. Informatica y Gestion S.A.*, Centre of Arbitration and Conciliation of the Chamber of Commerce of Bogotá, 17 Oct. 2006, 16.
23. *See* E. Rengifo García, *Propiedad Intelectual: El Moderno Derecho de Autor* (Bogotá, Universidad Externado de Colombia, 1996), 47.
24. *See* Constitutional Court, judgment C-282, 5 Jun. 1997.
25. *See* Circular No. 1 of the National Direction of Copyright, 9 Oct. 2001. *See also* Council of State, judgment of 4 Dec. 1990.

It may be of a different nature of that of a regular literary creation, but a literary work can be 'any intellectual original creation, expressed in a reproducible medium'.[26] This position was adopted by Decree 1360 of 1989 that defines software as a literary creation,[27] allowing protection under the regime established by Law 23 even though the term software is not explicitly included in it. In the same sense, Article 23 of Decision 351 provides that 'computer programs are protected in the same way as literary works'.[28] This allows software creators to profit the same advantages of copyright: a well-established legal system, based on recognized international conventions that offer worldwide protection.[29] But copyright protection has also its downside: the monopoly over the creation is not as restrictive as in the case of patents, which makes its unlawful use easier.[30]

31. Moreover, as with literary works, the idea in which the software is based on cannot be protected. It is then possible to develop software with the risk of getting to the same solution of a problem that another software has already solved.[31] This is linked to the principle of independent creation according to which it is possible to protect two identical works as long as they were created independently from each other.[32] These two concepts were analysed by an arbitral tribunal in the case of *As Colombia Ltda. v. Informática y Gestión S.A.*, in which it was argued that the software developed by the respondent was essentially the same as another one belonging to the complainant. The Tribunal clarified that, even though both instruments solved the same problem, their elements were not the same and the paths the creator chose to arrive to the respective solutions had been different. The Tribunal also held that 'the

26. *See* World Intellectual Property Organisation, 'Glossary on Copyright and Neighbouring Rights', (Geneva, 1980), 268.
27. This is a regulatory decree and therefore its definition of software cannot be held as official. In any case, the Council of State considered in its judgment of 14 Dec. 1990, that it can be taken as a useful tool that develops the broad meaning of literary works contained in Law 23.
28. Even though software is protected in the same way as literary works, it is important to clarify the extent of moral rights because Art. 23 of the Decision only grants creators the right of paternity and integrity. Therefore, respecting moral rights in software, Art. 30 of Law 23 is not applicable.
29. *See* F. Chaparro et al., *Manual sobre la Propiedad Intelectual de Productos Derivados de la Actividad Académica en Universidades y Centros de Investigación*, (Bogotá, Universidad Nacional de Colombia, 1997), 54.
30. The suitability of protection through the copyright regime is not a unanimously accepted position; many still believe that patents would provide a better incentive for innovation and would be a better tool against piracy. This has been the position adopted by the United States as it has granted software patents in the past. In the case of Europe, it is still debating whether patents are the best system or if it should remain faithful to copyright, even though the European Patent Office has been granting patents for software, especially to non-European companies. *See* generally C. Miceli, 'Quietly Tying Down Gulliver. The Software Patent Fairy Tale', *Revista de Derecho Informático*, No. 098, September 2006, in <http://www.egov.ufsc.br/portal/conteudo/quietly-tying-down-gulliver-software-patent-fairy-tale> (last visited 28 Nov. 2017).
31. *See As Colombia. Ltda v. Informatica Y Gestión S.A*, Centre of Arbitration and Conciliation of the Chamber of Commerce of Bogotá, 17 Oct. 2006, 22.
32. *Ibid.*

fact that a program shares the same or similar functions with a previous one does not inhibit it from being original'.[33]

32. Also, as a literary work, the protection of copyright is not unlimited. Under these circumstances, it is subject to the following exceptions:

(1) Backup copy: Article 24 of the Decision establishes that the lawful owner of software can make a copy or adaptation of said software as long as such activities are essential for the use of the program. Furthermore, Article 25 provides that a copy can be made to replace the original when it has been damaged. According to said provision, this act does not require authorization from the right owner.
(2) Personal use: Article 26 of the Decision allows the owner of a legally acquired copy of software to introduce said software into his/her computer but only when it is for personal use. However, if more people were using the software, such use would not be contemplated in the exception and therefore would be an illegal use.[34]
(3) Adaptation of the software to the computer: Article 27 of the Decision prescribes that the adaptation of software for the exclusive personal use of the adaptor does not constitute a transformation.

33. As to the term of protection of software, it receives protection since the date of its creation, in the same way literary works do. Nevertheless, its inscription is advisable to facilitate further proof of the ownership of the software. Article 5 of Decree 1360 provides that in order to register software in the National Copyright Register, an application must be submitted containing the following information: (1) name, identification, and place of domicile of the applicant, who must state whether he is applying on his own behalf or as a representative of a third party, in which case evidence of such representation must be attached to the application; (2) name and identification of the author or authors; (3) name of the producer; (4) title of the work, year of creation, country of origin, brief description of its functions and, in general, any other characteristic which may enable it to be distinguished from another work of the same nature; (5) a statement to the effect that it is an original work or, alternatively, that it is a derived work; (6) a statement to the effect that the work is individual, collaborative, collective, anonymous, pseudonymous or posthumous.

B. Databases

34. Databases are the 'accumulation of stored information in such a way that it can be systematically searched and recovered by a computer. In the end it is any collection of registers in magnetic support that can be accessed by a computer'.[35] According to Article 28 of the Decision, 'databases are protected provided that the

33. *Ibid.*, 31.
34. *See* S. Rodríguez, *La era digital y las excepciones y limitaciones al derecho de autor*, (Bogotá, *Universidad Externado de Colombia*, 2004), 103.
35. *See* E. Rengifo García, *Propiedad Intelectual: El Moderno Derecho de Autor* (Bogotá, Universidad Externado de Colombia, 1996), 246.

selection or the arrangement of the subject matters shall constitute an intellectual creation'. In this same sense, Article 5 of the WIPO Copyright Treaty states:

> Compilations of data or other material, in any form, which by reason of the selection or arrangement of their contents constitute intellectual creations, are protected as such. This protection does not extend to the data or the material itself and is without prejudice to any copyright subsisting in the data or material contained in the compilation.

35. In turn, Article 5 of Law 23 sets forth that databases are protected as independent works but only when they represent an original creation. Therefore, it is necessary to verify that it is an original database.[36] The difficulty of an *a priori* determination thereto demands a case-by-case basis analysis that takes into account the skill, effort, and the contribution of the compiler in the selection, distribution, and systematic ordering of the information.[37] The subject matter of protection in regards to databases is not the information per se; the protection is over the external form of its composition.[38] On this point the Andean Tribunal stated that according to Article 58 of the Decision, in order to be protected, a database must be a selection or compilation of information that is original and constitute a personal creation.[39] Therefore, the selection, arrangement, and systematic order of the information must be an original creation; a simple mechanical ordering or accumulation of data without any selection criterion cannot be protected.

36. The protection given to databases does not exclude the creator's obligations to respect the copyrights of the information they use when it is part of a work not belonging to public domain. The incorporation of data into a database can be considered as a reproduction of the work,[40] which implies that any incorporation without authorization violates copyrights. This is also valid for summaries of protected works as they can be considered as a modification in the sense of Article 5(a) of Law 23.

37. Regarding the ownership of databases, these are collective works under the coordination of a natural or legal person. The former is the right owner and will hold the rights of disposition, reproduction, adaptation, and public communication. These rights are extended to the organized presentation of the work, and remain enforceable despite the update to which the database is subject to, as long as the initial order and disposition remain.[41]

---

36. Article 28 of the Decision establishes the same criterion when it states that 'data bases shall be protected insofar as the selection or arrangement of the contents constitute an intellectual creation'.
37. *Ibid.*, 248.
38. *See* Art. 10 of TRIPS.
39. *See* Andean Court of Justice, Legal Opinion No. 10-IP-1999 of 11 Jun. 1999, published in Gaceta Oficial del Acuerdo de Cartagena, No. 468 of 12 Aug. 1999.
40. *See* United Nations Education, Scientific and Cultural Organisation-Word Intellectual Property Organisation, Second Committee of Governmental experts (Geneva, 1982).
41. *See* E. Rengifo García, *Propiedad Intelectual: El Moderno Derecho de Autor* (Bogotá, Universidad Externado de Colombia, 1996), 259.

C. *Artistic Expressions of Traditional and Popular Cultures*

38. Given the pluri-ethnic composition of the Colombian population, very different traditions result in artistic expressions. Nonetheless, cultural traditional heritage in the form of artistic creations is not protected, as they may be deemed as belonging to public domain. In the terms of Article 189 of Law 23, 'indigenous art in all its manifestations, including dances, songs, handicrafts, drawings and sculptures, belongs to cultural heritage'. Therefore, as part of the cultural heritage and patrimony,[42] it belongs to the whole nation, as stipulated in Article 72 of the constitution.

39. Regarding arts and crafts of popular cultures, the National Direction of Copyright has defined them as 'hand-made art consisting in the production of hand-made objects in wood, rock, metals, or other elements, through the performance of different tasks such as carving, smithing, basketry, and pottery, among others'. The majority of these creations (jewellery designs, furniture, painted papers, ornaments, clothing, to name a few) qualify as works of applied art to the industry and receive protection as such.[43] In any case, arts and crafts could also qualify as other works protected by copyright and therefore a detailed analysis is required in each case to determine under which form the work will be protected.

D. *Works of Art Applied to the Industry*

40. According to Article 3.14 of the Decision, works of applied art are artistic creations with utilitarian functions incorporated in a useful article, whether a work of handicraft or one produced on an industrial scale. Examples of these works are jewellery, furniture, handicrafts and fashion designs, among others. The most important aspect of these creations is their artistic value and not their functional character, even though the latter determines that the term of protection is of the lifespan of the author, plus twenty-five years, and not eighty as in copyrighted works.[44]

The Decision does not specify the terms of protection of these creations. Hence, recourse shall be made to Law 23 in the aspects not regulated by it. However, since the Decision establishes that *all* works of applied art are subject of protection, the requirement provided for in Article 6 of Law 23,[45] according to which such artistic

42. Cultural patrimony is defined in Art. 4 of Law 397 of 1997 as follows: 'The cultural patrimony of the Nation is conformed by all the cultural goods and values that are an expression of Colombian nationality, such as traditions, customs and habits, as well as the gathering of immaterial and material goods, movable or immovable, that have a special historical, artistic, aesthetic, plastic, architectural, urban, archaeological, linguistic, musical, audiovisual, filmic, scientific, testimonial, documental, literary, bibliographic, and anthropologic interest and the manifestations, products and representations of popular culture.'
43. *See* National Direction of Copyright, Circular No. 10 of 5 Dec. 2003.
44. *See* Art. 7.4 of the Berne Convention.
45. According to the National Direction of Copyright, this article was suspended by the Decision. National Direction of Copyright, Concept (Oficio) No. 97003008, 25 Jun. 1997.

value must be able of being separated from the industrial character of the object in which the work is embodied, cannot be applied.[46]

§3. Conditions of Protection

41. Copyright protection is not subject to the same formalities as other forms of intellectual property.[47] Yet this apparent lack of formalities does not mean that each new text or image is worthy of protection; works have to fulfil two requirements: they have to be original and have to be fixed in some sort of material medium allowing its further communication. Once a work has fulfilled these requirements, it is suitable of receiving protection but, for proving purposes,[48] it should be entered into the National Copyright Register. Along this section we will explain the requirements for copyright protection as well as the procedure before the National Copyright Register.

42. As to the requirements, first of all, the work has to be original. In the terms of Article 3.12 of the Decision, a work will be considered as such when it is an 'original intellectual creation of artistic, scientific or literary character susceptible of disclosure or reproduction in any form'. This means that, in order to receive protection, the work in question cannot be a copy or a complete or partial simulation of another work,[49] as it is a manifestation of the personality of its creator.[50] Nonetheless, the latter has been an object of discussion among scholars and judges given that nowadays most of the works do not necessarily reflect the personality of the author, especially because of technological development. Thus, they have to involve certain level of creativity. In spite of this approach, by mandate of Article 1 of the Decision, copyright protection

46. Before the Decision entered into force, the *separability* criterion was understood as the possibility of ideal separation of the aesthetic characteristics from the object in such a way that the design could be applied to other objects; the practical function of the object was just an opportunity to enjoy its aesthetic components. Therefore, a design printed on a shirt would have the same aesthetic value as if it were printed in a purse, carpet, etc. However, if the design became so related to the object, in such a way that consumers could identify it just by looking at the design, then the artistic value could not be separated from the industrial application of the object. This was the case of Marlboro, in which the National Direction of Copyright stated that the design printed on the boxes (two horses holding a shield) was no longer a work of art in itself because customers were able to identify the cigarettes just by looking at it. Therefore, it became a graphic trademark since its artistic merit could not be separated from the object in which it was incorporated. *See* Resolution 1526 of 25 Oct. 1993. In the same sense, the Council of State held, in the case of Cola & Pola, that the work reproduced in the cans could not be considered a work of art applied to the industry because it was now an element of identification of the product, which made them inseparable. *See* Council of State, judgment of 3 Feb. 1995.

47. *See* Superintendence of Industry and Commerce, Resolution 8269 of 31 Mar. 2006.

48. *See* Art. 5 of the Berne Convention and Art. 18.2 of the G2, Free Trade Agreement between Colombia and Mexico. Regarding this last treaty, it is important to remember that it was initially integrated by the two mentioned countries and Venezuela, but this last country denounced the treaty in 2007.

49. *See* E. Rengifo García, *Propiedad Intelectual: El Moderno Derecho de Autor* (Bogotá, Universidad Externado de Colombia, 1996), 175.

50. *Ibid.*, 89.

in Colombia is granted regardless of the artistic merit of the work and its application in the industrial field.

43. The second requirement is that the work has to be fixed or incorporated in some physical medium. As per Article 3.9 of the Decision, fixation shall be understood as 'the incorporation of signs, sounds or images in a physical material that enables them to be perceived, reproduced or communicated'.[51] This might seem as a contradiction to Article 4 that grants protection to lectures, addresses, sermons and other works of the same nature. However, '[spoken] words are considered as a means of fixation of thought',[52] reason why Article 40 of Law 23 protects conferences or lectures in education, which cannot be reproduced or published without the consent of the lecturer.

44. Once a work complies with the preceding requirements, it will automatically receive copyright protection. Anyhow, its entry into the National Copyright Register is advisable as it is a mechanism to guarantee authenticity and legal certainty to the owner of the copyright or of related rights, and to the acts and contracts referring thereto. The other purpose of the registration is to give publicity to the rights of owners and to the contracts that transfer or modify the ownership of the works; to provide guarantees of authenticity and security to titles of copyright and neighbouring rights protection and to contracts referring thereto.[53]

I. Registration Process

45. The entry of a work in the National Copyright Register is carried out before the Registration Office of the National Direction of Copyright that is, in the wording of Article 1 of Decree 460, a Special Administrative Unit serving the entire Colombian territory. In order to enter a work into the register, the applicant can submit the work online[54] or as a hardcopy by filling certain forms published by the Direction for that purpose. Regardless of the way in which the application has been made, the registration process must be completed within fifteen working days following the filing date. All entries are public and therefore can be consulted by the public at a special request.[55]

Article 8 of Decree 460 provides that the applicant must provide:

51. In the same way, Art. 8 of Law 23 defines fixation as 'the incorporation of images and/or sounds on a sufficient permanent or stable material base that allows its perception, reproduction or communication'.
52. *See* E. Rengifo García, *Propiedad Intelectual: El Moderno Derecho de Autor* (Bogotá, Universidad Externado de Colombia, 1996), 92.
53. *See* Art. 2 of Decree 460 of 1995.
54. *See* <http://registroenlinea.gov.co/portal.htm> (last visited 28 Nov. 2017).
55. *See* Art. 5 of Decree 460. This special request shall be made in the form of a petition right (*derecho de petición*) set forth in Art. 23 of the constitution. According to this article, 'any person has the right to present respectful requests to the authorities in the name of public or private interest and to obtain prompt resolution'. This right is further regulated in the Administrative Procedure and Administrative Litigation Code, Decree 1 of 1984. According to Art. 14 of said Code, authorities must reply in a fifteen-day term, unless it is impossible to answer in such period, case in which the applicant must be informed.

(a) The name, nationality, identification document, and current residence of the author of authors of the work. Also, the date of death and pseudonym, as the case may be. If the name of the author is in the form of a pseudonym, the applicant must indicate the name of the editor to whom the economic rights correspond.
(b) Title of the work.
(c) The applicant must specify if the work has been edited or not, if it is original or derived, individual or collective, in collaboration, a translation, and in general whatever characteristics the work may have.
(d) Year of creation.
(e) Name, nationality, identification document, and current address of the applicant, indicating if he/she is a representative of the author or not. In such cases, the applicant must submit proof of the representation.
(f) If the owner of the economic rights is different from the author, his/her name or commercial name must be indicated. Also, the applicant must submit proof of how said person acquired the economic rights. This can be done by means of a public deed or a private document with acknowledgement of signature and content by notary public.

46. For edited literary works (works published and available to the public), the author is obliged to submit a copy meeting the requirements established in Article 125 of Law 23. These requirements are: (a) the indication of the title of the work; (b) the name or pseudonym of the author(s) and of the translator, unless they have chosen to remain anonymous; (c) the indication to the effect that copyright has been reserved, and the year of the first publication (such indication must be preceded by the symbol ©); (d) the year and place of publication and of previous publications if any; and (e) the name and address of publisher and printer.

47. If it is a musical piece, Article 11 of Decree 460 provides that the applicant must also mention the genre to which the piece belongs and the musical notation of it. If the piece has lyrics, the applicant must attach the notation because otherwise the piece will be protected as a literary work and not as a musical creation. If it is a visual work, Article 12 establishes that the applicant must also indicate the name and address of the director, of the author of the script, of the author of the incidental music, and of the author of the drawings if it is an animated work. Also, he/she must indicate the name and address of the producer, of the principal performers, the nationality of the piece as well as its date of conclusion and length. Finally, the application must include the plot of the story, a short excerpt of the dialogues and a brief description of the scenery and music. Regarding artistic works, including paintings and sculptures, the application must also include a complete and detailed written description of the piece.[56]

48. Applications to register works can be filed personally or sent by mail by the author, or by the owner of the economic rights if there has been an assignment. In the case of legal entities, they must act through their legal representatives, attaching certificate of legal existence and representation, or by an attorney, who must file the corresponding power of attorney. The process takes up to fifteen working days counted as from the filing date and no official fees are charged.

56. *See* Art. 13 of Decree 460.

49. Books and other literary creations must also comply with the following requirements:

(1) Inscription in the International Standard Book Number:
The International Standard Book Number (ISBN) is an international system that gives a sole numeric identification code to all books published in each country, region or idiomatic area. It is a 'short and clear identifier that is potentially machine-readable. The ISBN denotes a particular monographic publication uniquely and should, therefore, be associated with it from early production stages'.[57] It was designed precisely to facilitate national and international exchange and commerce. When assigned to a given book, the ISBN becomes the international identification card of the work, which facilitates the identification, not only of a title, but also of an edition, a publisher, and a country. It is a useful tool for inventory control and for the organization of books in libraries.[58]
The use of the ISBN in Colombia[59] is mandatory by virtue of Law 98 of 1993, which dictates the provisions for the democratization and promotion of Colombian books. Article 11 states that 'All books edited and printed in Colombia must bear their international standard book number (ISBN) without which the author cannot invoke the benefits of this law.' In the same way, books (non-periodical printed publication comprising at least forty-nine pages, excluding cover pages) and brochures (short printed publications consisting of four to forty-eight pages providing accurate and specific information) must have an ISBN. Publications consisting of less than four pages, namely, periodicals, leaflets, corporate statements, and by-laws, transport guides, maps, blueprints, postcards, and strictly advertising material do not require ISBN.

(2) Legal Deposit:
As per Article 2 of Decree 460, editors of printed works and audiovisual and phonogram producers in Colombia, as well as importers of the same works must deliver free samples to the *Librería Nacional* (National Library), to the library of the Congress and to the library of *Universidad Nacional de Colombia* (National University of Colombia). The purpose of this deposit, according to the same provision, is to keep a record of Colombian literary, audiovisual, and phonographic production and thus increase the country's cultural heritage. With respect to works that have been edited in a place other than the Department of Cundinamarca, a copy must also be delivered to the library of the department where the publisher's main seat is located.[60]

57. *See* International ISBN Agency, 'The International Standard Book Number System: ISBN's Users Manual', International Edition (Sixth Edition), London 2012, at <https://www.isbn-international.org/sites/default/files/ISBN%20Manual%202012%20-corr.pdf> (last visited 28 Nov. 2017).

58. *Ibid.*

59. According to Art. 31 of Decree 460, the Colombian Chamber of Books runs the National ISBN Office in Colombia. It must deliver a tri-monthly report to the National Library indicating a list of the registered works during that period.

60. *See* Introduction for an explanation on the political division of Colombia.

§4. Ownership

I. The Author (Initial Authorship)

50. Initially, the owner of copyrights over certain work is the author, who is, according to Article 3 of the Decision, the individual who carries out the intellectual creation.[61] As per Article 8 of the Decision, 'in the absence of proof in the contrary, the person whose name, pseudonym or other identifying mark is visibly shown on the work shall be presumed to be the author thereof'. Additionally, Law 23 considers that artists that interpret a piece hold the rights over such interpretation,[62] the producer over the phonogram, the broadcasters over the broadcast, the inheritors of the above-mentioned right owners, and natural or legal persons that acquire by means of a contract the production of a scientific, literary or artistic work made by one or several authors.

II. Works in Collaboration and Joint Works

51. Consistent with Article 18 of Law 23, a collaborative work is that produced jointly by two or more individuals whose contribution to the work cannot be separated from each other. In order to consider a work as one made in 'collaboration', it must be produced by a number of people working together and it cannot be divided without altering the nature of the work. Therefore, as a work that cannot be divided without losing its spirit, none of the collaborators can dispose freely of his/her contribution, unless such faculty was expressly agreed to at the time the work was first started.[63]

52. As to joint works, in accordance with Article 19, they are works produced by a group of authors on the initiative and under the direction of a single individual or legal entity which coordinates, disseminates, and publishes it under his or its name. This provision has to be read in conjunction with Article 83 of the same law according to which 'the director of a collective work is the right owner of the copyrights over it'.

III. Works Made for Hire

53. Works made for hire are those performed under a contract which allows persons different than the author to be right holders of copyrights. This contract is contemplated in Article 20 of Law 23, according to which where one or more authors

61. In the Preferential Trade Agreement negotiated between Colombia and the United States, which at the present time is fulfilling the internal constitutional procedures in both countries, Colombia rejected the United States proposal to allow legal entities to be original right holders. Accordingly, Art. 16.5 of the draft states that the 'authorship of a literary or artistic work will initially be in the head of the author or authors of the work'.

62. These artists hold rights in the realm of the neighbouring rights. This subject will be thoroughly addressed in s. 9.

63. *See* Art. 18 of Law 23.

prepare a work under a service agreement, following a plan set forth by and for the account and risk of an individual or legal entity, they will only receive the fees agreed to in the contract. By virtue of this act, it is understood that the author or authors transfer the rights over the work, but they will keep the prerogatives set forth in Article 30 of this Law, in letters (a)[64] and (b).[65]

In other words, authors transfer economic rights but they retain the moral rights of paternity and integrity.[66] This is consistent with Article 10 of the Decision, which states that 'natural persons or legal entities shall exercise original or derived ownership, according to national legislation, of economic rights in works created for them on commission or by virtue of employment relations'.

54. For the assumption established for works made for hire to operate, the following circumstances must be present:[67]

- A service agreement must exist between the author and the person ordering the work, indicating the corresponding fees. Consequently, the contract cannot have an employment nature; it must be the agreement between two persons by virtue of which a determined service, in this case the creation of a work, will be carried out and a determinate fee will be paid.[68]
- The work must be prepared to the account and at the risk of the person ordering it; the person ordering the work must assume the costs and furnish the elements required to develop the creation.
- The work must be prepared as per the plan designed by the person ordering it, who previously indicates its conditions, characteristics and attributes and establishes guidelines as to the time, form, and place for its development.[69] If this requirement were not complied with, the economic rights would not be transferred to the person ordering the work.

55. The presence of the above-mentioned conditions suffices to assume that the economic rights are in the head of the person ordering the work.[70] Thus, acts of alienation in regards to a work made for hire do not have to fulfil the conditions set forth in Article

64. According to Art. 30(a), the author shall have rights to 'claim at all times authorship of the work, and in particular, to have his name mentioned or pseudonym appear'.
65. Part B of said provision states that the author may 'oppose to deformation, mutilation or other modification of the work where such acts might o do cause damage to his/her reputation or good name, or which may render the work undeserving on such account'.
66. Economic and moral rights will be thoroughly explained in s. 5.
67. These requirements were established by the National Direction of Copyright in its Legal Opinion (*Concepto*) on the Transfer of Economic Rights, No. 1-2005-14246 of 18 Jul. 2005.
68. *See* National Direction of Copyright, Legal Opinion (*Concepto*) No. 1-2005-8134 of 16 May 2005. On the assignment regime, *see also* National Direction of Copyright, Legal opinion (*Concepto*) No. 1-2005-23251 of 21 Nov. 2005.
69. *Ibid.*
70. *See* E. Rengifo García, *Propiedad Intelectual: El Moderno Derecho de Autor* (Bogotá, Universidad Externado de Colombia, 1996), 50.

183 of Law 23.[71] Article 20[72] is a special provision and therefore it applies preferentially over any other general provision such as Article 183.[73] In any case, the parties in the contract can agree not to transfer the economic rights and such stipulation would be valid.[74]

IV. Works Made Within the Framework of an Employment Relationship

56. Works made within the framework of an employment relationship are not expressly contemplated in the Decision or in the domestic legislation. Nonetheless, this notion is of growing importance and therefore it deserves a special mention.

This type of works are developed under a relationship of subordination in which the employer instructs the employee about how specific tasks will be performed. However, economic rights remain in the head of the employee, as neither the Andean legislation nor Law 23 contemplate otherwise. Therefore, the assignment of economic rights has to abide by the stipulations of Article 183 of the Decision.[75] Also, the assignment has to be over completed works as, in the terms of Article 129 of Law 23, 'future production of the intellect may not be subject matter of a contract'. In short, the employee cannot transfer his/her economic rights over all the works done during the employment relationship when the contract is signed. The only way in which the transfer is valid is if there is a clear stipulation in the contract as to the nature of the work and the specific characteristics that it must observe.[76] This stipulation is not necessary when several people made the work and it is not possible to separate the contribution made by each one of them. In that case, the right holder of the copyright would be the employee for whose account and risk the work was carried out.[77]

57. The differences with the works made for hire are that: (1) works made for hire should be developed within a service contract; (2) in works made within the framework of an employment relationship there is not an assumption as to the assignment of economic rights; (3) in works made for hire the author retains only the right of paternity and integrity over the work. In works made within the framework of an employment relationship the author retains all of the moral rights[78] and only transfers the economic ones; and (4) transfers of rights over works made within the framework

71. Article 183 reads as follows: 'Any act of alienation of the copyright whether partial or total shall be attested by a public deed, or in a private document acknowledged before a notary public, such instruments requiring for their enforceability before third parties, to be recorded before the Copyright Office, with the formalities established herein.'
72. The compliance of this article with the Constitution was analysed by the Constitutional Court in its judgment C-276 of 1996.
73. *See* National Direction of Copyright, Legal Opinion (*Concepto*) on Works Made for Hire, No. 1-2005-21288 of 13 Oct. 2005.
74. *See* National Direction of Copyright, Legal Opinion (*Concepto*) on the implementation of Art. 20 of Law 23 of 1982, No. 1-2004-21716 of 22 Dec. 2004.
75. The transfer of economic rights will be thoroughly explained in s. 6.
76. *See* Art. 129 of Law 23.
77. *See* Art. 92 of Law 23.
78. *See* s. 5.

of an employment relationship, have to comply with the requirements established in Article 183 of the Decision, while the transfer in works made for hire is not subject to any formalities.

§5. Scope of Exclusive Rights

58. Copyrights confer to the author of a work certain exclusive rights from the very moment of the creation of the work, without the fulfilment of any legal formalities. Article 3 of Law 23 grants authors the right to dispose of their work, derive profit from it, and to exercise the prerogatives granted by the law to defend moral rights. In other words, the exclusive rights granted to authors, which can be grouped into moral and economic rights, give authors the possibility of protecting and claiming paternity over their work, but also of claiming economic revenues derived from the use of it. During this section, we will explain subsequently the two categories of exclusive rights.

I. Moral Rights

59. Moral rights are inherent to the author's personality and are, in the opinion of the National Direction of Copyright, a human right detaching from the Universal Declaration of Human Rights.[79] Similarly, the Constitutional Court expressed in its judgment C-155 of 1998 that moral rights are of fundamental nature as they allude to the creativity of men; the possibility of expressing ideas or feelings in a particular; their inventive capacity, talent and in general all forms of manifestations of the spirit. [The latter] are inherent prerogatives to the rational condition characterizing human nature and to the free dimension derived therein. Denying individuals rights over the product of their own creativity, of the exclusive manifestation of their spirit or talent, is the same thing as denying them their condition of individuals that think and create, and that express such rationality as a manifestation of their own nature. For this reason, moral rights must be protected as rights that are drawn from the very human condition'.[80]

Consequently, and pursuant to Article 30 of Law 23, moral rights are characterized for being perpetual, because their duration is unlimited; non-alienable which means that transfers over the rights over certain work do not include transfer of moral rights; and non-waivable, reason why the right holder cannot relinquish these rights.[81]

60. Article 30 of Law 23 contains the moral rights to which the author is entitled. They comprise the following powers:

79. *See* Legal Opinion (*concepto*) of the National Direction of Copyright on the Generalities of Copyright of 13 Aug. 2003.
80. *See also* Constitutional Court, judgment C-1490 of 2000.
81. *See* generally Constitutional Court, judgments C-334 of 1993 and C-226 of 1996. This has to be read in conjunction with Art. 15 of the Civil Code according to which 'the rights conferred by laws can be renounced, as long as they only concern the individual interest of the person that renounces and that such act is not forbidden by the law'.

(a) *Right to the authorship of the work*: often called the right of paternity, it allows the author to vindicate at all times the paternity of his/her work and to demand that his/her name is indicated if the work is reproduced, translated, adapted, transformed, or communicated.

(b) *Right to the integrity of the work*: it allows authors to oppose deformation, mutilation, or any other modification of the work, when such acts can cause prejudice to his/her honour or reputation or demerit the work. The author is entitled to urge respect for the integrity of the work, when he/she may feel that his/her wealth, honour or reputation has been affected. In this way, the right of integrity seeks to 'preserve the essential elements of the work and to impede that no person or authority, on purpose or for lack of understanding, alters its contents'.[82] Incidentally, the right of integrity can be limited by means of a contract that allows the work to be modified. In any case, if the modification done to the work harms in any way the integrity of the work, the author will be able to oppose it. This rule has an exception regarding architectural pieces where the author cannot oppose modifications. As per Article 43 of the Decision, he/she cannot impede that the owner of the building modifies the work, but he/she could impede that his/her name is associated with the altered work.

(c) To maintain the work unedited or anonym, until the author's death, or even after when that was his/her will expressed through a testamentary provision. The anonymity of a work has to be expressly indicated by the author,[83] in the same way the indication of the use a pseudonym by using a name different from his/her civil name must be done.

(d) To modify the work prior or after its publication. This provision has to be read in the light of Article 111 of Law 23 according to which authors can introduce any correction they deem necessary during the stage destined to such purpose. If the author decides to introduce corrections after the work has been published, he/she shall reimburse the editor the expenses generated by the corrections. This is applicable to other cases in which the author had already transmitted the economic rights before the modification.

(e) The *Right of repenting*: by virtue of this right, the author can withdraw the work from circulation or suspend any use of it even though it had been previously authorized. This right is exercised in a discretional manner by the author and it does not require any formalities. In any case, it is limited to collecting the edition, that is, to withdraw from bookstores the copies that are not sold. The author cannot exercise this right in regards to the copies that were already purchased.

---

82. *See* Constitutional Court, judgment SU-056 of 1995.

83. For further reference of moral rights in a digital scenario, *see* generally R. Antequera, *El comercio electrónico, puesta a disposición de contenidos y transmisiones digitales, Revista de Derecho Privado*, No. 26, (August) 2001, 101.

II. Economic Rights

61. Economic rights are the retribution to which the owner of such rights is entitled when the work is disclosed by any means.[84] This 'pecuniary retribution stimulates creators to make new works and contributes, obviously, to the cultural and intellectual progress of people'.[85] According to Article 11 of Law 23, these rights are protected during the life of the author and eighty years after he/she is deceased. In the case of collaborative works, this period is counted from the date of death of the last co-author. Economic rights are laid down in Article 13 of the Decision and will be explained subsequently in this section.

A. The Reproduction of the Work by Any Means or Process

62. In the terms of Article 14 of the Decision, reproduction is to be understood as 'the fixation of the work on a medium that permits it to be communicated or copies of all or part of it to be made by any means or processes'. Our legislation grants this right to copyright owners as well as to owners of neighbouring rights, in a way that they can all carry out, authorize, or prohibit reproduction of the work, of the phonogram or of the artistic presentation by any mean or procedure. The reason behind the right of reproduction is that almost anyone can acquire a copy of the work, but this is not an authorization to reproduce the creation there contained since 'the person that acquires the material object is not the owner of the economic exploitation rights of the work'.[86]

This right may be infringed if the work is reproduced, regardless of the material form the new copy is in. In the same way, an unauthorized transformation of the work (i.e., a translation) would also constitute a violation since the 'reproduction right does not only cover the work in its original form, but also the transformations to which it can be subjected'.[87]

B. The Communication of the Work to the Public by Any Means Serving to Convey the Words, Signs, Sounds or Images Thereof

63. In accordance with Article 15 of the Decision, communication of the work to the public 'shall be understood to mean any act by which two or more persons, whether or not they are gathered together in the same place, may have access to the work without the prior distribution of copies to each one of them'. Article 15 also contains the following examples of public communication:

(1) stage presentations, recitals, dissertations, and public performances of dramatic, dramatic-musical, literary, and musical works by any means or process. As per Article 11 of the Berne Convention, this type of communication can be delivered

84. *See* Art. 72 of Law 23.
85. *See* Legal Opinion (*concepto*) of the National Direction of Copyright on the Generalities of Copyright of 13 Aug. 2003.
86. *See* Legal Opinion (*concepto*) of the National Direction of Copyright on the Generalities of Copyright of 13 Aug. 2003, 165.
87. *Ibid.*, 167.

through live performances or broadcasts of the work. In sum, all public display of the work is considered as a public communication of it. When it is done within a private domicile, it will not be a violation of this right unless such communication is also being propagated to the exterior. Similarly, the communication of a work will not be considered to be public when it is done for educational purposes within the facilities of the educational entity and there is no entrance fee.[88] Moreover, Article 159 of Law 23 states that public performances of musical works 'are those given in theatres, cinemas, concert and dance halls, bars, clubs of any kind, stadiums, circuses, restaurants, hotels, commercial, banking and industrial establishments and in general wherever musical works are interpreted, performed or transmitted by radio or television, whether by artists or with the use of mechanical, electronic, sound or audiovisual processes';

(2) the public projection or display of cinematographic and other audiovisual works;
(3) the transmission of any work by broadcasting or any other means of wireless distribution of signs, sounds or images; the concept of transmission shall likewise include the sending of signals from a ground station to a broadcasting or telecommunication satellite;
(4) the transmission of works to the public by wire, cable, optic fibre or other comparable process, whether free or on subscription;
(5) the retransmission, by any of the means specified in the foregoing subparagraphs and by a broadcasting organization different from the original one, of the work broadcast by radio or television;
(6) the emission or transmission in or to a place accessible to the public and by means of any appropriate apparatus, of a work broadcast by radio or television;
(7) the public display of works of art or reproductions thereof;
(8) public access to computer data bases by means of telecommunication, insofar as the said databases incorporate or constitute protected works;
(9) in general, the dissemination of signs, words, sounds or images by any known or future process.

C. *The Translation, Adaptation, Arrangement or Other Transformation of the Work*

64. This right gives the author the possibility of authorizing the creation of derived works from his/her own in such a way that it can be translated, adapted, revised, summarized, and so forth. A transformation will occur if the work is changed within the same form of expression, or if it is changed as in the case of a novel that is adapted into a movie.[89] In the case of translations, the translator of a protected scientific, literary or artistic work, duly authorized by the author, must cite the author and title of the original work but will acquire copyrights over the translation. As to adaptations, a person who, with the express permission of an author, transports, modifies, makes abstracts, compendia or parodies of a work in the private domain, has the copyright

88. *See* Art. 149 Law 23.

89. *See* Legal Opinion (*concepto*) of the National Direction of Copyright on the Generalities of Copyright of 13 Aug. 2003, 172.

over such adaptation. The title of original work and the author must be mentioned, unless otherwise is agreed.

III. Other Rights: Droit de Suite

65. Article 16 of the Decision provides that the authors of works of art and, on their death, their successors in title shall have the inalienable right to be granted a share in the successive sales of the work by public auction or through a professional art dealer. The Member Countries shall enact provisions on the said right.

The text of this article is different from Article 14*ter*.1 of the Berne Convention, which provides that the author, or after his death the persons or institutions authorized by national legislation, shall, with respect to original works of art and original manuscripts of writers and composers, enjoy the inalienable right to an interest in any sale of the work subsequent to the first transfer by the author of the work.

The latter means that the protection given by the communitarian legislation is more restricted, limiting it only to works of art.[90] The underlying rationale of this restriction is that it is considered that the economic value of works of art will increase with time and in consequence the author or his/her heirs should be entitled to receive a part of that increased value, reason why this right cannot be transmitted.[91] But this faculty is only triggered when the work is sold in a public auction and can be exercised all throughout the author's life and as long as the economic rights are protected after his/her death.[92]

§6. Transfer

I. Assignment of Copyright

66. In the words of Article 182 of Law 23, 'the owners of copyright and neighbouring rights may transfer their rights to third parties either in whole or in part, universally or in a particular work. The transfer of rights, whether whole or partial, shall not include the moral rights'. When copyrights are transferred by means of assignment, the assignee is accredited as owner of the right and is deemed empowered to act in his/her own name, even for purposes of instituting judicial actions against infringers. If the assignment is partial, the authors retain the economic prerogatives not expressly assigned.

90. It is important to clarify that Art. 16 does not grant this right to authors of applied art in the sense of Art. 3.14 of the Decision, which reads as follows: 'a work of applied art means an artistic creation with utilitarian functions or incorporated in a useful article, whether a work of handicraft or one produced on an industrial scale'.
91. *See* Constitutional Court, judgment C-155 of 1998.
92. *See* Legal Opinion (*concepto*) of the National Direction of Copyright on the Generalities of Copyright of 13 Aug. 2003, 175.

67. The main characteristic of this contract is that the author transmits his/her economic rights and the buyer becomes a derivative owner. The assignment is a solemn act given that it must be formalized by means of public deed or of a private document acknowledged before a public notary.[93] In accordance with Article 5 of Law 44 of 1993, these acts must be registered before the National Copyright Register so they can be opposed against third parties.

II. Licences

A. Copyright Licence Agreement

68. There are no specific provisions relating to copyright licence agreements. These are not deemed a technology transfer agreement, which is the case of industrial property licence agreements. A public register for copyright licence agreements does not exist.

B. Edition and Publishing Agreements

69. This is the best known and most used type of agreement in the copyright field. Article 105 of Law 23 establishes that by means of this agreement, 'the owner of copyrights protecting a literary or scientific work is obliged to deliver the work to an editor, who is in turn obliged to publish it in the manner of a graphic printing and to distribute it at his own risk and account'. Law 23 has limited the purpose to the reproduction of the work in the manner of a 'graphic printing', which includes only the so-called paper *edition*.[94] The reproduction includes preparation of a support that can be paper, silk or any other material, provided that the concept of 'graphic printing' is maintained. The reproduction can be done through any means, whether known or to be known, such as typography, lithography, chalcography, polychrome, any kind of photographic process, electric process, but excluding reproduction of sound, audiovisual or Internet means.

70. The purpose of the agreement is to reproduce or disseminate the work. To accomplish it, the parties must comply with certain obligations. As to the copyright owner, he/she must deliver the originals within the term and as per the conditions agreed.[95] In the event of breach on behalf of the owner of the copyright with respect to the date and form of delivery of originals, the editor may rescind the agreement; return the originals for adjustment of their presentation to the terms agreed; or make the relevant corrections at the account of the owner. When the originals are not delivered as agreed, the editor could make the relevant corrections to the account of the copyright owner.[96] It is also the obligation of the copyright owner to refrain from contracting

93. *See* Art. 183 of Law 23.
94. However, by virtue of Art. 138 of Law 23, the same provisions regulating this contract are applicable to contracts for publishing musical works.
95. *See* Art. 113 of Law 23.
96. *See* Art. 114 of Law 23.

new editions of the work with third parties before the term of the edition contracted expires or before the run is exhausted.

71. As to the editor, the principal obligation is to pay royalties to the right owner, which, in the wording of Article 106 of Law 23, shall be agreed to between the parties. In the absence of such stipulation, the right holder shall receive 20% of the price of the sale to the public of the edited copies. If the remuneration is a royalty, it must be paid on the date and in the form stipulated in the agreement. The editor is also obliged to publish the work, strongly advertise it, furnish some gratuitous samples to the right owner, and the other obligations stipulated in the agreement.[97] In regards to the number of printings, Article 109 of Law 23 provides that the editor must make the number of printings agreed to in the contract. In the absence of such stipulation, it shall be understood that he/she can only print one edition.[98] In the same way, Article 122 authorizes the editor to print a maximum of 3,000 copies, unless otherwise is agreed.

72. During the validity of the edition agreement, the editor has the right to demand through judicial means recall of work samples edited fraudulently, without prejudice of the author's right to bring actions, which can be done in conjunction with the editor or separately. The edition agreement ends at the expiration of the term established by the parties[99] or due to the physical exhaustion of the samples. Moreover, Article 135 of Law 23 provides the possibility for the editor to terminate the agreement when less than 30% of the copies have been sold after five years of publication. In this case, the right owner has the priority to buy the remaining copies, but at a discounted price of 40% less than the price offered to the public. In addition, Article 133 instructs that in the presence of death or disability of the author, the editor may choose between publishing the finished part, reducing proportionally the agreed remuneration or to terminate the agreement. The editor, with the authorization of the author or his/her heirs and if the nature of the work allows it, may also ask a third party to finish the work, mentioning this event in the edition. Finally, the agreement can terminate due to the disappearance of the sole original at the editor's fault. In this case, the copyright owner has the right to receive the agreed remuneration. If the right holder has a copy of the disappeared sample, he/she must make it available to the editor.[100]

C. Artist Contracts

73. Pursuant to Article 139 of Law 23, a performance contract 'is one by which the author of a dramatic, musical-dramatic or choreographic work or of a work of similar nature authorizes a manager to have his/her work performed in public'. Such public performance shall be understood as one that is given outside a private domicile, or even inside if it is projected outside, or when mechanical means are used,[101] unless the performances are given for educational purposes.[102] This shall be done within the period stipulated for the compliance of the obligations, which in no case can exceed

97. *See* Art. 125 of Law 23.
98. *See* Art. 108 of Law 23.
99. *See* Art. 107 of Law 23.
100. *See* Art. 117 of Law 23.
101. *See* Art. 140 of Law 23.
102. *See* Art. 149 of Law 23.

one year.[103] The author has the right to receive remuneration in this contract, which can be agreed to by the parties. In the absence of an agreement, Article 143 provides that he/she shall receive at least 15% of the amount of the admission tickets of the opening performance, and 10% of the amount of the admission tickets collected in each show or performance done after that.

The manager is also obliged to present the work as many times as stipulated in the contract. If there was no stipulation, the frequency will be determined by the amount of public attending the functions. The manager's obligations will cease in the moment attendance stops.[104] If the manager fails to observe with his/her obligations, he/she shall return the copy of the work given by the author and provide an indemnity for the damages caused.

D. *Contract of Inclusion in Sound Recordings*

74. By virtue of the contract of inclusion of phonograms or sound recordings the author of a musical work authorizes an individual or entity to fix the work on a disk, tape, film, paper reel or on any other device for such purposes.[105] It is important to clarify that this is neither an authorization to make public performances of the work, nor it extends to any other use of the work.[106] As per Article 155 of Law 23, future production may not be subject matter of this contract, except when the production is limited to a maximum number of five works. Any stipulation whereby the author commits in a general or unspecified manner his/her future work shall be null and void.

§7. Limitations or Exemptions to the Scope of Copyright Protection

75. Authors have exclusive power to authorize, previously and expressly, any use of their works. However, these rights are not absolute; Colombian legislation, in accordance with the Berne Convention, the TRIPS Agreement and the WIPO Convention on Copyright, limits this right in order to keep a balance between the individual interests of the author and the collective interests of society while using such works.[107] Said limits strictly determine the cases where, under certain circumstances, the use of a work is allowed without prior and express authorization of the author or owner and without making any payments for this use. The different forms of limitations and exceptions to copyrights will be explained next.

---

103. *See* Art. 141 of Law 23.

104. *See* Art. 146 of Law 23.

105. *See* Art. 151 of Law 23.

106. *See* Art. 154 of Law 23. In the terms of Art. 157, the provisions regarding this contract are also 'applicable to literary works, which may be used as texts of a musical work, or for their declamation or reading, if the author of said work has authorized the producer of the sound recording to fix or record it on a disk, tape, or any other device or analogous mechanism for the reproduction, dissemination or sale of the work'.

107. *See* Legal Opinion (*concepto*) of the National Direction of Copyright on the Generalities of Copyright of 13 Aug. 2003.

I. Quotation Rights

76. The possibility of quoting the work of an author is provided for in Article 22 of Decision 351, according to which it is lawful to quote within a work a published piece, without the authorization of the author and without any payment, provided that any such quotations are made pursuant to honest use and to the extent justified by the purpose pursued. The quotation must mention the original author and the title of the published work.[108] Otherwise, the quotation will be considered as plagiarism which implies the use of another work in such a way that it seems to belong to someone different than its original author.[109]

As to the honest use of a work, quotations cannot be so many or so frequent that they might reasonably be considered as a reproduction in disguise.[110] In the same sense, Article 3 of the Decision provides that the exercise of this quoting right cannot interfere with the normal exploitation of the right or unreasonably prejudice the legitimate interest of the right holder.

As to the purpose pursued by the quote, it is usually accepted that the main purpose of quoting a work should be to illustrate an idea, concept or thesis, or even to criticize the work quoted. Based on this purpose, the justified extent seeks basically to determine the broadness of the quote. Our legal regime does not contemplate a quantitative limitation (extent of the quotation)[111] for which the qualitative aspect must be taken into account. Nowadays, judges have to establish to their discretion if a work has been quoted lawfully or whether it has been reproduced without authorization for what they will analyse the context of the quote. There are not absolute criteria to determine an adequate proportion of a quote; this will be determined on a case-by-case basis.[112] There is a tool, however, contained in the TRIPS Agreement that can help judges determine if the quotation does not constitute an exception of copyrights but a violation of these. The so-called three-step rule of Article 13 of TRIPS provides that the exception must be: (1) done only for a special case; (2) that it does not interfere with the normal exploitation of the right; and (3) that it does not cause an unjustified prejudice to the legitimate interests of right holders.

II. Educational Purposes

77. Article 32 of Law 23 sets forth the possibility for literary or artistic works, or parts thereof to be used as illustrations in books for teaching purposes, such as

108. *See* Legal Opinion (*concepto*) of the National Direction of Copyright on the Generalities of Copyright of 13 Aug. 2003.

109. *Ibid.*

110. *See* National Direction of Copyright, Legal Opinion (*Concepto*) on the Plagiarism of a Literary Work of 9 Jun. 2003.

111. Contrary to what happened in our former legislation. Art. 15 of Law 86 of 1946 limited the quotation right to 1,000 words for literary or scientific works and to 4 compasses for musical pieces.

112. *See* Legal Opinion (*concepto*) of the National Direction of Copyright on the Generalities of Copyright of 13 Aug. 2003, 59.

publications, broadcasts or sound or visual recordings, within the limits as may be justified by the stated purpose of the use; or the work may be broadcasted for teaching purposes in schools, universities or other educational or professional training activities not undertaken for gain, provided the name of the author and the title of the work are mentioned.

Accordingly, lectures or lessons given in establishments of higher education, secondary or primary institutions may be recorded and collected freely by students to whom they are addressed to; but publication or reproduction thereof in whole or in part is prohibited, without the written permission from the author.[113]

III. News of General Interest

78. Daily news, or events solely having press information are not protected by copyright. Pursuant to Article 22(e) of the Decision, it is lawful to reproduce and distribute through the press, or to emit through radio broadcasting or through a public transmission by cable, any articles on current events, economic, political, or religious discussions published in periodicals or periodical collections, or works radio broadcasted having the same character, in cases where the reproduction or the public transmission have not been expressly reserved.

From the foregoing, it may be concluded that a third party is authorized to utilize an article on a current event, on an economic, political or religious discussion without the need of prior and express authorization from its creator whenever it is done through a communication means and:

(1) It is a reproduction or a distribution.
(2) Such uses are carried out through the press, radio broadcasting or public transmission by cable.
(3) The article reproduced or distributed was published in periodicals or periodical collections or was a radio broadcasted work.
(4) The reproduction, radio broadcasting or public transmission was not prohibited.

IV. Private Copies

79. Article 37 of Law 23 ascertains that it is lawful to reproduce by any means any literary or scientific work ordered or obtained in one single copy by an interested party for exclusive personal use. The constitutionality of this article was questioned in 1987 before the Supreme Court of Justice.[114] The Court argued that this article establishes a simple limitation to copyrights that responds to the need of the prevalence of public over private interest. That is why the law authorizes the reproduction of literary and artistic works by any means when this activity is not destined to produce

113. *See* Art. 40 of Law 23.
114. Before the Constitution of 1991, the guard of the constitutional order was assigned to the Supreme Court of Justice. After 1991, this function was conferred to the newly created Constitutional Court.

profit, therefore accomplishing the social function of property established in Article 58 of the former Constitution.[115] This is also consistent with Article 44 of Law 23 according to which scientific, literary, and artistic works can be used freely within a private domicile when this is not for profit.

V. Public Libraries

80. Consistent with Article 38 of Law 23, public libraries may, for the exclusive use of their readers and whenever necessary for conservation or for lending to other libraries, make one copy of protected works in their collections or files if no longer available on the local market. These copies may themselves be reproduced once by the library receiving them, if necessary for conservation and only for the use of its readers.

VI. Limitations Related to Artistic and Architectural Works

81. As per Article 39 of Law 23, reproductions by painting, drawing, photography or film may be made of works permanently placed in public passages, streets or squares, and such reproductions may be distributed and communicated publicly. In the case of architecture, this licence applies only to exteriors.

Beyond this, the author of an architectural piece cannot impede the owner of the building from introducing modifications to it, but can oppose being related to the altered piece.[116]

VII. Reproduction of Legal Texts and Norms

82. Article 41 of Law 23 grants the possibility for anyone to reproduce the constitution, any laws, decrees, orders, agreements, regulations, and other administrative acts and judicial decisions, if this is done following the textual publication in the official edition, where not prohibited.

§8. Duration of Protection

83. Copyright protects works during the lifetime of the author and for eighty years thereafter.[117] When the ownership of the rights accrues to a legal entity, the term of protection is of fifty years counted from the making, disclosure or publication of the work, as the case may be.[118] The protection for compilations, dictionaries,

115. *See* Supreme Court of Justice, judgment of 23 Apr. 1987.
116. *See* Art. 43 of Law 23.
117. *See* Art. 11 of Law 23.
118. *See* Art. 29 of Law 23, as modified by Art. 2 of Law 44 of 1993. Before this modification, the protection awarded to legal entities was of thirty years.

encyclopaedias, and other collective works shall last for eighty years calculated from the date of publication, and it shall accrue to the editors.

As to performers, phonogram producers, and broadcasting organizations, they shall receive protection for eighty years from the death of the right owner, when such owner is a natural person; when the owner is a legal entity, the term shall be thirty years from the date on which the performance, or the first fixation of the phonogram, or when the transmission of the broadcast took place.

§9. Neighbouring Rights

84. Neighbouring rights concern those that participate in the diffusion and not in the creation of literary or artistic works.[119] These are rights that grew up *around* copyrighted works, and provide similar, although often more limited[120] and of shorter duration, rights to: performing artists (such as actors and musicians) in their performances; producers of sound recordings (e.g., cassette recordings and compact discs) in their recordings; [and] broadcasting organizations in their radio and television programmes.[121]

85. In regards to artists, interpreters, and performers, Article 34 of the Decision grants them the possibility to authorize or prohibit the communication to the public in, any manner whatsoever, of their interpretations and performances. Article 35 also confers right owners of neighbouring rights the possibility of demanding that their names appear in, or are associated to each interpretation or performance made, and of opposing to any deformation, mutilation or any other act against their interpretation or performance which may damage their prestige or reputation. This is consistent with the text of Article 171 of Law 23, which grants artists, interpreters, and performers the moral rights laid down in Article 30 of said law. The duration of these rights should not be less than fifty years, counted as from the first day of January of the year following that one when the interpretation or performance took place, or of its fixation, as the case may be.[122]

In 17 July 2010, the Colombian Congress amended the neighbouring rights regime by approving the 'Fanny Mickey Law', which seeks to protect the royalties and economic rights of actors involved in audiovisual productions that are later sold and broadcast in Colombia and abroad. This marked the end of a long struggle of over fifteen years, started by the CICA (Colombian Artists Circle) and AISGE (Performers Management Society), and provides for the payment of royalties to artists and performers of broadcast works and audiovisual recordings, in which they have participated, for their purchase and rent, a right that artists in other countries have been able to claim and enjoy for decades. This new law is of great importance, given the significant export of Colombian dramas, soap operas and movies that have been produced in recent years. This payment for the contribution that actors and Colombian artists have made to the

119. *See* Constitutional Court, judgment C-040 of 1994.

120. For this reason, copyrights prevail over neighbouring rights. *See* Constitutional Court, judgment C-053 of 2001.

121. *See* World Intellectual Property Organisation, *Copyright and Related Rights*, in <wipo.int/about-ip/en/copyright.html> (last visited 28 Nov. 2017).

122. *See* Art. 36 of Law 23.

quality of exported products was not supported or protected in any way nationally until the enactment of the Fanny Mickey Law.

The law refers exclusively to audiovisual performances. It is, therefore, a rule that does not affect other owners, who already enjoy protection under the Copyright Law since 1982.

86. As to phonogram producers, in the terms of Article 37 of the Decision, they are entitled to: (a) authorize or prohibit the direct or indirect reproduction of their phonograms; (b) prevent the importation of copies of the phonogram made without authorization of the owner of the rights; (c) authorize or prohibit the public distribution of the original and every copy thereof to the public by sale, rental or any other means; (d) charge remuneration for every use of the phonogram or copies thereof for commercial purposes, which remuneration may be shared among the performers. The rights of phonogram producers shall last fifty years counted as from the first day of January of the year following that when the fixation was made.[123]

87. Analogously, Article 39 provides that radio broadcasting bodies enjoy the exclusive right to authorize or prohibit the retransmission of their broadcasts by any means or processes; the fixing of their broadcasts on a physical medium; and the reproduction of a fixation of their broadcasts. As per Article 40, the broadcast includes the production of programme-carrying signals destined to a radio broadcasting or telecommunications satellite, and comprises the diffusion to the public by an entity emitting or diffusing emissions from any others, received through any of the mentioned satellites. The duration of the protection of the copyrights of radio broadcasting organizations is of fifty years, counted as from the first day of January of the year following such when the emission shall have been made.[124]

§10. Collective Administration Associations

88. As stated in Section 5, copyright holders[125] have economic rights in regards to their work, which allows them to oppose the reproduction of it without their consent. In the same sense, they are entitled to receive royalties when their work is used, even if authorization was given for it. Normally those royalties would be collected directly by the author, but in the case of musical creations, some legal entities especially designed for that purposed have been designated to collect royalties.

89. Article 173 of Law 23 provides that when a phonogram or a reproduction of it is published for commercial purposes and used directly for broadcasting or any other form of communication to the public, the user thereof shall credit an equitable and single amount to the producer intended both for the artists interpreters or performers and the producer of the sound recording, sum which shall be paid by the user to the interpreting or performing artists and to the producers of phonograms, through collective administration associations constituted in accordance with the law, and distributed in equal parts.

123. *See* Art. 38 of the Decision.

124. *See* Art. 41 of the Decision.

125. What is said in this section is totally applicable to holders of neighbouring rights.

In other words, users of protected works are to pay an amount to the right holder and this shall be done through a collective administration association.

90. Collective administration associations in Colombia exist since 1946 when SAYCO (*Sociedad de Autores y Compositores* – authors' and composers' association) was founded and got legal recognition through Resolution 1537 of the then Ministry of Justice.[126] In 1982, Law 23 established its functioning structure, which was recognized by the National Direction of Copyright in Resolution 001 of 1982. After the entry into force of Decision 351, the direction granted SAYCO the permit to run operations through Resolution 070 of 1997. The primary objective of SAYCO is to collect and distribute the economic revenues derived from the public execution and reproduction of the works of its affiliates, which can only be authors or composers.[127] The collection of the economic rights of holders of neighbouring rights is done by ACINPRO (*Asociación Colombiana de Intérpretes y Productores de Fonogramas* – Colombian Association of Interpreters and Phonogram Producers), a non-profit collective administration association created by Resolution 002 of 1982 enacted by the National Direction of Copyright.[128]

91. SAYCO collects copyrights for the communication, radio diffusion, public execution, and other uses of musical works done on the radio, television, TV cables, satellite television, parabolic antennas, multimedia, Internet, and others. Likewise, it collects for the reproduction and synchronization of music in audiovisual pieces in general (movies, videos, soap operas, short and long films, etc.), radio and television commercials.[129]

In turn, ACINPRO collects for the public execution corresponding to the interpreter over his/her performance and to the phonogram producer when the phonogram (CD, cassette, LP) is used.[130] The SAYCO-ACINPRO Organization[131] only collects public communication revenues for the use of phonograms in public establishments such as bars, discotheques, taverns, restaurants, hotels, and music stores, among others.

92. The rights collected by these organizations are not considered as taxes. In the opinion of the Constitutional Court, they are neither a tax nor part of public income since they satisfy the individual rights of copyright and neighbouring right owners.[132] Also, because these organizations can only collect rights when the work that is being used belongs to one of their affiliates who can be Colombian authors, producers, interpreters, or foreign parties having the same qualities when they belong to an association with which SAYCO has reciprocal representation contracts.[133] About 60% of those rights will be distributed among the right owners; 30% will be destined to

126. *See* Official website of SAYCO, *What is SAYCO?*, in <sayco.org/publicaciones.aspx?cat_id=1047> (last visited 16 Aug. 2007).
127. *Ibid.*
128. *See* Official website of ACINPRO, *About ACINPRO*, in <acinpro.org.co/empresa.htm> (last visited 16 Aug. 2007).
129. *See* Constitutional Court, judgments C-334 of 1993 and C-226 of 1996.
130. *Ibid.*
131. The SAYCO-ACINPRO Organization is different from SAYCO, on the one hand, and ACINPRO on the other. It is a private legal person incorporated in 1985 by the two societies.
132. *See* Constitutional Court, judgment C-533 of 1993.
133. *See* Constitutional Court, judgments C-334 of 1993 and C-226 of 1996.

cover administrative costs; the remaining 10% will be destined to social welfare of the association.

In the event that an obliged party dismisses the obligation to pay economic rights, Article 54 of Law 44 of 1993 authorizes the police to suspend the public execution of the work and to collect the copies used for that purpose. Also, the police could seal the establishment off and suspend or cancel the functioning licence.

§11. Infringements

93. For a complete explanation on infringements, *see* Chapter 12.

Chapter 2. Patents

§1. Sources and Legislation

94. Patent protection in Colombia has been a long-standing issue that goes as back as 1848 when the Congress of the Nueva Granada[134] promulgated the first patent law.[135] Eleven years later, the Congress of the United States of Colombia[136] enacted the law on invention, improvements or introduction of invention patents,[137] which granted patent holders the exclusive right of using the invention or improvement for five to twenty years. In 1911, the Congress of Colombia amended this regulation, increasing the term of protection from ten to twenty years.[138] In 1925, the Congress modified this law once again, limiting the patent protection to twenty years and establishing other patent requirements.[139] Until 1971, when the Colombian Code of Commerce entered into force, this law remained the applicable statute for patents.[140]

95. This legislative evolution was influenced by Colombia's participation in the international scenario in the intellectual property arena, which started with the ratification of the Montreal Treaty on Patents of Invention of 1889. Since then, several conventions have been negotiated, including the Industrial Property Convention with France of 1901,[141] the Bolivarian Convention on Invention Patents approved by Colombia on 1913, the Paris Convention for the Protection of Industrial Property of 1883,[142] among others. Colombia also became a member of international organizations such as the WIPO,[143] 'a specialized agency of the United Nations dedicated to developing a balanced and accessible international intellectual property system, which rewards creativity, stimulated innovation and contributes to economic development while

134. Former political name of the Republic of Colombia.
135. *See* Senate and the Chamber of Representatives of the Nueva Granada, Law of 15 May 1848 on invention or improvement of machines or industrial products patents. The fundaments of this law can be found on Art. 67.13 of the Constitution of 1843 that called for the protection, and encouragement of science and arts.
136. Former political name of the Republic of Colombia.
137. *See* Congress of the Unites States of Colombia, Art. 2 of Law 35 of 1969 on patents of invention, improvement or introduction of new industries. The Presidential Decree No. 218 of 1900 and 475 of 1902 regulated this law.
138. *See* Congress of Colombia, Law 49 of 1911, Art. 2.
139. *See* Congress of Colombia, Law 31 of 1925 on industrial property protection and by virtue of which a provision on the income tax is promulgated.
140. *See* Code of Commerce, Decree-Law 417 of 1971.
141. Promulgated by Decree 597 of 7 Jul. 1904.
142. Ratified by Law 178 of 1994.
143. Colombia ratified the Treaty Establishing the WIPO by means of Law 46 of 1979.

safeguarding the public interest'.[144] In 1994, it also became a member of the WTO[145] and hence of the Agreement of Trade-Related Aspects of Intellectual Property (TRIPS Agreement), which sets minimum standards for Member Countries as to intellectual property rights.

96. Moreover, as a member of the ACN,[146] Colombia must follow the decisions of the Commission in terms of patent regulation. The first Decision on the matter was Decision 85 of 1978,[147] which approved the Regulation for the Application of Norms on Industrial Property. In 1991, this Decision was replaced by Decision 311, which in turn was replaced by Decision 313 of 1992.[148] Subsequently, the Commission promulgated Decision 344 of 1993 on the Common Regime of Industrial Property,[149] and then replaced it with Decision 486 of 2000 (the Decision), which is the current industrial property regime in the Andean Community. Decision 486 was inspired on the on the TRIPS Agreement and on the Paris Convention. Consequently, the Andean legislation is now compatible with the international standards in terms of patent protection, providing Colombia a clear and solid legal framework in the matter.

The Decision also allows Member Countries to subscribe other international treaties in the matter, as long as they do not oppose its regulations. This is the case of the Patent Cooperation Treaty (PCT), a treaty administered by WIPO, whose primary objective is 'to simplify and to render more effective and more economical – in the interests of the users of the patent system and the Offices which have the responsibility for administering it – the previously established means of applying in several countries for protection of inventions'.[150] The PCT uniforms the patent prosecution rules of international applications, which later on, can be entered into national phases in the countries of interest of the applicant, which could lead to patent protection in several States but with only one application.

97. Apart from these regulations, there are more national and international provisions that are relevant in terms of patents. For instance, the Criminal Code establishes sanctions for infringements of intellectual property rights. However, we consider that at this stage further explanation is not needed. These provisions will be addressed throughout this chapter as the need arises.

144. *See* Official Website of WIPO, 'What is WIPO?', in <wipo.int/about-wipo/en/what_is_wipo.html> (last visited 15 Jun. 2007).
145. Colombia approved the Marrakech Agreement establishing the WTO by means of Law 170 of 1994 and deposited the instrument of ratification in 31 Mar. 1995.
146. *See* Ch. 1.
147. Until the entry into force of this Decision, domestic legislation was applicable to patents. After Decision 85 entered into force, domestic legislation was suspended in application of the principle of immediate application of communitarian legislation. For further information, *see* the introductory chapter.
148. *See* Decree No. 575 of 1992 on the regulation of this Decision.
149. *See* Decree No. 117 of 1994 on the regulation of this Decision.
150. *See* Franklin Pierce Law Centre in Cooperation with the World Intellectual Property Organization (WIPO), Ninth Comprehensive PCT Seminar, Concord, New Hampshire, 27–28 Apr. 2007, 2.

§2. Patentable Subject Matter

98. Pursuant to Decision 486, Colombia will grant a patent to any invention of a product or a process, in all fields of technology, if they are new, involve an inventive step and are liable to industrial application.[151] According to Article 27 of the TRIPS Agreement, national authorities shall grant patents regardless of the field of technology and whether products are imported or locally produced. This express prohibition of discrimination is absolute when the invention in question is susceptible of being protected by means of a patent. The latter means that, in order for a product or a process to be subject matter of patent protection, it must be considered as an invention as will be explained in this section.

99. An invention, for the purpose of becoming the object of a patent, 'includes all new products or procedures that, as a consequence of the creative activity of human beings, imply a technological advance – and therefore are not derived from the "state of technique" in an obvious manner – and that can be used or produced in any type of industry'.[152] In other words, inventions refer to products or procedures as long as they provide a useful result, solving a problem that the available technique could not resolve before. In that sense, inventions of products are conformed by a determinate good destined to fulfil an industrial necessity; and inventions of procedures are conformed by a series of operations that affect matter (solid, liquid or gas) directed to obtaining a determinate thing or result.[153]

§3. Conditions of Patentability

100. Article 14 of the Decision provides that, in order for an invention to be patentable, it has to be novel, involve an inventive step and be industrially applicable, and not be excluded from patentability. In this section we will thoroughly explain each one of these requirements.

I. Novelty

101. Article 16 of the Decision establishes that 'an invention may be deemed new when not included in the state of the art. The state of the art comprises everything that has been made available to the public by written or oral description, use, marketing, or any other means prior to the filing date of the patent or, when appropriate, of the

151. *See* Art. 14 of the Decision. *See also* Superintendence of Industry and Commerce, Concept No. 02038289, 26 Jun. 2002.
152. *See* Andean Court of Justice, Proceeding No. 21-IP-2000 of 21 Oct. 2000, published in *Gaceta Oficial del Acuerdo de Cartagena*, No. 631 of 10 Jan. 2001.
153. *See* Andean Court of Justice, Proceeding No. 43-IP-2002 of 16 Oct. 2002, published in *Gaceta Oficial del Acuerdo de Cartagena*, No. 870 of 9 Dec. 2002.

priority claimed'.[154] According to said provision, the state of the art will also comprise the contents of a previous pending application before the Superintendence, when the filing date of such application, or the claiming of its priority, is prior to the filing date of the application under study and the contents of the previous application were published. In the wording of the Andean Court of Justice (Andean Court), something novel is something that is not comprised in the state of the art (qualified disclosure) or that has not been disclosed or made available to the public in any place (simple disclosure and absolute novelty). Furthermore, novelty has an objective character that is not determined by the specific characteristics of the inventor or the applicant; it is determined by the objective conditions of state of the art in a specific time. Also, the novelty of an invention has a universal character; it is determined by the existing knowledge in and outside the country. Therefore, patent protection cannot be granted to a product or process that is unknown within a country but known elsewhere. The reason is that once the information is disclosed, it irreversibly loses its novelty,[155] affecting all future applications.

102. The disclosure mentioned in the preceding paragraph can be done in an oral or written manner, can result from the use or exploitation, or result from any other means. Said disclosure has to provide detail and, in any case, be sufficient so that a professional in the area can use such information to execute or exploit the invention.[156] However, not every disclosure affects the novelty of an invention; Article 17 of the Decision mentions situations in which the subject to be patented can be revealed to the public in the year before the filing date of the application or during the year before the date of priority, if claimed, and not affect the novelty. Said disclosure must be attributable to:

(1) the inventor or the inventor's assignee: any of these persons could be interested in marketing the product or process immediately, instead of waiting to do so after the patent is granted. This could be done to determine the market's reaction to the invention and to recover some of the research and development invested. Therefore, since the information that would become part of the state of the art comes from the inventor himself/herself or the assignee, it should not be an obstacle to patent protection, as long as this disclosure is done in the year prior to the filing of the application;

---

154. The right of priority is recognized in Art. 9 of the Decision in the following way: 'The first application for an invention or utility model patent or for the registration of register an industrial design or a trademark that is validly filed in another Member Country or with a national, regional, or international authority to which the Member Country is linked by a treaty establishing an analogous right of priority to that established in this Decision, shall confer on the applicant or the applicant's assignee the right of priority in filing for a patent or registration on the same subject-matter in the Member Country … In order to qualify for that right, an application claiming priority shall be filed within the following non extendible periods to be counted as from the filing date of the application whose priority is claimed: a) twelve months for patents on inventions and utility models.'

155. *See* Andean Court of Justice, Proceeding No. 07-IP-2004 of 17 Mar. 2004, published in *Gaceta Oficial del Acuerdo de Cartagena*, No. 1057 of 21 Apr. 2004.

156. *See* Andean Court of Justice, Proceeding No. 6-IP-89 of 6 Nov. 1989, published in *Gaceta Oficial del Acuerdo de Cartagena*, No. 50 of 17 Nov. 1989.

(2) a competent national office that publishes the contents of a patent application filed by the inventor or the inventor's assignee in contravention to the applicable provision: in this case, the inventor did not authorize the disclosure so he/she should not suffer the consequences of the revelation of information;
(3) a third party who obtained the information directly or indirectly from the inventor or the inventor's assignee:[157] The reasoning is the same as that explained in the preceding paragraph.

103. According to the Andean Court, in order to establish whether an invention is new or not, the examiner must undergo four steps. First, he/she must determine the applicable technical rule to the patent application, which will be determined by the extent of the claims. Second, specify the date according to which the invention has to be compared against the state of the art. This date can be the filing date of the application or the recognized priority. Third, determine the contents of the state of the art (precedents) on the date of the priority, which is the nearest field that intends to solve the same problem as the invention in question. According to the Superintendence, the state of the art comprises the set of information that, to the filing date of the patent application or of the claimed priority, had been accessible to the public by any means. For public it shall be understood the people or group of persons that are not obliged to maintain the confidential information in the sphere of the invention that is subject of examination.[158]

The Superintendence (Patent Office) has to perform a search 'using all the available resources (patent documentary funds, patent offices databases on the Internet or in CD-ROM collections, specialized magazines, scientific publications, and bibliographical in general) to find patent or non-patent documents that are related with the object of the invention that is being claimed'.[159] Finally, the invention has to be compared to the technical rule.[160] In order to do so, the examiner shall perform a novelty test comparing the elements of the invention with the ones present in the state of the art. It is important to clarify that the examiner cannot compare the invention against every document present in the state of the art; the examiner's task will be to compare the invention with only one document of the state of the art and verify if all the elements of the invention are present in said document. The invention will be novel if all of the elements examined together are not present in the document.[161] If the elements in the claim were not new, the examiner shall file a written report giving due account of where that element can be found within the state of the art.

---

157. In this case, the Decision does not mention how such information was acquired. In consequence, the methods used for obtaining the information can be very different.
158. *See* Superintendence of Industry and Commerce, Legal Opinion (*Concepto*) 03005202, 28 Feb. 2003.
159. *See* International Bureau of WIPO, *Manual for the Examination of Invention Patent Applications in the Industrial Property Offices in the Andean Community Countries* (Secretariat-General of the Andean Community, WIPO, European Patent Office, Quito-Ecuador, 2004), 53.
160. *See* Andean Court of Justice, Proceeding No. 105-IP-2000 of 21 Mar. 2001, published in *Gaceta Oficial del Acuerdo de Cartagena*, No. 660 of 10 Apr. 2001.
161. *See* Andean Court of Justice, Proceeding No. 43-IP-2000 of 16 Oct. 2002, published in *Gaceta Oficial del Acuerdo de Cartagena*, No. 870 of 9 Dec. 2002.

II. Inventive Step

104. The second requirement for an invention to be patented is the need for it to involve an inventive step. In conformity with Article 18 of the Decision, 'an invention shall be regarded as involving an inventive step if, for a person with average skills in the technical field concerned, the invention is neither obvious nor evidently derived from the state of the art'. To verify this requirement, the examiner must determine if, with the knowledge available in the state of the art (this time the examiner can compare the invention against two documents), the invention would have been obvious. Therefore, the invention must involve a qualitative jump in the elaboration of the technical rule and be the result of a creative activity performed by the inventor.[162]

105. The examiner has to complete three steps to evaluate the inventive step of an invention, which is also known as the problem-solution method. According to said method, the examiner must first identify the nearest state of the art; second, identify the technical characteristics of the invention that are different from pre-existing knowledge; and finally, determine the technical problem to be solved on the basis of the nearest state of the art.[163] The state of the art does not necessarily have to be the one known by the applicant. It will depend on the search performed by the Superintendence. Also, the technical problem will not always be the one thought by the applicant; it will be the result of the definition of the state of the art.

III. Industrial Application

106. After verifying if an invention is new and involves an inventive step, in order for it to be patentable, it should be susceptible of industrial application. According to Article 19 of the Decision, 'an invention shall be regarded as industrially applicable when its subject matter may be produced or used in any type of industry, industry being understood as that involving any productive activity, including services'. The Andean Court of Justice has explained that this requirement means the 'possibility of an invention to be used, that is to say, that it is materially feasible in a practical situation. The means proposed by the inventor should be capable of providing, with more or less perfection, the intended industrial result'.[164] The rationale behind this requirement is that a product or process that cannot be industrially applicable to any type of industry will never be more than a creation with aesthetical or scientific value, which would not tantamount to patent protection.[165] Therefore, the industrial application of an

162. *See* International Bureau of WIPO, *Manual for the Examination of Invention Patent Applications in the Industrial Property Offices in the Andean Community Countries* (Secretariat-General of the Andean Community, WIPO, European Patent Office, Quito-Ecuador, 2004), 53.
163. *See* International Bureau of WIPO, *Manual for the Examination of Invention Patent Applications in the Industrial Property Offices in the Andean Community Countries* (Secretariat-General of the Andean Community, WIPO, European Patent Office, Quito-Ecuador, 2004), 77.
164. *See* Andean Court of Justice, Proceeding No. 26-IP-99 of 23 Jul. 1999, published in *Gaceta Oficial del Acuerdo de Cartagena*, No. 475 of 1 Sep. 1999.
165. *See* Andean Court of Justice, Proceeding No. 43-IP-2000 of 16 Oct. 2002, published in *Gaceta Oficial del Acuerdo de Cartagena*, No. 870 of 9 Dec. 2002.

invention will be verified when 'the technical effect induces to the obtaining of an industrial result or product, understanding by industry the activity that seeks, by means of a conscious act of men, to make the natural forces useful for the satisfaction of human needs'.[166] Moreover, this requirement also implies that the invention is useful.[167]

107. In Resolution 26260 of 6 October 2006,[168] the Superintendence denied patent protection to a process used to predict the quantitative values of the properties of a rock or fluid in a subterranean oil deposit through the integrated use of seismic data and geological models, among other things. According to the Superintendence, the objectives of the application were related to methods to predict quantitative values through the use of other data, which implied the use of mere intellectual and abstract processes. The object of the application was related only to the management of data and values, and therefore did not tantamount to patent protection because it lacked industrial applicability. According to the Superintendence, the scientific management of information, although useful, does not have industrial applicability by itself; in order for that to happen, the information must undergo some sort of physical or chemical transformation.

IV. Not Be Excluded from Patentability

108. The Decision allows members to exclude certain products or procedures from patentability because they are not considered as inventions. The underlying reason is that these products or procedures cannot be industrially applicable. In that sense, Article 15 of the Decision provides that the following items are not considered as an invention:

A. Discoveries, Scientific Theories, and Mathematical Methods

109. A 'discovery is a revelation of something already existent but previously unknown to men'.[169] Thus, something that already exists cannot be considered as an

166. *Ibid.*

167. In Resolution 07167 of 28 Feb. 2002, the Superintendence denied patent protection to a machine that was not useful because, despite the fact that it could be produced by the metal-mechanic industry, it could not work under certain circumstances specified by the applicant. This is similar to what happens under patent law in the United States and Australia, where the usefulness of the invention is another patentability requirement. However, under these legislations this requirement is different from the one referred to the industrial application of the invention in such a way that an invention that patent protection could be granted to useful creations, but that are not necessarily industrially applicable. On the contrary, where the criterion of the industrial application is adopted (as in the Andean Community, the European Union or Japan), these creations would not be protected. For further details *see* generally M. Escobar and J.D. Martínez, *Análisis de las diferencias existentes entre la utilidad y la aplicación industrial como requisito de patentabilidad*, Pontificia Universidad Javeriana, (Bogotá) 2006, 69.

168. *See* Superintendence of Industry and Commerce, Resolution No. 26260 of 6 Oct. 2006.

169. *See* International Bureau of WIPO, *Manual for the Examination of Invention Patent Applications in the Industrial Property Offices in the Andean Community Countries* (Secretariat-General of the Andean Community, WIPO, European Patent Office, Quito-Ecuador, 2004), 45.

invention. The inventor's work shall undergo an intellectual process by means of which something is created to solve a technical problem.[170] For example, neither the isolated organic matter for closer study, nor the material or phenomenon already in nature is an invention. However, the process carried out to isolate organic material or to recognize the existence of a material in nature could be considered as an invention and could be subject matter of patent protection if it complies with the patentability requirements.

110. This reasoning is also valid for scientific theories and mathematical methods, which are not inventions because they are abstract concepts where no technical contribution can be given.[171] According to the Superintendence, a mathematical method takes measurable abstract data, tries to rationalize the achieved results and intends to find a perfect pattern that can be useful to understand nature; in general, a mathematical method tries to explain the world.[172] However, such theories and methods can be used as part of a process or production of a product that solves a technical need. In that case, they might receive patent protection.

B. Any Living Thing, Either Complete or Partial, as Found in Nature, Natural Biological Processes, and Biological Material, as Existing in Nature, or Able to Be Separated, Including the Genome or Germ Plasma of Any Living Thing

111. This prohibition results from the fact that living things can neither be considered as inventions and nor can biological processes that happen spontaneously in nature where human intervention does not alter the final result.[173]The simple isolation of a biological material cannot be considered as an invention. The Andean Court has established that any isolation of matter previously existent in nature, even if it possesses microbiological character, does not qualify as an invention.[174] The Court has also referred to the genome or germ plasma of a living thing and stated that 'the proteins that integrate the human being, the genes or the DNA sequences are not susceptible of patent protection'.[175]

Along the same line, the Andean Tribunal established that, in order to decide if an invention is against public order, a morality test is required, as reasons of an eminently ethical nature prevent the human body and even its minimum components, such as genes, from being the object of exclusive appropriation for profit and industrial purposes. Therefore, when interpreting and applying to a specific case the prohibition on the patenting of matters which make up the human body and its genetic identity,

170. The WIPO manual provides an illustrative example of a previously known element that was given a new application that was patentable. This is the case of diamonds, which cannot be patentable by themselves. However, the diamond-point scalpel was a revolutionary device in medicine that was in fact patented. *Ibid.*, 46.
171. *See* International Bureau of WIPO, *Manual for the Examination of Invention Patent Applications in the Industrial Property Offices in the Andean Community Countries* (Secretariat-General of the Andean Community, WIPO, European Patent Office, Quito-Ecuador, 2004), 46.
172. *See* Superintendence of Industry and Commerce, Resolution No. 26260 of 6 Oct. 2006.
173. *See* Superintendence of Industry and Commerce, Resolution No. 26260 of 6 Oct. 2006.
174. *Ibid.*
175. *Ibid.*

the judge or the competent national office must take into account, primarily, the moral, ethical, and public order implications that may arise.

Included within the prohibition on patenting elements that form part of the human body and its genetic identity, are: the genome or germ plasm, genetic modification procedures, as well as other techniques that may be contrary to the dignity of the person or public order, such as cloning, the manipulation of human embryos or creation of individualized human beings in the laboratory.[176]

C. Literary and Artistic Works or Any Other Aesthetic Creation Protected by Copyright

112. These creations cannot be protected by a patent because they do not fulfil the patentability requirements. The aim of these creations is to interact with people's intellects and not to solve a technical need, reason why they are protected by copyright law. Nonetheless, an invention can have aesthetic value;[177] it could be patented if it constitutes a new creation and if the patentability requirements are complied with.

D. Plans, Rules, and Methods for the Pursuit of Intellectual Activities, Playing of Games, or Economic and Business Activities

113. The items mentioned in this article are not patentable since they are intellectual creations of abstract character.[178] Examples of this can be methods to solve a crossword puzzle, the rules of a game or the plans to organize a commercial operation.[179]

E. Computer Programs and Software

114. Computer programs and software cannot be considered as an invention since they do not have technical character. They are the instructions a machine needs to accomplish a result.[180] They are protected by means of copyright legislation[181] because they do not have a technical character. However, according to the inventor's manual of the Superintendence, software acquires said technical character when it is

176. *See* Andean Court of Justice, Proceeding No. 21-IP-00 of 27 Oct. 2000, published in *Gaceta Oficial del Acuerdo de Cartagena,* No. 631 of 10 Jan. 2001.

177. It is important to differentiate aesthetically appealing inventions from works of applied art. The first ones are creations that satisfy an industrial necessity and are protected by means of the patent legislation. The second ones are artistic creations incorporated to an article. Their aesthetic value can be separated from the article itself and therefore are protected by copyright law as a work of art. For further information, refer to Ch. 2.

178. *See* International Bureau of WIPO, *Manual for the Examination of Invention Patent Applications in the Industrial Property Offices in the Andean Community Countries* (Secretariat-General of the Andean Community, WIPO, European Patent Office, Quito-Ecuador, 2004), 47.

179. *Ibid.*

180. *See* International Bureau of WIPO, *Manual for the Examination of Invention Patent Applications in the Industrial Property Offices in the Andean Community Countries* (Secretariat-General of the Andean Community, WIPO, European Patent Office, Quito-Ecuador, 2004), 47.

181. *See* Ch. 2 for further information regarding the protection awarded to software and the discussion as to the most appropriate form of protection.

a part of an industrial process, or that a product requires it to accomplish its functions;[182] therefore, it could be protected by means of a patent.

Accordingly, the Superintendence has followed the software patentability criteria established by the European Patent Office, and grants patent protection to inventions related to software based on the type of technical evidence provided by claims submitted:[183]

> Inventions involving programs for computers can be protected in different forms of a 'computer-implemented invention', an expression intended to cover claims which involve computers, computer networks or other programmable apparatus whereby at least one feature is realised by means of a program. Claims directed to computer-implemented inventions may take the forms described in F-IV, 3.9 and sub-sections.

In light of the above since 2011, the Colombian Patent Office has granted several patents protecting different forms of 'computer implemented inventions'[184] following the guidelines for the Examination of Patent in the European Patent Office and in 2012 issued its own guidelines for the examination of Invention Patent and Utility Models, which state that in order to decide whether or not an invention can get patent protection as a 'computer-implemented invention' the examiner must identify that the claim meets the following criteria:

(a) The claim is about a product or about a procedure,
(b) The invention is or not excluded from patentability.
(c) The invention has a real practical application.[185]

F. Methods for Presenting Information

115. The patentability exclusion applies if the claim is directed to the presentation per se of the information (e.g., an acoustic signal, an oral or written speech, a visual display), to the stored information in a media (e.g., a book characterized by its contents, a recording tape characterized by the musical piece recorded, a compact disc characterized by the data or program recorded), or a process or device for the presentation of the information (e.g., a recorder characterized only by the information recorded, a computer characterized by the data stored).[186]

---

182. *See* Superintendence of Industry and Commerce, *Inventor's Manual*, (Bogotá) 2007, 16.
183. *See* European Patent Office, guidelines for the Examination of Patents, 2017.
184. *See* Salas Pasuy Brenda, Software o programa de ordenador y el concepto de invención patentable, Universidad Externado de Colombia, Bogotá, 2017, 431.
185. *See* Superintendence of Industry and Commerce, guidelines for the Examination of Patents and Utility models, (Bogotá), 2012, 233.
186. *See* Andean Court of Justice, Proceeding No. 43-IP-2002 of 16 Oct. 2002, published in *Gaceta Oficial del Acuerdo de Cartagena*, No. 870 of 9 Dec. 2002.

116. After this explanation on what is not considered an invention as such by the Andean legislation, we now turn to the products and processes that, despite being inventions, are not subject matter to patent protection. In this sense, Article 20 of the Decision provides that the following shall not be patentable:

1. Inventions Whose Prevention of Commercial Exploitation Within the Territory of the Respective Member Country Is Necessary to Protect Public Order or Morality, Provided That Such Exclusion Is Not Merely Because the Exploitation Is Prohibited or Regulated by Legal or Administrative Provision

117. The notion of public order or morality is not defined in the Decision or in the TRIPS Agreement. Therefore, recourse may be made to other sources, such as the decisions of the WTO's Dispute Settlement Body, which addressed this issue in the US-Gambling case. In its report, the panel defined public morals as a notion that 'denotes standards of right and wrong conduct maintained by or on behalf of a community or nation'.[187] The panel further found that the definition of the term public order 'refers to the preservation of the fundamental interests of a society, as reflected in public policy and law'.[188] Applying this definition to the Colombian case, it can be stated that a patent that goes against the values and social principles established in the Constitution[189] shall not be subject to patent protection. In this sense, the Superintendence denied patent protection over a gun because it considered it to be a menace to constitutional principles and values.

2. Inventions Whose Commercial Exploitation Within the Respective Member Country Is Necessary to Be Prevented to Protect Human or Animal Life or Health or to Avoid Serious Prejudice to the Environment, Provided That Such Exclusion Is Not Merely Because the Exploitation Is Prohibited or Regulated by Legal or Administrative Provision

118. Protection for inventions that constitute a menace to human or animal health within a Member Country will be prohibited at all times. For this purpose, the Superintendence established a list of examples of the type of biotechnological inventions

187. *See* WTO Dispute Settlement Body, United States – Measures Affecting the Cross-Border Supply of Gambling and Betting Services, Panel Report, para. 6.465. It is important to clarify that in this case, the panel examined claims under the General Agreement on Trade and Services (GATS), whose principles are different to those established under TRIPS. Nevertheless, reference to this case is useful as the terms public order and public morals are invariable regardless of the area of trade in question.

188. *Ibid.*, para. 6.467.

189. Article 1 of the constitution establishes that the Colombian State is based on the respect of human dignity, in the solidarity of the people that integrate it and on the prevalence of public interest.

that examiners must consider excluded from patentability:[190] procedures to clone human beings; procedures to modify the genetic identity of humans; use of human embryos for industrial or commercial purposes; and procedures to modify the genetic identity of animals that may cause them suffering without a substantial medical benefit for mankind or for the animal. The human body, in different stages of development, and every simple discovery of its elements, including the genetic sequence, may not constitute patentable inventions.

Also, if the invention is a potential environmental hazard, it shall not be susceptible to patent protection even if it is an idea that could solve a technical problem.

3. Plants, Animals, and Essentially Biological Processes for the Production of Plants or Animals Other that Non-biological or Microbiological Processes

119. According to the Andean Court, plant varieties and species and animal breeds are not patentable, for example in the case of transgenic animal and plants.[191] However, 'the non-biological or microbiological procedure for their obtaining could be patentable (when they are not the mere result of isolation activities). Also, the biological material object of a transformation could be subject matter of a patent if it does not constitute a plant or an animal'.[192] The latter because such procedures involve a technical stage that alters the final result and makes the new being different from the others already existing in nature. Accordingly, the non-biological procedures that imply genetic modifications can be patented, as long as they comply with the patentability requirements.[193]

4. Diagnostic, Therapeutic, and Surgical Methods for the Treatment of Humans or Animals

120. Diagnostic, therapeutic, and surgical methods for the treatment of humans or animals are generally not patentable as they are not susceptible of industrial application. However, this is not applicable to the instruments used for diagnostic procedures or certain methods used to gather information that do not have the capability of curing a disease. Such procedures shall be able to be operated by a technician who does not decide the course of the patient's treatment or gives any assertion as to the extent of the disease or the existence of it.[194] Examples of this could be radiology methods.

---

190. *See* Superintendence of Industry and Commerce, guidelines for the Examination of Patents and Utility models, (Bogotá), 2012, 64.

191. *See* International Bureau of WIPO, *Manual for the Examination of Invention Patent Applications in the Industrial Property Offices in the Andean Community Countries* (Secretariat-General of the Andean Community, WIPO, European Patent Office, Quito-Ecuador, 2004), 48. *See also* Ch. 7.

192. *Ibid.*

193. *See* Superintendence of Industry and Commerce, Legal Opinion (*Concepto*) No. 03093878 of 30 Dec. 2003.

194. *See* European Patent Office, T 385/86 (OJ EPO 8/1988. 308).

As to therapeutic methods, these not only include those used for curing diseases, but also preventive treatments. A difference shall be made with cosmetic methods that, according to the Andean Court, are patentable since they are intended to produce only aesthetic effects[195] and if the cosmetic effect can be distinguishable from the outside.[196] However, the Superintendence does not accept this opinion and does not grant patent protection for cosmetic procedures either.

In regards to prosthetic elements that are built using the body's dimensions, they are not excluded from patentability given that the process of fabrication is performed outside the body. With respect to methods performed on animals, some of them would not be excluded from patentability when they are used for agricultural purposes. For example, a method to increase fertility or weight in animals could be subject of a patent. However, since many of these processes (i.e., the increased weight in the animal) could also be observed under any health condition in the animal, it is important that the claim explicitly states that the method is non-therapeutic.

121. It is now important to address a significant issue within the Decision: the patentability of uses and second uses. As to the first issue, the TRIPS Agreement remains silent in the matter. The Decision, however, explicitly states that patents will only be granted to products and processes, excluding the possibility of patenting uses.[197] According to the Andean Court, it cannot be construed from the text of Article 1 of the 344 Decision (Members shall grant patents or the product or process inventions)[198] that members have the possibility to patent other class or nature of creations different from inventions, like for example uses or, particularly, second uses.[199] As to the second point, 'products and processes already patented and included in the state of the art within the meaning of Article 16 of the Decision may not be the subject of new patents on the sole ground of having been put to a use different from that originally contemplated by the initial patent'.[200] The debate over the patentability of second uses has been more active in the pharmaceutical sector given that in the development of new products, many previously known substances can be mixed, achieving different results from the one originally intended. A clear example of this is the Viagra case, a medicine that sought

195. *See* Andean Court of Justice, proceeding 11-IP-1995 of 7 Apr. 1998, published in *Gaceta Oficial del Acuerdo de Cartagena*, No. 349 of 19 Jun. 1998.

196. *See* European Patent Office, T 290/86 (OJ 1992. 412).

197. This was the opinion of the Superintendence in the Viagra case where it stated that, in the event that the intention of the law is not clear, recourse should be made to the grammatical criterion of interpretation. Therefore, as the Decision only grants patent protection to invention of products or processes, without mentioning uses, it should be understood that they are excluded from patentability. *See* Superintendence of Industry and Commerce, Resolution 112 of 13 Feb. 2000.

198. Even though this interpretation was issued under the validity of Decision 344, it is totally applicable to the actual regime enacted by Decision 486.

199. *See* Andean Court of Justice, Proceeding 89-AI-2000 of 11 Sep. 2002, published in *Gaceta Oficial del Acuerdo de Cartagena*, No. 838 of 22 Sep. 2002.

200. *See* Art. 21 of the Decision. This issue was addressed in the negotiations of the PTA between Colombia and the United States but nothing was agreed. Colombia did not accept the United State's proposal of extending patent protection to second uses. *See* L.A. Madrid, *La salud pública y la discusión de propiedad intelectual en el TLC Colombia-Estados Unidos*, Centro de Documentación TLC Colombia, Sergio Arboleda University, in <usergioarboleda.edu.co/tlc/tlc_salud.htm> (last visited 3 Oct. 2007).

to treat heart diseases but as time went by, a new use was discovered to combat erectile dysfunction. In the Superintendence's opinion, this use could not be patented, therefore assimilating it to a process; a process is a sequence of stages performed to achieve a final product while the use is an inherent quality of the product.[201]

§4. Formalities

122. If the applicant considers that the invention is novel, involves an inventive step and can be industrially applicable, he/she could apply for a patent. In order to do so, the application must comply with certain formal and substantial requirements. In this section we will explain the formalities regarding the process set forth in the Decision. Details will be provided as to contents of the application and the steps of the process for each one, as well as for the administrative actions an applicant has to contest a resolution from the Superintendence. In this point it is also important to mention the PCT procedure as it allows applicants that have filed an international application to enter into national phase before the Superintendence and obtain patent protection in Colombia.

Through this procedure applicants can start the international phase before the Superintendence, as it was appointed as a receiving office with the USPTO since 2012, with the Spanish Patent and Trademark Office in 2013 and with the Japanese Patent Office since 2014. The most recent the implementation of the PCT was in 2016 with South Korea, Prosur,[202] and the Pacific Alliance.

I. PCT Procedure

123. As stated in Section 1, the PCT is an agreement that allows an applicant to file for protection for inventions in the contracting States designated in an international patent application that is previously filed in the offices authorized for this purpose. This agreement is currently applied in more than 100 countries and in Colombia it has been in force since 28 February 2001. It must be clarified, however, that the PCT does not constitute a means of granting international patents; patent protection will be granted individually by each country in which the process is carried out, but many processes in different countries can start with the filing of only one international application.[203] The procedure set forth in this treaty is divided into two phases: the international and the national phase. Up next we will explain each of these phases.

124. As for the international phase, it begins when the applicant files the international application. Article 3 of the PCT establishes that said applications must

201. *See* Superintendence of Industry and Commerce, Resolution 112 of 13 Feb. 2000.
202. PROSUR is an agreement between Argentina, Brazil, Chile, Colombia, Ecuador, Paraguay, Peru, Suriname, and Uruguay that aims to facilitate and optimize processes-related intellectual property and entrepreneurship in the region.
203. *See* Superintendence of Industry and Commerce, Legal Opinion (*Concepto*) No. 0108164 of 16 Nov. 2001.

contain a request, a description,[204] one or more claims,[205] one or more drawings (when required),[206] and an abstract, which will only serve the purpose of providing technical information.

Pursuant to Article 4 of the PCT, the request in the application must contain the following elements:

(1) a petition to the effect that the international application be processed according to the PCT;
(2) the designation of the Contracting State or states in which protection for the invention is desired on the basis of the international application ('designated States');
(3) the title of the invention;
(4) the name of and other prescribed data concerning the applicant and the agent (if any); and
(5) the name of and other prescribed data concerning the inventor where the national law of at least one of the designated States requires that these indications be furnished at the time of filing a national application.

125. The applicant must furnish three copies of the application, one of which will remain at the receiving office, another one will be transmitted to WIPO's International Bureau in Geneva, and the last one will be transmitted to the competent administration to perform the international search.[207] After all of the copies are received, the receiving office shall accord as the international filing date the date in which it received the application,[208] provided that the following is complied with:[209]

(1) The applicant does not lack, for reasons of residence or nationality, the right to file an international application with the receiving office.
(2) The international application is in Spanish.
(3) The international application contains at least the following elements:

    (a) an indication that it is intended as an international application;
    (b) the designation of at least one Contracting State;
    (c) the name of the applicant, as prescribed;

204. According to Art. 5 of the PCT, 'the description shall disclose the invention in a manner sufficiently clear and complete for the invention to be carried out by a person skilled in the art'.
205. According to Art. 6 of the PCT, 'the claim or claims shall define the matter for which protection is sought. Claims shall be clear and concise. They shall be fully supported by the description'.
206. According to Art. 7 of the PCT, 'drawings shall be required when they are necessary for the understanding of the invention'. When the drawings are not necessary to understand the invention, the applicant has the option to include them or not. In the same sense, the designated office has the faculty to ask the applicant to submit said drawings.
207. *See* Art. 12 of the PCT. For further information *See* Superintendence of Industry and Commerce, Unique Circular, Chapter 5: Instructions on the Application of the Patent Cooperation Treaty (PCT), modified by Circular No. 003 of 28 Apr. 2003.
208. According to Art. 11.3 of the PCT, this date will be considered the filing date in each designated State.
209. *See* Art. 11.1 of the PCT.

(d) a part which on the face of it appears to be a description;
(e) a part which on the face of it appears to be a claim or claims.

126. If the application does not fulfil the preceding requirements, the receiving office will ask the applicant to correct the application within the next month of said request. If the application is not completed, it will be considered withdrawn. It will also verify if the application does not contain the defects laid down in Article 14 of the PCT. These defects are that the application: (1) is not signed as provided in the regulations; (2) does not contain the prescribed indications concerning the applicant; (3) does not contain a title; (4) does not contain an abstract; or (5) does not comply to the extent provided in the regulations with the prescribed physical requirements. If the application contains one of the aforementioned defects, the Superintendence will request the applicant to correct them within the next month, which can be extended for a reasonable period of time at the request of the applicant. The failure to correct the defects will result in the withdrawal of the international application, which will be notified to the International Bureau.[210]

127. After the application is accorded a filing date, it will undergo a process of international search to verify the existence of priorities that could affect the patentability of the invention. As per Article 15 of the PCT, the purpose of the international search is to discover the relevant prior art, taking the claims as the starting point. The chosen authority will have nine months to perform the search, at the end of which it must issue a report. After receiving the report, the applicant will have the opportunity to amend the claims of the application by filling the amendments before the International Bureau. As per Article 19.2 of the PCT, such amendments 'shall not go beyond the disclosure in the international application as filed'. Subsequently, the application must be published within a term of eighteen months from the priority date of the application. This step will be omitted if the applicant chooses to withdraw the application, or if it is considered withdrawn before the technical preparations for its publication are completed.[211]

128. To continue with the procedure, the applicant must request that the application is submitted for the international preliminary examination. Pursuant to Article 31.3 of the PCT, the demand for the examination must be done separately from the international application and it must indicate the State or States in which the applicant intends to use the results of the examination ('elected states'). Furthermore, the receiving office has to designate an Examining Authority to perform the exam.[212] At this point, the applicant could modify any element of the application. According to Article 33.1 of the PCT, 'the objective of the international preliminary examination is to formulate a

210. *See* Superintendence of Industry and Commerce, Unique Circular–Chapter 5: Instructions on the Application of the Patent Cooperation Treaty (PCT), modified by Circular No. 003 of 28 Apr. 2003.

211. *See* Art. 21.5 of the PCT.

212. By Resolution 007 of 14 Dec. 2009, the Superintendence of Industry and Commerce formalized the possibility of this entity to act as a receiving office for PCT applications. Before, if applicants wanted to enter into national phase in Colombia, the international preliminary examination would have to be lodged through the European Patent Office, the Austrian Patent Office, or the Russian Patent and Trademark Agency.

preliminary and non-binding opinion on the questions whether the claimed invention appears to be novel, to involve an inventive step (to be non-obvious), and to be industrially applicable'. Before the Examining Authority issues the preliminary examination, the applicant may amend the claims, the description and the drawings. In any case, the amendments cannot go beyond the disclosure in the international application as it was filed. As per Article 35.2, the report of the preliminary examination will not contain any declarations as to the patentability of the invention according to any national law; the report will declare, in regards to each claim, whether it satisfies the criteria of novelty,[213] inventive step,[214] and industrial applicability.[215]

129. In accordance with Article 22 of the PCT, if the applicant decides to continue with the process and enter into the national phase, he/she shall submit copies for each one of the designated offices within a term of thirty months from the priority date. However, if Colombia is one of the designated States, the applicant will have thirty-one months[216] as from the date of the priority to submit the copies. This period was unilaterally established by Colombia in agreement to what is established in Article 22.3, according to which any national may fix time limits that expire later than the time limit of thirty months.

To enter into the national phase to obtain patent protection in Colombia, the applicant must file an application before the Superintendence before the expiration of the thirty-one-month period mentioned in the preceding paragraph. The applicant will have to pay the filing fees established by the Superintendence, but does not need to claim priority if it was already recognized in the international application. Failure to comply with these to requirements will cause the application to be withdrawn.

130. Once the Superintendence receives the documents, it will accord the application a filing date, in the same way it does with national applications. Subsequently, the Division of New Creations of the Superintendence will verify if the application contains all the requirements established in Articles 26 and 27 of the Decision.[217] Then, the Division of New Creations continues the procedure in the same way as it would if the application was filed under the procedure provided for in the Decision.

---

213. According to Art. 33.2 of the PCT 'for the purposes of the international preliminary examination, a claimed invention shall be considered novel if it is not anticipated by the prior art as defined in the Regulations'.

214. According to Art. 33.3 of the PCT, 'for the purposes of the international preliminary examination, a claimed invention shall be considered to involve an inventive step if, having regard to the prior art as defined in the regulations, it is not, at the prescribed relevant date, obvious to a person skilled in the art'.

215. According to Art. 33.4 of the PCT, 'for the purposes of the international preliminary examination, a claimed invention shall be considered industrially applicable if, according to its nature, it can be made or used (in the technological sense) in any kind of industry. "Industry" shall be understood in its broadest sense, as in the Paris Convention for the Protection of Industrial Property'.

216. *See* Superintendence of Industry and Commerce, Unique Circular–Chapter 5: Instructions on the Application of the Patent Cooperation Treaty (PCT), modified by Circular No. 003 of 28 Apr. 2003.

217. *See* Superintendence of Industry and Commerce, Unique Circular–Chapter 5: Instructions on the Application of the Patent Cooperation Treaty (PCT), modified by Circular No. 003 of 28 Apr. 2003. *See infra* for an explanation of Arts 26 and 27 of the Decision.

II. Procedure under the Decision

131. If the applicant wishes to obtain patent protection in the Colombian territory, he/she shall file an application following the requirements set forth in the Decision. Accordingly, the application should contain the following requirements:

(1) The application brief:
As per Article 27 of the Decision, the application brief has to be contained in a form elaborated by the Superintendence and it shall include: (a) the application for the grant of the patent, meaning that the applicant must specify that he/she is applying for an invention patent; (b) the name and the address of the applicant; (c) the nationality or domicile of the applicant. When the latter is a legal person, the place of incorporation shall be stated; (d) the name of the invention. According to Article 6 of the Regulatory Decree 2591 of 2000, the name of the invention shall reflect the object and industrial field to which the invention is related to and be in conformity with the claims and description. It cannot be a personal name, the trademark of a product or a fantasy name; (e) the name and domicile of the inventor, when not being the same as the applicant; (f) as the case may be, the name and address of the legal representative of the applicant; (g) the signature of the applicant and of his/her legal representative. When the applicant is a legal person, the examiner must receive proof of the existence and legal representation of it. This can be verified with a certificate issued by the pertinent Chamber of Commerce; and (h) when required, the date, number, and the filing office of filing of any application for patent or other patent protection that may have been filed or obtained abroad by the same applicant or its successor when it refers totally or partially to the same invention claimed in the application.

(2) The description:
The description of the invention has to be clear and readable. In accordance with Article 28, it 'shall be sufficiently clear and complete to be understood and for the invention to be carried out by a person skilled in the art. The description shall contain the name of the invention and the following information'. The purpose of the description is that when the information is disclosed, it is comprehensible to all of those who might be interested, whether it is for opposition purposes or for plain curiosity. Also, the description must be useful to easily identify the technical problem the invention seeks to solve. As for the expert, 'this person shall be qualified in the matter to which the invention refers to. His level of knowledge is higher to that of the public in general, but does not exceed what can normally be expected of a qualified person'.[218]
In conformity with Article 28, the description must specify: (a) the technological sector to which it refers or to which the invention is applied. The language of the description should be the one commonly used in that determined area of technology;[219] (b) the prior technology known by the applicant which may be

218. *See* International Bureau of WIPO, *Manual for the Examination of Invention Patent Applications in the Industrial Property Offices in the Andean Community Countries* (Secretariat-General of the Andean Community, WIPO, European Patent Office, Quito-Ecuador, 2004), 32.

219. *Ibid.*, 33.

useful for understanding and examining the invention, and the references to previous documents and publications relating to the relevant technology; (c) a description of the invention in terms that allow the understanding of the technical problem and the solution given by the invention, setting forth the potential differences and advantages with respect to the prior technology; (d) a description of the drawings, when available. These drawings should be briefly described at the beginning of the description so the examiner can understand them. Furthermore, the signs and conventions used should be consistent throughout the description;[220] (e) a description of the best manner known by the applicant of executing or putting into practice the invention, using examples and references to the drawings, if being relevant; and (f) an indication as to the manner in which the invention satisfies the condition of being industrially applicable, if that is not evident from the description or from the nature of the invention.

This description might not be enough in all cases though. In the cases of products or processes relating to biological material, the sole description could not allow the examiner to fully understand the invention and its purpose. In such cases, Article 29 prescribes that the description shall be complemented with a deposit of the related material in such a way that it allows that any interested person obtains samples of said material. This deposit can be made with a recognized international authority pursuant to the Budapest Treaty on International Acknowledgement of Deposit of Microorganisms for Purposes of Processes in Patent Related Matters of 1977, or another institution recognized by the national competent office for such purposes. The Superintendence will only require the certificate of deposit of the biological material.

(3) One or more claims:

The claims are the most important part of the application. They define the matter to be protected through the patent and the scope of such protection.[221] For that reason, Article 30 of the Decision establishes that claims should be clear and concise, and thoroughly supported by the description. This is the most important characteristic of the claims because if they are not clear and concise, the Superintendence will not be able to perform the substantial examination and establish the extent of patent protection. Claims must include all the technical characteristics of the invention that make them different from the previous state of the art. Other things, such as the commercial importance of the invention, may be included but this can be done for the sake of clarity; the examiner will not take those considerations into account when deciding if the invention is worthy of patent protection.

There are two categories of claims: of product and procedure. The first one 'includes basic substances and composition, as well as physical entities as such like machines, devices, systems, systems of apparatus that cooperate among each other as a combination of apparatus, etc.'.[222] The second one applies to 'all sort

220. *Ibid.*

221. *See* Art. 51 of the Decision.

222. *See* International Bureau of WIPO, *Manual for the Examination of Invention Patent Applications in the Industrial Property Offices in the Andean Community Countries* (Secretariat-General of the Andean Community, WIPO, European Patent Office, Quito-Ecuador, 2004), 37.

of activities that suppose the use of any material product to perform the process. Said activities can be over material products, energy or other processes, or over living things'.[223] The application must indicate the category for which the invention seeks protection. Otherwise, it can be objected for lack of clarity. Moreover, there are two types of claims as defined in Article 30: independent and dependent claims. According to this provision, the former is the one that defines all the essential characteristics of the invention and is self-standing. The latter is the one that makes reference to one or several previous claims. However, not every claim that refers to another one is a dependent claim since this reference could be done without including all the characteristics from the previous claim.

As explained at the beginning of this section, claims define the scope of protection. Consequently, they should define the invention by its characteristics and not by the result pursued since this would grant the applicant protection not only over the invention, but also for all the other possible solutions of the technical problem that the invention seeks to solve.[224]

The examiner's task should be the comprehensive interpretation of the claims. In order to complete it, he/she must use the description to give full meaning to each and every claim, as long as they are clear and concise. Therefore, the claims and the description have to be consistent with each other. When there is an inconsistency between the wording of the limits of the claims and those of the description, either the claims or the description can be amended. However, the inconsistency cannot be only linguistic; the essential elements present in the description could be lacking in the claims. Introducing those characteristics into the claims can solve this irregularity.

(4) One or more drawings, when required for understanding the invention, which shall be deemed to form an integral part of the description:
The complexity of certain inventions sometimes requires more than an explanation in words. For example a machine that has many parts may be difficult for the examiner or a third party to understand by just reading the description and claims. In such cases, a drawing illustrating the parts of the machine is needed. Hence, the drawing must have a direct relation with the description, which is accomplished by introducing references in both instruments.[225]

(5) The summary:
The summary, to which Article 31 refers to, is 'a synthesis of the technical disclosure contained in the patent application. Such summary shall serve only for technical information purposes and shall bear no effect whatsoever on the interpretation of the scope of the protection afforded by the patent'. The examiner will merely verify that the application contains a summary that indicates the technical field pertaining to the invention.[226]

(6) The powers of attorney required:
The examiner shall verify the existence of a power that complies with the requirements established in Article 65 of the Colombian Civil Procedure Code.

223. *Ibid.*
224. *Ibid.*, 41.
225. *Ibid.*, 44.
226. *Ibid.*

(7) The payment receipt of the established fees.
(8) As the case may be, the copy of the access agreement, when the products or processes whose patent is applied for have been obtained or developed from genetic resources or from their by-products of which any Member Country is the country of origin.
(9) If such is the case, the copy of the document proving the licence or authorization to use the traditional knowledge of indigenous, Afro-American or local communities of the Member Countries, when the products or processes whose protection is being applied for have been obtained or developed from such knowledge, when any of the Member Countries is the country of origin, pursuant to the provisions of Decision 391 and its amendments and enforceable regulations.
(10) If such is the case, the certificate of deposit of the biological material.
(11) As the case may be, the copy of the document attesting to the assignment of the patent right from the inventor to the applicant or his successor.

132. Once the application is completed, the applicant shall file it before the Superintendence for processing. But, if the applicant decides to change something in the application, divide it, or merge two applications into one, he may do so in light of the authorization given by Articles 34, 36, and 37 of the Decision, respectively. However, that modification cannot imply an extension of the protection sought in the first application. Likewise, at any time of the procedure, the applicant can request that his/her patent application is converted into a utility model application if all the requirements are complied with.[227]

133. If the applicant chooses to file the application through the system set forth in the Decision, he/she shall file it before the Superintendence where the application must undergo the procedure established in the Decision. In compliance with Article 33, the date of filing the application shall be that of its receipt by the Superintendence. The steps of said procedure are explained below.[228]

134. When the application arrives at the Superintendence, the assigned examiner verifies the presence of at least the identification data of the applicant, the description of the invention, the drawings when relevant, and the payment of the established fees. Article 33 is clear in stating that the failure to include any of these requirements causes the inadmission of the application and, consequently, will not be appointed a filing date.

135. Then, the examiner will determine within thirty days, counted as from the filing date, if the application complies with the formalities set forth in Articles 26 and 27. If those formalities are not complied with, by virtue of Article 39, the Superintendence

227. According to the Superintendence, the applicant could request the amendment, conversion, division or fusion of the application at any time during the procedure, as long as this petition is done before it issues the resolution resolving whether or not it grants patent protection. *See* Superintendence of Industry and Commerce, Memorandum No. 04127967 of 22 Dec. 2004.

228. *See* International Bureau of WIPO, *Manual for the Examination of Invention Patent Applications in the Industrial Property Offices in the Andean Community Countries* (Secretariat-General of the Andean Community, WIPO, European Patent Office, Quito-Ecuador, 2004), 19–20.

shall request the applicant to correct the application within two months.[229] That period can be extended once for another two months if the applicant so requests, which would not cause losing the right of priority. Conversely, if after said period the applicant does not deliver the rest of the documents, the Superintendence will consider that application was abandoned.

136. Up until the period referred to in Article 31, the contents of the application shall be undisclosed, but, after eighteen months have elapsed since the date of the application or since the priority was claimed, it will become public meaning that the application will be published and anyone can consult it. In any case, pursuant to Article 40, the applicant may request that the application is published before that date if the examination of the formal requirements has concluded. The Superintendence then classifies the application according to the International Patent Classification. Also, the Superintendence must verify that the excerpt to be published contains the all the data supporting the application, as well as the summary and the claims.[230]

137. Once the application is published, whoever has a legitimate interest has sixty days to file a well-founded opposition to the patentability of the invention.[231] The period to submit arguments is extendable for another sixty days, at the request of an interested party. When the opposition is received, the Superintendence shall notify the applicant so he/she can counterargument, as established in Article 43. Consequently, during the following sixty days, the applicant will have access to the file of the opposition, including the annexes, therefore allowing him/her to contest the opposition. That period is also extendable for sixty days at the request of the applicant. This extension has to be requested at any moment before the allotted period is over and it will proceed automatically.

138. Article 44 provides that 'within the term of six months counted as from the publication of the application, independently from whether or not oppositions have been filed, the applicant shall request that examination of merits for patentability be made'. If the applicant does not request this examination, the Superintendence will reckon the application to be abandoned. Before starting this exam, the Superintendence will verify the general situation of the file. According to the Andean Patent Manual, this includes the following:

(1) that the application was published;
(2) that the applicant did not abandon the application;
(3) that the applicant requested the examination of the merits and paid the respective fee;
(4) if the case involves the right of priority, the examiner will verify that the applicant claimed such right and that the application, in accordance with Article 9 of the

229. According to the Council of State, the observations made by the Superintendence shall be very clear, in such a way that the applicant can know exactly what to correct. *See Henkel Kommanditgesellshaft auf Aktien v. Superintendence of Industry and Commerce*, Council of State, File No. 11001032400020010006101 (6864), 9 Mar. 2006.

230. *See* International Bureau of WIPO, *Manual for the Examination of Invention Patent Applications in the Industrial Property Offices in the Andean Community Countries* (Secretariat-General of the Andean Community, WIPO, European Patent Office, Quito-Ecuador, 2004), 28.

231. *See* Art. 42 of the Decision.

Decision, was filed within the twelve-month lapse starting from the day after the first application was filed, providing proof of said application and the date of presentation. Also, that the documents mentioned are in fact those corresponding to the first application and that the applicant paid the corresponding fee. Finally, the examiner will evaluate if the technical contents of the application correspond to those claimed in the first one;

(5) that the oppositions, if there were any, notifications and answers are present in the file;

(6) that the file contains the amendments or modifications, if there were any; and

(7) if the application was divided into more than one application or not.[232]

139. Once the examiner completes the preceding steps, he/she will continue to study the description, claims, drawings, and modifications, if it were the case. If the examiner concludes that the invention is not patentable or does not meet the requirements established in the Decision, he/she shall serve process upon the applicant so the application can be complemented or modified.[233] The examiner must indicate the reasons of the objection, specifying if it is for lack of clarity, novelty, inventive step, and so forth.[234] The applicant shall respond to the objections within sixty days counted as from the date of the notification. Again, this period is extendable, but this time only for thirty additional days. The Superintendence may serve the applicant for two or more times. If the applicant does not answer, Article 45 allows the Superintendence to deny the patent. Article 48 prescribes that if the examination results favourable, the patent shall be granted. If it were not favourable, the patent would be denied, unless it was only partially unfavourable case in which the patent would only be granted over the accepted claims. Once the patent is granted, in accordance with Article 49, the examiner shall classify it according to the International Classification for Patents of Invention established by the Strasbourg Agreement relating to the International Classification of Patents of 1971. The protection of the patent should last twenty years counted from the filing date of the application.[235]

140. After the Superintendence grants a patent, the patent holder may request the modification of it, in such a way that information as the date, address, residence, etc. that appeared on the application can be changed.[236] Also, Article 71 allows that

232. *See* International Bureau of WIPO, *Manual for the Examination of Invention Patent Applications in the Industrial Property Offices in the Andean Community Countries* (Secretariat-General of the Andean Community, WIPO, European Patent Office, Quito-Ecuador, 2004), 31.

233. *See* Art. 45 of the Decision.

234. This obligation is only complied with when the invention is found to be not patentable or the application does not fulfil the requirements set forth in the Decision. This because nothing in the Decision, or in the rest of Colombian legislation for that matter, obliges the Superintendence to specify the reasons to grant a patent. When protection is granted, the Superintendence issues a resolution by which the patent is granted. It does not state its reasons to believe that the invention is novel, involves an inventive step or that it is industrially applicable. On that account, neither applicants nor interested third parties know exactly why the application was adequate according to the Superintendence so the new applications they intend to present in the future are done in conformity with such parameters.

235. *See* Art. 50 of the Decision.

236. *See* Art. 70 of the Decision.

the patent owner withdraws one or more claims or the patent as a whole. This withdrawal shall be effective on the date the Superintendence receives the declaration. This provision is complemented by Article 566 of the Code of Commerce according to which the patent holder can resign to patent protection by means of a written request addressed to the Superintendence. If a licence was granted over the patent, the resignation will not be effective until the licence consents in it.

141. If the Superintendent denies the patent, the applicant can file a reconsideration petition in order to contest that Decision. This petition is provided for in Article 74 of the Administrative Procedure and Administrative Litigation Code, according to which it is to be filed before the officer that made the Decision so he/she can clarify, modify or revoke such Decision. In terms of Article 51 of the Code, the applicant will have five days to file the petition in writing before the Superintendent, counted from the date of the Decision.

III. Invalidation of the Patent

142. If a mistake was done in regards to the compliance with patentability requirements, or if an interested party considers that the invention was not patentable, the Council of State could declare the patent null and void. Article 75 of the Decision prescribes that this can be done in the following cases:[237]

(1) The subject matter of the patent is not an invention according to the requirements stipulated in Article 15.
(2) The invention fails to comply with the requirements for patentability set forth in Article 14.
(3) The patent was granted for an invention covered by Article 20.
(4) The patent fails to disclose the invention, as required by Article 28 and, if pertinent, Article 29.
(5) The claims included in the patent are not fully substantiated by the description provided.
(6) Use of the patent granted has been broader than the one indicated in the original application and requires having to extend its scope of protection.
(7) When pertinent, the products or processes in respect of which the patent is being filed have been obtained and developed on the basis of genetic resources or their by-products originating in one of the Member Countries, if the applicant failed to submit a copy of the contract for access to that genetic material.
(8) When pertinent, the products or processes whose protection is being requested have been obtained or developed on the basis of traditional knowledge belonging to indigenous, African-American, or local communities in the Member Countries, if the applicant has failed to submit a copy of the document certifying the existence

237. The cases established in the Decision as to when a patent can be declared null and void are not the only ones that can lead to said declaration. The Superintendence can also refer to domestic legislation to verify if the patent does not conflict with the provisions established therein. In any case, the applicable legislation to establish if a patent is null and void must be the legislation in force at the time of the application, whether it is communitarian or domestic legislation.

of a licence or authorization for use of that knowledge originating in any one of the Member Countries.

(9) There are grounds for absolute invalidation according to domestic legislation covering administrative acts.

The Council of State will examine the arguments and determine if the grounds above are applicable to one or more claims. If they are, the affected claims, or the patent as a whole, will be declared null and void as from the filing date of the patent application.

143. Article 77 provides that in the case the patent was granted to someone who was not entitled to it, the Superintendence will be able to annul the patent. However, this can only be done if the person who was righteously entitled to receive patent protection initiates the invalidation proceedings within five years counted as from the date the patent was granted, or two years following after he/she learned about the use of the invention, whichever period elapses first. Pursuant to Article 78, the patent holder will be able to present arguments and submit proof within the next two months, counted from the Superintendence's notification, period which can be extended for another two months. The Superintendence shall rule and inform the parties after this period expires.

§5. Ownership and Transfer

144. The inventor is the person entitled to claim patent protection. This right could be assigned or transferred by succession to another person who would act as patent holder. Article 22 provides for two special cases regarding the ownership of the patent: the community over patents and when several persons make the same invention. As to the first case, if several people jointly make an invention, they will share the right to patent it. In accordance with Article 554 of the Code of Commerce, each one of the patent holders will be entitled to exploit the invention and attack false copies. Licences to exploit this type of patents can only be granted if all of the patent holders agree or with the authorization of a civil judge. Moreover, each patent holder can yield his/her quota but the other patent holders will be preferred to acquire that part during the next three months following the notification from the patent holder that wishes to yield his/her part. Turning to the second case, if several people make the same invention, each one independently from the others, the patent shall be granted to the person or the assignee with the first filing of the application date or, where the date priority was claimed.

145. Incidentally, an invention can be the result of an employment relationship, as provided for in Article 23 of the Decision. In that case, 'the employer, whatever its form and nature, may transfer part of the economic benefits deriving from the innovations to the employee inventors in order to promote research activity'. Article 539 of the Code of Commerce provides that an invention made by an employee belongs to the employer, unless otherwise is agreed. Accordingly, 'a patent can be subject to registration on behalf of the employer provided that the function of performing activities directed to the completion of the invention is included among those assigned to the employee, or that such invention is carried out by virtue of the means provided by the labour itself'.[238] In this case, the employee will be awarded a compensation that will be established according to the monthly payment, importance of the invention, benefit for the company, etc. These provisions are automatically incorporated in the labour contract. In any case, it is advisable to include an explicit clause about this issue in the contract.

146. Once the patent has been granted, or when it is undergoing the approval process, it can be assigned or transferred by succession. In compliance with Article 56 of the Decision, all the assignments and transfers have to be registered at the Superintendence so it can be valid with respect to third parties. Also, 'the owner of a patent or a patent application that is being processed may license to one or more third parties the exploitation of the invention it covers'.[239] Again, the licence has to be registered at the Superintendence so it can be enforced against third parties. This provision has to be read along with Article 556 of the Code of Commerce according to which a licence does not prohibit that the patent holder grants more licences or that he/she exploits the invention. The licensee will be able to exploit the licence all throughout the Colombian territory for the period of time established in the licence, but he/she will not be able to yield the licence or sublicense it.

§6. Scope of Exclusive Rights and Obligations of the Patent Holder

147. The importance of the protection granted by a patent is the possibility to exclude others from performing certain actions over the patented invention. Those exclusive rights, according to Article 28 of TRIPS, are the possibility to prevent others from the acts of making, using, offering for sale, selling or importing the product subject of the patent. When the patent is over a process, the patent holder will be able to prevent third parties from using the process and from the acts of using, offering for sale, selling or importing for these purposes the product obtained directly by that process. Article 52 of Decision 486 is a replica of TRIPS in this matter.

148. However, those exclusive rights are only enforceable within the Colombian territory[240] and are not absolute. According to Article 53 of the Decision, a patent owner cannot oppose these following acts:

(a) acts carried out in a private circle and for non-commercial purposes;
(b) acts carried out exclusively to experiment with the subject matter of the patented invention;
(c) acts carried out exclusively for the purposes of teaching or scientific or academic research;

238. *See* Superintendence of Industry and Commerce, Legal Opinion (*Concepto*) No. 00068772 of 19 Oct. 2000.
239. *See* Art. 57 of the Decision.
240. *See* Superintendence of Industry and Commerce, Legal Opinion (*Concepto*) No. 04121719 of 17 Jan. 2005.

(d) acts referred to in Article 5*bis* of the Paris Convention for the Protection of Industrial Property;[241]

(e) where the patent protects biological material that is capable of being reproduced, except for plants, using that material as a basis for obtaining a viable new material, except where the patented material must be used repeatedly to obtain the new material.

149. Also, patent holders cannot exercise their rights against third parties who were using or exploiting the invention in good faith and before the priority date or the filing date of the application, or had made serious preparations for such use or exploitation.[242] In the same sense, the patent owner will not be able to 'proceed against a third party making commercial use of a product protected by a patent once that product has been introduced into the commerce of any country by the owner or another person authorized by the right holder or with economic ties to that patent owner'.[243] The latter since the Decision adopted the international system of exhaustion of rights according to which the first sale, irrespective of the country where it is done, will exhaust the rights of the patent holder in such a way that he/she will not be able to oppose the acts contained in Article 52.[244]

150. Along with the rights conferred by a patent, the right holder has to perform a set of acts in order to maintain the protection alive. Article 59 of the Decision establishes that patent owners have to 'exploit their patented inventions in any Member Country, either directly or through a person they authorize to do so'. Said exploitation, in the terms of Article 60, is understood as the industrial manufacture of the patented product or the full use of the patented process, including the distribution and marketing of the results thereof on a scale sufficient to satisfy the demands of the market. Exploitation shall also be understood to mean the importation of the patented product, including its distribution and marketing, where this is done on a scale sufficient to satisfy the demands of the market.

151. The Superintendence is very keen in the examination of the fulfilment of this obligation. In the case of Glaxo Group Limited, the Superintendence denied the request for the extension of the patent protection[245] for the 'process for the preparation of INDOL derivates'. The Superintendence had already granted the patent but the right holder had not been able to commercially exploit it since it had not received the

241. Article 5*bis* of the Paris Convention reads as follows: All Industrial Property Rights: *Period of Grace for the Payment of Fees for the Maintenance of Rights*; Patents: *Restoration.*

242. *See* Art. 55 of the Decision.

243. *See* Art. 54 of the Decision.

244. The doctrine of exhaustion is not regulated under TRIPS. Article 6 states that none of the provisions shall be used to address the issue of the exhaustion of intellectual property rights. Therefore, it will be up to each country, or region in the case of the Andean Community, to establish what doctrine to adopt.

245. This patent was granted under Decision 85. Article 29 of said Decision allowed the extension of the five-year period of patent protection up to five more years if adequate exploitation was proven.

approval from the sanitary authority.[246] The Superintendent denied the extension of the patent on the grounds that the applicant had not timely delivered the necessary documents to prove the exploitation. The Superintendent argued that the fact that the applicant had not received sanitary approval could not constitute a case of force majeure since it could have had foreseen that the approval process was bound to last a considerable time.[247] This idea is still useful even though Decision 486 did not include the extension provision. It shows the importance of the obligation of exploiting the patent and that the criteria for accepting an excuse are rather strict.

152. Beyond this obligation, Article 80 of the Decision states that the patent owner has to pay annual fees established by the Superintendence 'in order to keep a patent in force or to maintain a pending patent application, as the case may be'. The non-compliance with this provision shall result in the legal lapsing of the patent or patent application.

§7. Compulsory Licences

153. The rights conferred to the patent holder are quite extensive yet they are not unlimited. As stated earlier, Article 53 establishes a series of situations to which the patent owner cannot oppose. In addition, there are further restrictions, such as compulsory licences, that are licences granted by the government without the consent of the patent owner.[248] Within the Decision, Articles 61 and above set forth the regime, establishing four types of licences: (i) licences when the patent holder has not properly exploited the patent; (ii) existence of public interest, an emergency, or national security

246. In Colombia, the INVIMA (National Food and Drug Surveillance Institute), has the jurisdiction to certify the safety of a drug and that it is suitable for consumption. However, this process is independent from the process before the Superintendence by virtue of which a patent is granted. Therefore, even if a pharmaceutical patent is granted by the Superintendence, the patent holder might still not be able to commercially exploit the invention due to the lack of permission from the INVIMA. In the Glaxo case, the applicant used this argument to excuse the lack of exploitation.

247. *See* Superintendence of Industry and Commerce, Resolution No. 2314 of 28 Oct. 1996.

248. *See* Official website of the WTO at <wto.org/english/tratop_e/trips_e/public_health_faq_e.htm> (last visited 16 Dec. 2017). Under TRIPS compulsory licences are normally issued under Art. 31, which contains several provisions in order to ensure the licences are granted in the best interest of society without completely depleting the patent holder's rights. According to this article, compulsory licences are only granted after the proposed user has made efforts to obtain authorization on reasonable commercial terms or without such authorization when there is a situation of national emergency or extreme urgency. On the same line, it establishes, among other things, that licences should be limited and provide adequate remuneration for the patent holder. Despite this, developing and least-developed countries argue that the adequate provision for compulsory licences is Art. 30 of TRIPS. In accordance with this provision, 'Members may provide limited exceptions to the exclusive rights conferred by a patent, provided that such exceptions do not unreasonably conflict with a normal exploitation of the patent and do not unreasonably prejudice the legitimate interests of the patent owner, taking account of the legitimate interests of third parties.' For these countries this provision is more favourable and consequently more suitable for their special situation.

considerations; (iii) to remedy anticompetitive practices; and (iv) when the licence is required for the exploitation of another patent.

154. To begin with the first type of licences, Article 61 instructs that at the expiry of a period of three years following a patent grant or of four years following the application for a patent, whichever is longer, the competent national office may grant a compulsory licence mainly for the industrial manufacture of the product covered by the patent, or for full use of the patented process, at the request of any interested party, but only if, at the time of the request, the patent had not been exploited in the manner specified in Articles 59 and 60, in the Member Country in which the licence is sought, or if the exploitation of the invention had been suspended for more than one year.

In any case, prior to the granting of the licence, the proposed user has to make efforts to obtain a contractual licence on its own account and these were not successful within a reasonable period of time.

155. Once the Superintendence receives the compulsory licence request, it has to notify the patent holder within the next sixty days. During this period, the patentee can submit the reasons why the invention was not being exploited at the time of the application. The Superintendence will only accept valid reasons, which may be of force majeure or an act of God. If it is not satisfied, it will grant the licence and define its scope, coverage, period for which it is granted, remuneration and the conditions for the payment of it.[249] These conditions can be changed at the request of the patent holder or licensee when new circumstances affect the licence, especially if the patent owner granted a licence on more favourable terms. The licensee shall exploit the licence within a period of two years counted from the day the licence was granted.[250] Nevertheless, if such exploitation does not take place, the licensee, according to Article 64, can give 'valid reasons for inaction consisting of force majeure or an act of God' or else, the patent holder can request that the licence is revoked.

156. The request for this type of licences shall comply with the provisions established in the Administrative Procedure and Administrative Litigation Code[251] and in the Unique Circular of the Superintendence. Specifically, the request must contain:

(a) name, identification, and domicile of the applicant, as well as of his/her attorney, depending on the case;
(b) annexes: (i) power of attorney, depending on the case; (ii) documents that prove the existence and legal representation of the legal person of the applicant; and (iii) proof that the applicant tried to obtain a licence from the patent holder on reasonable commercial terms and conditions;
(c) a complete identification of the patent, indicating at least the number of the certificate, the title of the invention and the name of the right holder;
(d) the applicant's express indication of the lack of exploitation of the patent;

249. *See* Arts 61 and 62 of the Decision. According to Art. 64 of the Colombian Civil Code, a case of force majeure or an Act of God will occur when the event is unpredictable or impossible to resist, as a shipwreck, an earthquake, the acts of authority exercised by a public official, etc.
250. *See* Art. 63 of the Decision.
251. The Administrative Procedure and Administrative Litigation Code regulates the actions before administrative entities such as the Superintendence. Article 16, in particular, regulates oral and written petitions.

(e) indication of the royalties that the applicant considers adequate; and
(f) request of other proof that the applicant deems necessary.

157. Turning to the second type of licences and after having explained the above, a significant element of the Decision must be address: the exceptions or flexibilities to the patent system which were mentioned initially in the Paris Convention of 1883, aiming to strike a balance between the progress of developing countries and the rights granted by the intellectual property systems.[252]

Accordingly, Article 31 of the TRIPS Agreement established the following exceptional circumstances that allow countries to grant compulsory licences: (a) national emergency; (b) abuse of the rights granted to the right holder; (c) anticompetitive practices; (d) for non-commercial exploitation and (e) in the interest of public health.

The WTO held in Doha a ministerial Conference in 2001 to clarify ambiguities on the TRIPS Agreement, several aspects of the TRIPS were debated, among them concerns related to the access to affordable medicine for populations in developing countries and their right to grant compulsory licences and their freedom to determine the grounds upon which said licences are granted, in the interest of public health.[253]

Article 65 of the Decision dictates that a patent can be licensed at any time following the declaration of the existence of public interest, an emergency, or national security considerations. The Superintendence will 'specify the scope or extent of the compulsory licence and, in particular, the term for which it is granted, the subject matter of the licence, and the amount of remuneration and the conditions for its payment'.[254] The patent holder shall be notified of the granting of the patent as soon as reasonably practicable.

Finally, Colombia has only one case regarding compulsory licences, known as the Kaletra case, which is an antiretroviral medicine containing ritonavir and lopinavir used for treating HIV/AIDS, produced by the multinational company Abbott Laboratories. The Colombian patent for Kaletra was valid until the end of 2016.

Initially the Superintendence fined the laboratory for selling the drug at a price three times higher than the maximum price allowed and despite the recommendation issued by the Ministry of Health to stick to the price of reference. In 2008 a coalition of NGOs made a request directly to the laboratory for a compulsory licence. No response to the request was made. Further, the same request was submitted to the Superintendence and was also denied. In July of the same year, the coalition requested the ministry to declare the high price an issue of public interest. The request was denied by the ministry as there was not a proven problem to access the drug.[255]

In 2009, a lawsuit was filed against the Ministry of Health, the Superintendence, and the Invima (Sanitary authority). In 2012, the judge ruled in favour of the petitioners, and declared the price of the drug violated collective rights. The Court also recognized

252. *See* Herrera Sierra Luisa. Las patentes y las flexibilidades del acuerdo sobre los ADPIC, Universidad Externado de Colombia, Bogotá, 2017, 615.
253. *See* World Trade Organization. Article 17 of the Doha Declaration. 2001.
254. *See* Superintendence of Industry and Commerce, Regulatory Compilation (Circular Única) published in the Official Gazette 44511 of 16 of Aug. 2001.
255. *See* Balancing wealth and health, Edited by Rochelle C. Dreyfuss and Cesar Rodriguez Garavito, Oxford 2014, 190.

that in this case the lack of state control affected the access to a structure that guarantees public health and ruled that the ministry was in charge of the price control of drugs and this duty could not be transferred to a private company[256]

At the time of writing, a similar case is awaiting resolution; this time the patented product is Imatinib, which is used as part of the treatment of leukaemia and manufactured by the Novartis Laboratory. Along the same lines of Kaletra, it was subject to price control and after negotiations between the laboratory and the Ministry of Health the price of Imatinib in Colombia was reduced by 50%. However, due to the resolution issued by the ministry in February of 2016, the pharmaceutical product was declared of public interest and, in that light, the Superintendence will have to decide whether to grant or deny the compulsory licence based on the evidence shown above.[257]

158. Compulsory licences for emergency reasons have been widely developed in the international arena, especially in the WTO, whose constant developments show the will of the international community to help cure serious diseases afflicting developed and least-developed countries. In that sense, in 2001 Members adopted the Doha Declaration on the TRIPS Agreement and Public Health whereby they agreed 'that the TRIPS Agreement does not and should not prevent members from taking measures to protect public health'.[258] Nonetheless, the principles and values of Doha are very important for Colombia and were upheld in the framework of the negotiation of the Free Trade Agreement with the European Free Trade Association (EFTA), where Colombia aimed at preserving the special concessions of the Doha Declaration.

159. As to the licences granted to remedy anticompetitive practices, Article 66 provides that the Superintendence can grant compulsory licences, either ex officio or at the request of a party 'where practices are noted to be detrimental to the exercise of free competition, especially where they constitute an abuse by the patent owner of a dominant position in the market'. Consequently, these licences will remain in force as long as the anticompetitive practice is taking place, or if it is likely to recur.

160. Finally, regarding the licences needed for the exploitation of another patent, the patent owner of the dependent patent can request that the Superintendence grants a licence when it was impossible to obtain it on reasonable commercial terms. As per Article 67, this licence has to abide by the following conditions:

(a) the invention claimed in the second patent shall involve an important technical advance of considerable economic significance in relation to the invention claimed in the first patent;
(b) the owner of the first patent shall be entitled to a cross-licence on reasonable terms to use the invention claimed in the second patent; and
(c) the licence authorized in respect of the first patent shall be non-assignable except with the assignment of the second patent.

256. *See* Cundinamarca Administrative Tribunal, ruling No. 2009-00269-01, 27 Sep. 2012.
257. *See* Herrera Sierra Luisa. Las patentes y las flexibilidades del acuerdo sobre los ADPIC, Universidad Externado de Colombia, Bogotá, 2017, 640.
258. *See* WTO Website, Fact Sheet: TRIPS and Pharmaceutical Patents. Obligations and Exceptions at <wto.org/english/tratop_e/trips_e/factsheet_pharm02_e.htm#health> (last visited 16 Dec. 2017).

161. In addition, compulsory licences have to comply with the requirements set forth in Article 68, regardless of their form or purpose. This article establishes that licences:

(a) shall be non-exclusive and may not be sublicensed;
(b) shall be non-assignable, except with the part of the business or goodwill, which permits its industrial use. This shall be evidenced in writing and registered with the competent national office. Otherwise, those assignments or transfers shall not be legally binding;
(c) shall be liable, subject to adequate protection of the legitimate interests of the persons so authorized, to be terminated if and when the circumstances which led to them cease to exist and are unlikely to recur;
(d) IEL Intellectual Property Law: Colombia – FM their scope and duration shall be limited to the purposes for which they were authorized;
(e) in the case of patents protecting semiconductor technology, a compulsory licence shall be authorized only for public non-commercial use or to remedy a practice declared by the competent national authority to be anticompetitive in accordance with Articles 65 and 66;
(f) provide for payment of adequate remuneration according to the circumstances of each case, taking into account the economic value of the licence, without prejudice to the stipulations of Article 66; and
(g) shall be used predominantly for the supply of the domestic market.[259]

§8. Infringements

162. For a complete explanation on infringements, *see* Chapter 12.

259. On this point, para. 6 the Doha Declaration on the TRIPS Agreement and Public Health allows members to issue compulsory licences to supply other countries' markets, as long as the requirements set forth in the Decision Implementing para. 6 of the Doha Declaration are complied with. For further information on this matter, please refer to the WTO website.

Chapter 3. Utility Models

§1. Sources and Legislation

163. Utility models were recognized for the first time within the Andean Community in Decision 311, which came into force for the five Member Countries of the Cartagena Agreement in 12 December 1991, becoming the second international organization in recognizing protection for such creations.[260] Decision 311 was replaced by Decision 313, which in turn was replaced by Decision 344. In 2000, this Decision was also replaced by Decision 486 (the Decision), the current industrial property regime in the Andean Community. Consequently, what was explained in regards to patents is completely applicably regarding utility models and therefore, it will not be explained in this chapter.

§2. Protection of Utility Models

164. According to Article 81 of the Decision, utility models shall be protected by patents. This same provision defines utility models as 'any shape, configuration, or arrangement of components of any device, tool, implement, mechanism or other object, or any part thereof, that permits improved or different operation, use, or manufacture of the object incorporating it, or that endows it with any utility, advantage, or technical effect that it did not have previously'. In other words, utility models can be defined as a 'minor invention or an industrial creation demanding less inventive degree, that constitute a technical improvement over what was previously known'.[261] Furthermore, Article 82 of the Decision prescribes that sculptures, architectural works, or objects that are purely aesthetic in nature are not considered as utility models, and that the same processes and materials excluded from patent protection are also excluded from the protection granted by utility models.

165. Utility models are considered as inventions. Hence, they must comply with the requirements of novelty, inventive step, and industrial applicability applied to patent protection. In the opinion of the Andean Court of Justice, a utility model 'must involve novelty and an inventive step in regards to the new advantage, benefit, improvement, usefulness or technical effect that is translated in the artefact, instrument,

260. The other being the African Organization for Industrial Property that recognizes utility models in Annex II of the Bangui Agreement of 1977. This organization, along with the Andean Community, is one of the few entities that accords protection to such models. *See* Andean Court of Justice, Proceeding 43-IP-2001 of 24 Aug. 2001, published in *Gaceta Oficial del Acuerdo de Cartagena*, No. 716 of 18 Sep. 2001.

261. *See* Andean Court of Justice, proceeding 43-IP 2001 of 24 Aug. 2001, published in *Gaceta Oficial del Acuerdo de Cartagena*, No. 716 of 18 Sep. 2001.

tool or mechanism that is added to the existent object'.[262] The latter implies that utility models cannot protect processes or substances since they have to refer to a specific object, which they intend to improve. Therefore, the claims should be over a defined form in such a way that it can be distinguished from any other. In regards to the industrial applicability of the utility model, this aspect has to be verified by proving that the incorporated element actually provides an additional benefit to the object. As to the inventive step, this can be verified if the content of the utility model is not obvious or it is not evidently derived from the state of the art[263]

166. The application for a utility model patent shall be carried out in the same way as that of a patent.[264] According to Article 85 of the Decision, the only exception is in regards to the processing periods of the application, which are reduced to one-half of what was originally provided for patents. However, the eighteen-month period provided in Article 40 after which the information in the application is disclosed is only reduced to twelve months. In any case, if the application was initially filed to obtain patent protection, the applicant can request the conversion of it into an application for a utility model, if the nature of the subject matter so allows it.[265] In the terms of Article 35, this can only be done once and the converted application keeps the original filing date.

167. As per Article 84 of the Decision, the duration of the protection granted by the utility model is ten years, counted from the filing date of the application or the claiming of priority.

§3. Infringements

168. For a complete explanation on infringements, *see* Chapter 12.

262. *See* Andean Court of Justice, proceeding 43-IP 2001 of 24 Aug. 2001, published in *Gaceta Oficial del Acuerdo de Cartagena*, No. 716 of 18 Sep. 2001.
263. *Ibid.*
264. *See* generally Ch. 2, s. 4 on the procedure to obtain patent protection. The procedure under the PCT is also applicable to utility models.
265. *See* Art. 83 of the Decision.

Chapter 4. Trademarks

§1. Sources and Legislation

169. Colombian legal sources on trademarks are composed of a wide body of international and national provisions, as well as decisions of domestic judges and from the Andean Court of Justice. Regarding international provisions, Colombia has ratified several treaties related to the protection of trademarks. It is also a member of different international organizations such as the WIPO[266] and the WTO,[267] which sets forth minimum standards of trademark protection through TRIPS, one of its backbone agreements. As for other international instruments related to trademarks, Colombia is part of the following:

- Convention concerning Industrial Property with France (the Colombian-French Convention), promulgated by Decree 597 of 7 July 1904.[268]
- General Inter-American Convention on Protection on Marks and Trade Names (the Washington Convention), approved by Law 59 of 25 March 1936.
- Free Trade Agreement between Republic of Colombia and Mexico (the G2), approved by Law 172 of 20 December 1994.[269]
- Paris Convention for the protection of Industrial Property (the Paris Convention), approved by Law 178 of 28 December 1994.
- Preferential Trade Agreement between Republic of Colombia and United States of America (the PTA).[270]
- Trademark Law Treaty, approved by Law 1343 of 27 October 2009.

170. Regarding other provisions, the ACN has regulated intellectual property aspect by means of Decision 486 of 2000, which constitutes the applicable regulation for trademarks in Colombia. In addition to Decision 486, Colombia has enacted several domestic laws and decrees in that matter, including:

(1) Law 14 of 15 March 1979, concerning the protection of the Spanish language.
(2) Decree 3466 of 2 December 1982, regarding consumer protection.

---

266. *See* the Convention establishing the World Intellectual Property Organisation, signed at Stockholm on 14 Jul. 1967 and amended on 28 Sep. 1979. Colombia by means of Law 46 of 1979 has been a member of the WIPO.

267. *See* the Agreement establishing the World Trade Organisation, signed in Marrakech on 15 Apr. 1994. Colombia by means of Law 170 of 1994 has been a member of the WTO.

269. Venezuela, which was also a party to this agreement, denounced the treaty effective on 19 Nov. 2006. Therefore, this treaty is only applicable to Colombia and México.

270. At the moment, the Preferential Trade Agreement is fulfilling the previous constitutional procedures to the ratification in both countries.

(3) Decree 2153 of 30 December 1992, which establishes the functions of the Superintendence of Industry and Commerce (the Superintendence).
(4) Decree 2269 of 16 September 1993, which contains some provisions related to certification marks.
(5) Decree 2591 of 13 December 2000, which regulates some important aspects of trademarks contained in Decision 486.
(6) Resolution 210 of 15 January 2001 of the Superintendence, which establishes some procedures that shall be followed for the granting of the protection.
(7) Unique Circular No. 10 of 2001 of the Superintendence, which provides some general formalities for the protection of trademarks.
(8) Decree 138 of 25 January 2005, which regulates Law 875 of 2004 concerning the use of the Red Cross emblem and other emblems protected by the Geneva Convention of 1949 and its additional protocols.
(9) Decree 729 of 13 of April of 2012, which regulates some elements of Decision 486 of 2000 and 689 of 2008.

§2. Subject Matter of Protection

I. Signs Which May Constitute Trademarks

171. A trademark is an intangible good used as a distinctive sign, which identifies certain products or services as those produced or provided by a specific person or enterprise.[271] Pursuant to Article 134 of Decision 486, any sign that is capable of distinguishing products and services on the market and capable of graphic representation may be registered as a trademark. The following signs can constitute trademarks, among others:

(1) combination of words;
(2) pictures, figures, symbols, graphic elements, logotypes, monograms, portraits, labels, and emblems;
(3) sounds and smells;
(4) letters and numbers;
(5) a colour or combination of colours demarcated in a specific shape;
(6) the shape of a product, its packaging or wrappings; and
(7) any combination of signs indicated above.

II. Different Categories of Trademarks

172. The categories of trademarks are not established in a specific law. Nevertheless, the case law of the Andean Court and the Colombian Council of State has continuously classified trademarks into different categories. The most important are: (1) word trademarks; (2) figurative or graphical trademarks; (3) combined trademarks; (4)

271. *See* <wipo.int/trademarks/en/trademarks.html> (last visited 31 Aug. 2007).

three-dimensional trademarks; (5) sound trademarks; (6) smell trademarks; (7) collective trademarks; and (8) certification trademarks. In turn, the preceding trademarks may also be classified as: (1) weak trademarks; (2) well-known or notorious trademarks; (3) famous trademarks; (4) derivative trademarks; (5) defensive trademarks; and (6) reserved trademarks. These classifications will be analysed in detail in the following sections.

A. Word Trademark

173. This category is also called nominative trademark, which consists of a phonetic element or a set of pronounceable words or a phrase.[272] These trademarks are visually and audibly perceivable, and are communicated through language. Word trademarks can be divided into four classes depending on the words they use:

(1) Fanciful trademarks are those composed of arbitrary or made-up words. According to the Andean Court, words in a foreign language are also fanciful trademarks,[273] for example, *ADIDAS* for shoes and clothes or *LEONISA* for underwear and swimwear.
(2) Arbitrary trademarks are those composed of words that have meaning but do not relate to the good or service they intend to identify, for example, *PUNTO BLANCO* (white dot). Trademarks consisting of personal names are also arbitrary, for example, *AC ARTURO CALLE* for clothing in general.
(3) Suggestive trademarks are those composed of words that evoke the good or service they intend to identify, but do not constitute a direct description, for example, *COPPERTONE* for sun care products.
(4) Descriptive trademarks are those composed of words that directly describe the characteristics of the good or service they intend to identify.

B. Figurative or Graphical Trademarks

174. These consist of graphic elements such as pictures, figures, symbols, logotypes, monograms, portraits, labels, and emblems, among others. They are signs perceivable by the eyes, evoking the shape of an image.

C. Combined Trademarks

175. These trademarks are composed of a denominative element (word or phrase) and a graphical one. According to the Andean Court, there is always a dominant element that prevails over the other. Usually, the nominative element in a combined trademark

272. *See* Andean Court of Justice, Proceeding No. 1-IP-87, 3 Dec. 1987, published in *Gaceta Oficial del Acuerdo de Cartagena*, No. 28, 15 Feb. 1988. The majority of the cases mentioned in this chapter are landmark decisions. However, this does not exclude the reference to other decisions of the Andean Court that have ratified such positions. Likewise, previous proceedings might have also approached these Issues and therefore may also be relevant.

273. *See* Andean Court of Justice, Proceeding No. 04-IP-97, 20 Jan. 1997, published in *Gaceta Oficial del Acuerdo de Cartagena*, No. 354, 13 Jul. 1998.

is the most prominent or determining element, due to the 'expressive strength of words, which, by definition, can be pronounced'. However, there are some exceptions because the graphic element can sometimes prevail given its size, colour, or position within the trademark arrangement.[274]

The Council of State, in the case of the trademark *DORMILUNA*, established that the graphic element prevails over the denominative element when it consists of a suggestive drawing rather that an abstract one.[275] The identification of the dominant element is useful to determine if two combined trademarks can result in confusion; there can be a case in which the graphic element prevails in one trademark, while the denominative element prevails in another one, therefore avoiding confusion among consumers. However, it might result that in both trademarks the same element prevails, case in which the Superintendence must compare the trademarks and determine if they could confuse consumers. In the case in hand, the Council of State held that the nominative element prevailed in all the trademarks under study: *DORMILUNA, PLUMA LUNA*, and *MARYLUNA*. Therefore, it proceeded to examine the trademarks applying the comparison rules established by the Andean Court,[276] and determined that the trademarks were not confusingly similar and consequently, they may coexist in the market.

D. *Three-Dimensional Trademarks*

176. A three-dimensional trademark is a sign consisting of a three-dimensional shape formed in a three-dimensional space; it is a body with volume. Consumers are capable of distinguishing the origin of a product by its packaging, wrapping, or container. In the past, these trademarks were considered as a subdivision of figurative or graphical trademarks. Decision 486 changed this perspective and became the first provision to recognize them as an independent category.[277]

177. In order for a three-dimensional sign to receive trademark protection, it must fulfil two requirements: first, the trademark shall not constitute a common or usual form and second, it shall not essentially impose a functional or technical advantage to it.[278] In that sense, the Andean Court mentioned that the three-dimensional form must show characteristics that would differentiate it from the usual or required form of the product or its bottling in such a way that consumers can identify the provenance of the product.[279] The three-dimensional forms must have a distinctive shape through the alteration of ordinary or common features or lines, allowing a difference to be

274. *See* Andean Court of Justice, Proceeding No. 4-IP-88, 9 Dec. 1988, published in *Gaceta Oficial del Acuerdo de Cartagena*, No. 39, 24 Jan. 1989.
275. *See Industrias Dormiluna Ltda. v. Superintendence of Industry and Commerce*, Council of State, File 7505, 27 Jul. 2006.
276. *See* the rules of comparison in para. 258.
277. *See* Andean Court of Justice, Proceeding No. 194-IP-2005, 25 Nov. 2005, published in *Gaceta Oficial del Acuerdo de Cartagena*, No. 1297, 16 Feb. 2006.
278. *See* R. Metke Méndez, *Lecciones de Propiedad Industrial* (First Edition, Medellín-Colombia, Editorial Diké, 2001), 68.
279. *See* Andean Court of Justice, Proceeding No. 23-IP-98, 25 Sep. 1998, published in *Gaceta Oficial del Acuerdo de Cartagena*, No. 379, 27 Oct. 1998.

made between the new shape and a typical one. In the same sense, it pointed out that the container must allow consumers to identify the product without taking into account the label as a distinctive element.[280]

178. 178. Accordingly, the Andean Court confirmed that shape must be the prevalent element when examining a three-dimensional trademark for distinctiveness. Therefore, there will be no protection of a three-dimensional sign printed on labels, since the labelling is not a part of the external form to be registered as a trademark.[281]

179. The Council of State has given guidance regarding three-dimensional trademarks in two renowned cases in which it was asked to declare null and void a resolution issued by the Superintendence refusing the registration of a three-dimensional mark in the shape of a bottle. In the first case, the Superintendence considered that the trademark consisted of the usual form of the bottle of the product, which was not eligible for registration under the Andean legislation. The plaintiff, *Postobón*, argued that the trademark had novel and distinctive characteristics, namely, the inclusion of veins, dots, and dashes placed on the upper side that simulated an engraving. The Council of State refused *Postobón's* claims since the applied-for mark lacked distinctive capacity. It stated that, even though the bottle included veins, dots, and dashes, these elements did not add a creation that could be deemed suggestive, arbitrary or fanciful and therefore could impede consumers to confuse it with another bottle.[282]

In the second case, the Council adopted the opposite position. Postobón filed another action against the Superintendence's resolution refusing the registration of another three-dimensional mark consisting of a bottle-shaped container. The Superintendence determined that the mark could not be registered because other beverages necessarily had to be bottled in container with same or similar shape. Therefore, exclusive rights over a bottle could not be granted, as competitors should also be allowed to use it. In this opportunity, Postobón argued before the Council of State, that the Superintendence could not refuse the registration of the trademark based on the fact that bottles are the natural containers for liquids reason why the mark would lack originality. In the plaintiff's opinion, the analysis should refer to whether the container had specific characteristics as to size, shape, and combination and distribution of geometric figures that could assure distinctiveness.

The Council of State took the plaintiff's side and indicated that the design of the bottle was original and sufficiently distinctive given its short-necked bottle with a square body and slightly rounded sides. The Council held that the existence of other registered three-dimensional marks consisting of the shape of a bottle indicated that such shapes were eligible for registration. It also clarified that this case was different from the first one involving *Postobón* given that, in that case, registration was refused on the grounds that the bottle did not add any fanciful creation and had no characteristics that would make it different from others.[283]

---

280. *Ibid.*

281. *See* Andean Court of Justice, Proceeding No. 149 – IP – 2007, 22 Nov. 2007, published in *Gaceta Oficial del Acuerdo de Cartagena,* No. 1586, 15 Feb. 2008.

282. *See Gaseosas Posada Tobón S.A. v. Superintendence of Industry and Commerce*, Council of State, File 7619, 4 Aug. 2005.

283. *See Gaseosas Posada Tobón S.A. v. Superintendence of Industry and Commerce*, Council of State, File 7620, 8 Jun. 2006.

180. The latter is not the only reference made by the Superintendence as to three-dimensional trademarks; it has also established that a trade dress may be registered as a combined or three-dimensional trademark. A trade dress is a combination of decorative elements that distinguish products or establishments; it involves the total image or a whole visual appearance. When the trade dress refers to an establishment, elements such as colours, lights, themes, packaging and architecture, among others, are part of the distinctive sign. In addition, when the trade dress involves products, elements such as sizes, shapes, containers, colours, and letters, among others, it can be combined to become a distinctive sign.[284] This type of trademark is not expressly regulated in Decision 486. Nonetheless, the Superintendence has registered some trade dresses as trademarks, in cases such as, petrol stations in the name of *SHELL BRANDS* and *PETROBRAS*. Furthermore, it has ascertained in several occasions that, since a trade dress is a combination of distinctive signs, it could be associated to a trademark or to an industrial design as well.[285]

E. Sound Trademarks

181. They consist of a sound or combination of sounds capable of distinguishing a product or service. This type of trademarks must be graphically represented in the form of a musical notation.[286] The Superintendence has registered several sound trademarks, in the name of *Celular Móvil de Colombia,*[287] *Banco Davivienda,*[288] *Productos Familia,*[289] *Twenty Century Fox,*[290] *Intel Corporation,*[291] and *The Clorox company.*[292]

F. Scent Trademarks

182. These consist of a scent capable of distinguishing a product or service. As with sound trademarks, it must be graphically represented. Taking into account the fundamental nature of a trademark, this category shall fulfil another condition: the possibility of reproducing the smell in an identical manner.[293] The Superintendence has not granted a registration of scent trademarks yet. However, in this matter, it is worth mentioning the application for a scent trademark to cover baby creams and lotions by the company *Productos Cero S.A.*[294] The Superintendence denied the registration given that the sign was not graphically represented and lacked distinctiveness.

284. *See* Legal Opinion (*Concepto*) 05014398. Superintendence of Industry and Commerce. (5 Apr. 2005).
285. *See* Ch. 3.
286. *See* Legal Opinion (*Concepto*) 03087905, Superintendence of Industry and Commerce. (17 Dec. 2003).
287. *See* Registration No. 292.580, Superintendence of Industry and Commerce.
288. *See* Registration No. 292.319, Superintendence of Industry and Commerce.
289. *See* Registration No. 291.636, Superintendence of Industry and Commerce.
290. *See* Registration No. 301.282, Superintendence of Industry and Commerce.
291. *See* Registration No. 325.521, Superintendence of Industry and Commerce.
292. *See* Registration No. 291.636, Superintendence of Industry and Commerce
293. *See* Registration No. 325.521, Superintendence of Industry and Commerce.
294. *See* Resolution No. 011956, Superintendence of Industry and Commerce (17 May 2005).

In this opportunity, the Superintendence established that a scent trademark cannot be represented through a chemical formula, a scent description, or a deposit of the scent sample. However, it was recognized that although in this moment scent trademarks cannot be graphically represented, some day it will be possible thanks to the advances in technology, which have developed different systems to graphically represent a scent. Regarding the chemical formula, it was stated that it does not represent the smell of the substance; it represents the substance or the product itself. As for the deposit of the scent sample, the Superintendence has argued that it might be troublesome as the clarity and precision of such sample may be affected by factors such as, time, temperature, and lightness of its components. Moreover, the Superintendence considered that the sign was not distinctive since the scent was common in those products (cosmetics, lotions, soaps) and it does not create a new concept in the market that allows consumer to identify the producer.

G. *Collective Trademarks*

183. As set forth in Article 180 of the Decision, a collective trademark is a sign that serves to distinguish the origin or any other common characteristics of goods or services from different businesses that use the sign under the owner's control. They identify an association of companies rather than one particular business organization. For this reason, the members of such association can jointly profit from the reputation created by the collective trademark and consumers may know that a company bearing such sign meets the standards set by the association. The standards are established in the application of the trademark, indicating the conditions and form in which the collective trademark shall be used in connection with the products or services.

H. *Certification Marks*

184. Certification marks owned by specific quality organizations, which allow other companies to use after the compliance with the standards prescribed for use of that mark. Article 185 of the Decision establishes that a certification mark is a sign applied to goods or services, whose qualities or other characteristics have been certified by the owner of the mark. According to Article 186, the owner of a certification mark may be a public or private business institution, or a state, regional, or international organization. The right holder is considered competent to certify the quality of the products and services that intend to use the mark. However, Article 188 establishes a prohibition for the owner to use the certification mark to market his/her own goods or services.

185. Certification marks may protect geographical indications (GIs) in those countries where such intellectual property right is not recognized, given that they both intend to protect the nature and quality of the products and affirm that they meet certain defined standards. This is not the case of Colombia, which legislation recognizes GIs as an independent intellectual property regime. However, countries such as the United States protect as a certification mark: Roquefort for cheese from France, Parma ham for ham products from Italy, and Swiss for Chocolate from Switzerland, as certification marks.[295]

186. According to WIPO, the main difference between collective trademarks and certification marks is that the former may only be used by a specific group of companies, while the latter may be used by anyone who complies with the standards defined by the owner of said mark.[296]

187. The eight categories of trademarks explained above, may also be classified as weak, well-known or notorious, famous or renamed, derivative, defensive, and reserved trademarks. This classification is explained as follows.

I. Weak Trademarks

188. Weak trademarks are considered those whose elements meet one of the following characteristics: (1) they are generic, meaning they are words used in the common language to identify a whole gender rather than a specific species of such gender; (2) they are composed of commonly used suffix or prefix; and (3) they evoke the quality or specific characteristics of the product or service. They are considered weak since other producers of the same goods or services use those elements frequently and, consequently, they cannot grant an exclusive right over its use.[297] On the contrary to well-known and notorious trademarks, this category does not enjoy of a special protection. Alternatively, they risk losing their distinctive force.

189. The Council of State has studied in several cases weak trademarks and its effects in the market. One illustrative case is the nullity action against the resolution that denied the registration of the trademark *NOVALAR*.[298] José María Fernández filed an application for registration of the expression Novalar. The company Fenolicos Colombianos Ltda. filed an opposition based on its previous registered trademark *NOVA* in the same class. The Superintendence initially found the opposition groundless and granted the registration of *NOVALAR*. Upon resolving the appeal filed by *NOVA*, however, the Superintendence retracted its position and denied the registration. The Council of State decided that the expression *Nova* could not be appropriated by anyone because it is a commonly used expression for qualifying something as new or for setting forth the idea that something has acquired temporarily a sparkling shine deeper than normal. Because commonly used expressions lack distinctiveness, they cannot be appropriated. Likewise, no one can claim exclusive use of them. The Council of State warned that the only way the expression *Nova* can acquire distinctiveness is if

295. *See* < http://www.wipo.int/edocs/mdocs/geoind/en/wipo_geo_sfo_03/wipo_geo_sfo_03_3-annex1.pdf> (last visited 16 Dec. 2017).

296. *See* <wipo.int/sme/en/ip_business/collective_marks/certification_marks.htm> (last visited 31 Jul. 2007).

297. *See* Andean Court of Justice, Proceeding No. 4-IP-95, 15 Dec. 1996, published in *Gaceta Oficial del Acuerdo de Cartagena*, No. 253, 7 Mar. 1997.

298. *See Fenolicos Colombianos Ltda. v. Superintendence of Industry and Commerce*, Council of State, File 5512, 13 Mar. 2003. Other relevant cases include: *Golden Brown International Limited v. Superintendence of Industry and Commerce*. Council of State, File 00250, 14 Apr. 2005.

certain expressions are added thereto that individualize the mark, such as in the case of *NOVACEL*, *NOVASOL*, *CORTINOVA*, *CADANOVA*, and *IPERNOVA*.

The Council of State had previously supported this reasoning in the proceeding initiated by the proprietor of the trademark *ECOGEL*,[299] where it held that the suffix *Gel*, which is common to trademarks such as *ECOGEL*, *DESCONGEL*, and *BIOGEL*, should be excluded for the purpose of establishing a comparison between trademarks because it was a commonly used expression that did nothing else that indicate a characteristic of the mode of presentation of the product (gel-like) and that it could not be appropriated by anyone.

190. Regarding a commonly used expression, it is important to address the treatment granted to trademarks of pharmaceutical products. In the case of the trademark *LACRISYN*,[300] the Council of State applied the statements made by the Andean Court regarding pharmaceutical trademarks. It was established that pharmaceutical trademarks are usually composed of prefix, suffix, or commonly used words that suggest an idea of the properties of the product or its principal components. In order to compare this kind of trademarks, the Superintendence must not take into account those commonly used elements. The distinctiveness of pharmaceutical trademarks is determined by the different element added to the sign, which usually consists of a fantasy word. The Andean Court has pointed out that the registrability exam of pharmaceutical trademarks must be very strict, in order to avoid mistakes and confusion, which may have serious or fatal consequences in consumers' health.

J. Well-Known or Notorious Trademarks

191. Decision 486 does not mention well-known trademarks as an independent category. Nevertheless, Article 224 of Decision 486, in accordance with Article 16(2) of TRIPS, defines the well-known distinctive signs. This definition is completely applicable to trademarks. Therefore, well-known or notorious trademarks are those recognized as such by the consumers of relevant sector in any Member Country of the ACN, regardless of the way or means by which the consumers became acquainted with the mark. According to Article 230, the relevant sectors are considered to be the following: (i) the real and potential consumers of the type of goods and services using the trademark; (ii) the persons involved in distribution or marketing channels of the kinds of goods or services using the trademark; and (iii) the commercial circles operating in lines of business connected with the kind of establishment, activity, goods, or services using the trademark.

192. Well-known or notorious trademarks enjoy a special protection since two important principles of ordinary trademarks do not apply to this category: speciality and territorial application.[301] The protection granted to well-known trademarks is

---

299. *See Ecogel. v. Superintendence of Industry and Commerce*, Council of State, File 6008, 7 Apr. 2000.

300. *See Allergan. Inc. v. Superintendence of Industry and Commerce*, Council of State, File 8180, 1 Jul. 2004. *See also* Andean Court of Justice, Proceeding No. 12-IP-2004, 14 Apr. 2004, published in *Gaceta Oficial del Acuerdo de Cartagena*, No. 1072, 28 May 2004.

301. *See* Andean Court of Justice, Proceeding No. 36-IP-99, 8 Oct. 1999, published in *Gaceta Oficial del Acuerdo de Cartagena*, No. 504, 9 Nov. 1999.

extended to other products regardless of the class of the products they intend to identify and regardless of the territory where their registration was claimed or granted. (For further information, *see* Section 6, Chapter 4.)

193. Even though the definition provided by Article 224 does not provide a clear understanding about what a well-known trademark is, it shows a key element required to establish the existence of a well-known trademark, which is the 'recognition in a sector'. This statement was made by the Andean Court which defined such trademarks as those known by a specific collective or group of consumers of a certain type of goods or services.[302]

194. There is no specific procedure in Colombia with regard to obtaining recognition of a well-known trademark. Therefore, in order to receive the qualification of a well-known trademark, the holder must present sufficient evidence before the Superintendence of Industry and Commerce, which must issue an administrative act, which may be opposed by third parties. In effect, this requirement entails a large probative procedure to obtain the status of broad recognition by consumers in the specific sector.

K. Famous Trademarks

195. This kind of trademark is not mentioned in any provision, but has been recognized as such by the Andean Court. Nowadays, famous trademarks are no longer a category of trademarks since they are considered well-known trademarks. However, they have a broader diffusion and appearance in the media allowing different groups of consumers to know the mark. In contrast to well-known and notorious trademarks, famous trademarks enjoy a higher distinction since they are recognized by different sectors or markets for the excellent quality of their products or services.[303] An example of a famous trademark may be *COCA-COLA* for a non-alcoholic beverage.

L. Derivative Trademarks

196. A derivative trademark is one that comes from a non-substantial variation of another registered trademark, or one that is used to refer to accessory elements of the principal trademark. According to the Andean Court, the owner of a registered trademark may use such trademark without its protection being diminished. Derivative trademarks do not have to be registered as an independent mark; the very slight variations regarding the principal trademark do not exclude the protection awarded to the principal trademark. In this sense, they must be included in the same class of products or services and they must not present substantial variations in regards to the trademark already registered. Otherwise, they would have to be independent and autonomously registered.[304]

302. *See* Andean Court of Justice, Proceeding No. 126-IP-03, 3 Dec. 2003, published in *Gaceta Oficial del Acuerdo de Cartagena*, No. 1040, 3 Mar. 2004.

303. *See* Andean Court of Justice, Proceeding No. 1-IP-87, 3 Dec. 1987, published in *Gaceta Oficial del Acuerdo de Cartagena*, No. 28, 15 Feb. 1988.

304. *See* Andean Court of Justice, Proceeding No. 84-IP-2000, 21 Mar. 2001, published in *Gaceta Oficial del Acuerdo de Cartagena*, No. 677, 13 Jun. 2001.

197. The Andean Court has made several statements regarding family of trademarks, which are composed of house or umbrella trademarks and their derivative marks. House or umbrella trademarks are not regulated in the Andean legislation. Although the Andean Court does not mention them as such, the Council of State has brought up the issue,[305] affirming that these trademarks consist in the corporate name of the manufacturer. Trademark regulation admits the existence of plural trademarks that share a common distinctive element allowing consumers to associate all of the products or services in the family. In this sense, consumers infer that products bearing common trademarks are manufactured by the same company.[306] Some examples of family of trademarks composed of umbrella trademarks and their corresponding derivative trademark are: *NESTLÉ – NESCAFÉ, NESQUIK, NESTEA*, and *NESTLÉ TRIX*, among others. *RENAULT – RENAULT CLIO, RENAULT TWINGO, RENAULT LOGAN*, and *RENAULT SYMBOL*, among others.

M. Defensive Trademarks

198. These trademarks are not mentioned in any provision as an independent category but are very frequent in practice. These trademarks are the ones registered without the intention of using them, for the sole purpose of impeding the registration of other trademarks. There are two kinds of defensive trademarks: (1) identical trademark registered in different classes; and (2) similar and well-planned variations of the main trademark registered in the same class.[307] They intend to protect the main trademark, so that other identical or similar trademarks cannot be registered, causing confusion among consumers. Decision 486 has established effective methods to avoid their registration, such as, the cancellation of registration when they have not been used for a period of three years. (For further information, *see* Section 9.)

N. Reserved Trademarks

199. In addition to defensive trademarks, the Court has also mentioned other kind of non-used trademarks: reserved trademarks. They consist of trademarks planned to be used in the future by the business organization, but which are not currently used.[308] They, however, can also be subject of cancellation of registration if they are not effectively used within three years after the registration. (For further information, *see* Section 9.)

305. *See Societé des Produits Nestlé S.A. v. Superintendence of Industry and Commerce*, Council of State, File 7337, 4 Aug. 2005.

306. *See* Andean Court of Justice, Proceeding No. 97-IP-2002, 5 Feb. 2003, published in *Gaceta Oficial del Acuerdo de Cartagena*, No. 912, 25 Mar. 2003.

307. *See* Andean Court of Justice, Proceeding No. 1-IP-87, 3 Dec. 1987, published in *Gaceta Oficial del Acuerdo de Cartagena*, No. 28, 15 Feb. 1988.

308. *See* Andean Court of Justice, Proceeding No. 1-IP-87, 3 Dec. 1987, published in *Gaceta Oficial del Acuerdo de Cartagena*, No. 28, 15 Feb. 1988.

O. Colour Trademarks

200. The trademark division of the Superintendence of Industry and Commerce has also granted protection to non-traditional trademarks which are characterized by grabbing the attention of consumers through different senses (e.g., sight or touch) or are represented in a different way such as musical chords, movements, and established colours.

Colour trademarks, as stated in the *Pink Postobon case,*[309] are not granted to the colour per se; there must be a clear delimitation with respect to the intended colour, so it cannot be understood that it is a colour in isolation. The protection is granted for the colour applied to the delimited specific form in this case a vase.

P. Texture Trademarks

201. In addition to colour trademarks, the Court has also mentioned another kind of non-traditional trademark: texture trademarks,[310] which are trademarks made up by the surface of an object together with its packaging, which when perceived through the sense of touch, can distinguish a product and its business origin.

According to the Court, in order for a texture trademark to be registered, the applicant must fulfil two conditions: the submission of a clear, complete, and precise description of the texture and also the submission of a sample, which will allow the examiner to determine if the packaging or surface has enough distinctiveness to receive trademark protection.[311]

§3. Conditions of Protection

202. The basic condition for the protection of a trademark is its effective registration of the sign for which it shall fulfil some conditions that are not expressly regulated by Decision 486, but can be inferred from the definition and from subsequent case law. The Andean Court has identified three important conditions: (i) perceptibility; (ii) distinctiveness, and; (iii) graphic representation.

- Perceptibility: the sign shall be perceptible, that is, it shall be capable of being apprehended through the senses. Since a trademark is an intangible good, it must be materialized to be identified by consumers.[312]
- Distinctiveness: it is the most important requirement that a sign has to fulfil in order to be registered as a trademark. In that sense, a sign will be considered

309. *See* Registrations No. 507.281 and 507.282, Superintendence of Industry and Commerce.
310. *See* Registration No. 345.30, Superintendence of Industry and Commerce.
311. *See* Andean Court of Justice, Proceeding No. 242-IP-15, published in *Gaceta Oficial del Acuerdo de Cartagena*, No. 753, 18 Sep. 2015.
312. *See* Andean Court of Justice, Proceeding No. 12-IP-97, 7 Jul. 2000, published in *Gaceta Oficial del Acuerdo de Cartagena*, No. 588, 2 Aug. 2000.

distinctive if it is able to distinguish the products or services which it intends to identify, from the similar or identical products or services in the market.[313]

– Graphic Representation: the graphic representation allows the construction of an image or an idea related to the characteristics and forms of the sign. It consists of a representation made with words, graphics, combined signs, colours, and figures among others. The sign must be visually represented to be identified.[314]

203. The sign must be distinctive, perceptible, and susceptible to graphic representation to be registered as a trademark. In addition, the sign must not fall in any of the causes of unregistrable signs mentioned in Articles 135 and 136 of the Decision. For methodological purposes, signs that cannot be registered as trademarks will be divided into four groups that will be individually explained next: (1) signs not capable of distinguishing products or services; (2) signs that can mislead or confuse consumers; (3) signs contrary to law, public morals, public order, or good manners, and; (4) signs that may affect the right of third parties.

I. Signs Not Capable of Distinguishing Products or Services

204. Pursuant to Article 135, signs lack distinctiveness when they:

(a) fail to constitute a trademark according to the requirements of perceptibility, distinctiveness, and graphic representation;
(b) are lacking distinguishable characteristics;
(c) consist solely of the usual shape of goods or their packaging, or of shapes or characteristics dictated by the nature or particular function of the product or service in question;
(d) consist exclusively of shapes or other elements that attribute a functional or technical advantage to the product or service to which they are applied;
(e) consist solely of a sign or statement that may serve in commerce to designate or describe, in respect of the goods and services for which they are to be used, their quality, quantity, purpose, value, geographic origin, or time of production, or that impart other details, characteristics, or information, including expressions of praise for those goods or services;
(f) consist exclusively of a sign or statement that is the common or technical name of the product or service concerned;
(g) consist solely of or have become a sign or statement which, in everyday language or normal use within the country, is the common or usual designation for the goods or services in question; or
(h) consist of a colour without any demarcation to give it a specific shape.

313. *See* Andean Court of Justice, Proceeding No. 1-IP-87, 3 Dec. 1987, published in *Gaceta Oficial del Acuerdo de Cartagena*, No. 28, 15 Feb. 1888.

314. *See* Andean Court of Justice, Proceeding No. 9-IP-97, 4 Feb. 1998, published in *Gaceta Oficial del Acuerdo de Cartagena*, No. 336, 27 Apr. 1898.

205. Notwithstanding, the signs stipulated under items (b), (e), (f), (g), and (h) may be registered as a trademark when it is continuously used by the applicant in a Member Country of the ACN, in such a way that endows it with distinctiveness regarding the products or services to which it is applied to. This is known as the secondary meaning. In this regard, the Superintendence has stated that products and services may be identified by expressions that at first glance are not distinctive but, for different reasons,[315] acquire a secondary meaning with distinguishing aptitude, and consequently, they may be registered as trademarks.[316]

206. Regarding item (e), descriptive signs are not distinctive and thus cannot be registered as trademarks. However, the Andean Court has stated that the descriptive nature of a sign is not a *sine qua non* condition to establish its unregistrability; the sign must refer exactly to common and generic qualities of the product. In this sense, adjectives may be accepted as trademarks if they do not have a close relation with the products or services they intend to identify.[317] Hence, adjectives that describe products or services can be registered as trademarks. However, it is important to clarify that when such adjectives can describe products or services of several classes, their distinctive force may be diminished, becoming weak trademarks.[318]

207. The case *Thomas Greg & Sons de Colombia S.A. v. Superintendence of Industry and Commerce* is illustrative in this matter. In this case, the service mark *HOLOGRAMA* (Hologram) was registered in Colombia to cover security services in Class 42.[319] Thomas Greg & Sons de Colombia S.A. filed a nullity action against said registration before the Council of State given that the trademark described the result of a service in which a laser-based photographic technique was applied. The result is the registration on a high-resolution photographic plate of a three-dimensional image formed by the interference between a coherent laser ray and the light dispersed by the object of which the image is obtained. According to the plaintiff, the registration of the mark *HOLOGRAMA* would prevent the producer of holograms from offering their product in the market, which would evidently damage their reputation and commercial use. The Court stated that the generic and descriptive nature of a denomination that prevents its registration as a trademark must be understood in its direct and material relationship with the product or service concerned. The Council of State based on the prejudicial interpretation of the Andean Court, established that the trademark did not have the minimum distinctive strength required to differentiate a product of the same description offered in the market by other competitors. Finally, the registration was declared null and void given that there is a close, substantial and unequivocal relationship

315. These reasons could include the prolonged use of the sign previous to registration or an advertising campaign of great diffusion.
316. *See* Legal Opinion (*Concepto*) 02043592, Superintendence of Industry and Commerce. (30 Jul. 2002).
317. *See* Andean Court of Justice, Proceeding No. 7-IP-95, 7 Aug. 1995, published in *Gaceta Oficial del Acuerdo de Cartagena*, No. 189, 10 Sep. 1995.
318. *Ibid.*
319. *See* Class 42: Scientific and technological services and research and design relating thereto; industrial analysis and research services; design and development of computer hardware and software; legal services.

between the mark *HOLOGRAMA* and the products and services that can result from the use of a hologram.[320]

208. Apart from descriptive signs, there are others that do not describe the product, but they evoke an idea or image of the product or service in the consumer's mind. There is a thin line separating descriptive and suggestive signs. The Superintendence is in charge of establishing the nature of the sign. Suggestive signs are accepted as trademarks when they are accompanied of a fantasy expression, which combined evoke a remote or indirect idea of the product or service in the mind of the consumer.[321] This is the case of trademarks such as LUKAFÉ for coffee (*café*) or CHOCO CRISPIS for a chocolate cereal.

209. Another illustrative case is the one of the trademark *CANAL SATELLITE.*[322] In this case, the company Canal Societe Anonyme applied for the registration of the trademark *CANAL SATELLITE* to distinguish services in Class 41.[323] The Superintendence refused the registration because it concluded that the mark consisted exclusively in the description of the services for which it is used. Canal Societe Anonyme applied for the nullity of said Decision arguing that its mark was not descriptive but suggestive because it was an expression of fantasy that suggest to consumers an idea regarding the services offered. The Council of State then decided that the mark, as a whole, is indicative of a substantial characteristic of television service, as it is rendered through channels that use satellites for functioning. Consequently, the Council of State determined that the Decision of the Superintendence to refuse the registration was valid.

210. Another important case is the one concerning the trademark *CEBAL AMERICAS.* In this case, Pechiney Plastic Packaging Inc. applied to register said trademark to cover products in International Class 20.[324] The Superintendence granted the registration despite the opposition filed by the company Induamercol based on its trademarks *AMERICA, AMERICAN, AMERICAN HOUSE, LADY AMERICANA,* and *POLIAMERICANA*. Induamercol filed an action for declaration of nullity and restoration of rights against the resolution of the Superintendence that disallowed the opposition. The Council of Stat held that a comparison of the trademark *CEBAL AMERICAS* and the trademarks of the opponent, did not reveal confusion, as the word *Cebal* had sufficient capacity to differentiate the opposed mark from any other trademark containing the word *America.* Indeed, the Andean Court stated that there is no risk of confusion when the words added to those words elements that coincide have a strong enough meaning to identify the source of the products, thus preventing consumers from making mistakes.

320. *See Thomas Greg & Sons de Colombia S.A. v. Superintendence of Industry and Commerce,* Council of State, File No. 5063, 30 Sep. 1999.

321. *See Thomas Greg & Sons de Colombia S.A. v. Superintendence of Industry and Commerce,* Council of State, File No. 5063, 30 Sep. 1999.

322. *See Canal Societe Anomyme v. Superintendence of Industry and Commerce.* Council of State, File 7005, 5 Oct. 2003 and Andean Court of Justice, Proceeding 60-IP-2003, 16 Jul. 2003, published in *Gaceta Oficial del Acuerdo de Cartagena,* No. 967, 18 Aug. 2003.

323. *See* Class 41: entertainment and cultural activities.

324. Plastic containers; tuber; non-metallic lids and capsules to be closed with a cork; containers with a body laminated in plastic; containers in the form of tubes; tubes for packaging products.

211. Concerning item (f) of Article 135, a generic name cannot be registered as a trademark when it has a close relation with the product or service. In this regard, the Andean Court conveyed that the generic term must be analysed taking into account its relation with the product or service it intends to identify. From the legal point of view, the grammatical criterion is not sufficient to determine the generic nature of a term. In this sense, just because a term is prescribed in a dictionary with several meanings, the Superintendence cannot consider it unregistrable. Generic words that serve as trademarks can be used in a figurative or metaphorical manner and therefore can acquire sufficient distinctiveness in relation to a product or service.[325] In any case, a generic term is unregistrable when competitors of the relevant economic sector need to use it to indicate such product or service.[326]

212. Trademarks containing descriptive and generic terms can also be registered. In the opinion of the Andean Court, a trademark must be analysed as a unit without separating its elements. In this sense, the combination of descriptive and generic terms may provide distinctive force to the sign.[327] However, trademarks composed of repeated generic or descriptive terms cannot be registered since there is not an additional element that provides distinctive force to the sign.[328]

213. In this matter, the case of the *COFFEE-CREM* trademark is illustrative.[329] *Compañia Nacional de Chocolates S.A.* applied for the registration of said trademark to cover products in Class 29. The Superintendence refused the registration, concluding that the expression was used in the market to describe a characteristic of the products to be covered. *Compañia Nacional de Chocolates S.A.* brought a nullity action against this Decision before the Council of State, arguing that the sign *COFFEE-CREM* has the characteristics necessary to be deemed a trademark. The Council of State requested a prejudicial interpretation from the Andean Court. Regarding generic denominations, in which the Court explained that they lack distinctive capacity, one of the basic requirements for a sign to become a trademark. Therefore, generic denominations do not allow for differentiation of one product from another product or service available in the market. The Council of State applied this interpretation to the case and determined that *CoffeE-Crem* was not distinctive because it was only the union of two generic words, coffee and cream, suggesting the idea that it is cream for coffee that softens its strength, colour or flavour. Hence, it ruled that the Decision of the Superintendence was correct.

214. Regarding signs composed of foreign words, the Andean Court has established that they are considered fanciful trademarks since it is presumed that the average consumer does not know those words. However, some foreign words are generally recognized by consumers, especially when they are frequently used or when

325. *See* Andean Court of Justice, Proceeding No. 2-IP-89, 19 Oct. 1989, published in *Gaceta Oficial del Acuerdo de Cartagena*, No. 49, 10 Nov. 1989.

326. *Ibid.*

327. *See* Andean Court of Justice, Proceeding No. 3-IP-95, 7 Aug. 1995, published in *Gaceta Oficial del Acuerdo de Cartagena*, No. 189, 10 Sep. 1995.

328. *See* Andean Court of Justice, Proceeding No. 33-IP-1995, 15 Nov. 1996, published in *Gaceta Oficial del Acuerdo de Cartagena*, No. 257, 14 Apr. 1997.

329. *See Compañia Nacional de Chocolates S.A. v. Superintendence of Industry and Commerce*, Council of State. File 5033, 17 Jul. 2003.

they are phonetically or orthographically similar to words in Spanish. In this case, the trademark must be examined taking into consideration its generic or descriptive nature, regardless of the language it is in.[330] Likewise, the Andean Court stated that words in another language whose use becomes usual in Colombia should be treated as local expressions.[331]

215. Regarding foreign words, it is worth mentioning the case of the trademark *LA FENETRE*.[332] In this case, the company Sodimac Colombia S.A. filed an action of nullity and restoration of rights against the resolution of the Superintendence refusing the registration of said trademark. According to the plaintiff, the expression *La Fenetre* is neither a descriptive term nor a commonly used expression in Colombia. The Council of State explained that the expression in question is a French word that means window (*Ventana* in Spanish). In this sense, the word describes the objective of the product, which is blinds and shades. The Council of State established that the Spanish Dictionary includes and recognizes expressions such as: (1) *finiestra* (coming from the Latin expression *fenestra* that means window; (2) *fenestraje* (combination of windows); (3) *defenestración* (action of throwing out of the window); and (4) *fenestra* (window). As those words are included in the dictionary, the Council of State establishes that the expression *La Fenetre* cannot be considered a fantasy expression but as a local descriptive expression. Consequently, the Council of State agreed with the Decision of the Superintendence.

II. Signs That May Mislead or Confuse Consumers

216. Regarding these signs, the Andean Court has declared that they do not fulfil the requirement of distinctiveness since they do not identify the real commercial source or origin of the products or services.[333] Furthermore, it was also established that misleading and confusion is produced when the sign creates a distortion of reality referred to the nature, characteristics, origin, production method, and other information about the product in the mind of the consumer.[334] As per Article 135 of the Decision, confusing signs are those that:

(a) can create a confusion in business circles or in the public in general, in particular as to the geographical origin, nature, manufacturing methods, characteristics, or qualities of the goods or services concerned, or their suitability for use;

330. *See* Andean Court of Justice, Proceeding No. 3-IP-95, 7 Aug. 1995, published in *Gaceta Oficial del Acuerdo de Cartagena*, No. 189, 10 Sep. 1995.
331. *See* Andean Court of Justice, Proceeding No. 63-IP-2002, 28 Aug. 2002, published in *Gaceta Oficial del Acuerdo de Cartagena*, No. 837, 20 Sep. 2002.
332. *See Sodimac Colombia S.A. v. Superintendence of Industry and Commerce*, Council of State. File 8907, 24 Aug. 2006.
333. *See* Andean Court of Justice, Proceeding No. 82-IP-2002, 4 Dec. 2002, published in *Gaceta Oficial del Acuerdo de Cartagena*, No. 891, 29 Jan. 2003.
334. *See* Andean Court of Justice, Proceeding No. 35-IP-98, 30 Oct. 1998, published in *Gaceta Oficial del Acuerdo de Cartagena*, No. 422, 30 Mar. 1999.

(b) reproduce, imitate, or contain a protected indication of origin that is liable to create confusion or a mistaken association with the indication in relation to the goods themselves or different goods, or that involve taking unfair advantages of the well-known character of that appellation among the public;
(c) contain a protected appellation of origin for wines and spirits;
(d) consist of a national or foreign geographical reference that is liable to create confusion in respect of its application to products or services;
(e) reproduce or imitate, as trademarks or elements of those trademarks, without the permission of the competent authority of the State or international organization concerned, heraldic elements, such as coats of arms, flags, and emblems, and the official signs and stamps used for the purposes of government control and guarantee and the coat of arms, flags, and other emblems, initials or designations of any international organization;
(f) reproduce or imitate signs denoting conformity with technical standards, except where the registration thereof is applied for by the national body responsible for standards and quality requirements in Member Countries of the ACN; or
(g) reproduce, imitate, or include the indication of a plant species protected in a Member Country of the ACN or any other country, where application of the sign to goods or services relating to that species of if its use is likely to cause confusion or a mistaken association with that variety.

217. Moreover, to avoid confusion regarding the place of origin of products, Article 160 establishes that when a trademark consists of a geographical name, the product may only be marketed bearing visible and clearly legible identification of its place of manufacture.

III. Signs Contrary to Law, Public Morals, Public Order, or Good Manners

218. As to signs contrary to the law, the Andean Court has stated that when communitarian provisions mention the concept 'law', it shall not be understood that domestic legislation can add more signs that are deemed unregistrable, different from those provided for in the Andean legislation. It was also pointed out that there are imperative provisions in every country that protect public interest and have their foundation on public order, peace, stability, public morals, and good manners.[335] These imperative norms shall be taken into account by the Superintendence when registering trademarks.

335. *See* Andean Court of Justice, Proceeding No. 30-IP-96, 12 Sep. 1997, published in *Gaceta Oficial del Acuerdo de Cartagena*, No. 299, 17 Oct. 1997.

IV. Signs That May Constitute an Infringement to the Right of Third Parties

219. All of the above-mentioned signs cannot be registered as a trademark in order to protect public interest. However, the signs included in this group are established in the specific interest of registration owners. In accordance with the Andean Court, the main function of a trademark is the identification of the products or services of a producer, so that they could be distinguished from other products or services of another producer. For these purposes, the owner of a trademark has an exclusive right at exploitation over the distinctive sign and therefore, he/she has the right to oppose the use or registration of similar or identical trademarks. The Court has mentioned that when two or more trademarks create confusion, the consumer may make a mistake, risking the liberty of choosing a specific product or service.[336] In addition, it pointed out that the confusion could be present in several degrees, going from a plain similarity between two trademarks, as far as the total identity of them. Consequently, a trademark is considered to be confusing when it involves an identical or similar sign that has already been registered to identify the same or similar kind of products or services. Such trademark lacks distinctive force.[337]

Article 136 of Decision 486 indicates that those signs that may infringe the right of third parties. The following may not be registered as trademarks when:

(a) They are identical, or similar to a trademark filed for registration or registered earlier by a third party for the same goods or services, or for goods or services in respect of which use of the trademark is likely to lead to confusion or mistaken association.
(b) They are identical or similar to a protected trade name, label, or emblem that, given the circumstances, their use would result in a likelihood of confusion or mistaken association.
(c) They are identical or similar to a filed for or registered advertising slogan that, given the circumstances, their use would result in a likelihood of confusion or mistaken association.
(d) They are identical or so similar to a distinctive sign belonging to a third party when, the applicant is or has been a representative or distributor such of the owner of the protected sign in a Member Country of the ACN or elsewhere or a person expressly authorized by that right holder, their use, given the circumstances, would result in a likelihood of confusion or mistaken association.
(e) Consist of a sign that is capable of affecting the identity or prestige of legal entities, whether non-profit or not, or natural persons other that the applicant or identifiable by the general public as being such a different person. Particularly in regard to a given name, family name, signature, title, nickname, pseudonym, image, portrait, or caricature, when no consent has been obtained from that person or, if deceased, the declared heirs of that person.

336. *See* Andean Court of Justice, Proceeding No. 159-IP-2005, 30 Nov. 2005, published in *Gaceta Oficial del Acuerdo de Cartagena*, No. 1297, 16 Feb. 2006.

337. *See* Andean Court of Justice, Proceeding No. 7-IP-97, 7 Jul. 1998, published in *Gaceta Oficial del Acuerdo de Cartagena*, No. 412, 26 Feb. 1999.

(f) Consist of a sign that may violate the intellectual property right or copyright of a third party, unless the consent of that party has been obtained.
(g) Consist of the name of indigenous, African-American, or local communities, or of such denominations, words, letters, characters, or signs as are used to distinguish their products, services, or methods of processing, or that constitute an expression of their culture or practice, unless the application is filed by the community itself or with its express consent.
(h) Consist of a total or partial reproduction, imitation, translation, transliteration, or transcription of a well-known sign belonging to a third party without regard to the type of product or service to which it shall be applied, when its use would lead to a likelihood of confusion or mistaken association with that party; taking unfair advantage of the prestige of the sign; or weakening its distinctive force or its use for commercial or advertising purposes.

220. Item (d) is not clear, however, it seems to indicate that the right holder's representative, distributor or any person authorized to use his/her distinctive sign cannot register a similar or identical trademarks, since it would result in a possible confusion or mistaken association.

§4. Formalities: Procedure for Obtaining Protection, Establishing and Maintaining Trademarks

221. A sign will only be protected after it is registered, which is, according to the Andean Court, an 'attributive system'.[338] The explanation of the procedure for obtaining the registration will be divided in four steps in order to clarify and simplify the whole process: (1) application for registration; (2) formal exam of the application; (3) publication of the application, and; (4) final exam for registration.

I. The Application for Registration

222. The application for registration of a trademark is filed before the Superintendence. Article 138 of Decision 486 establishes that one application shall be filed for each class of goods or services the trademark intends to identify, in accordance with the International Classification of Goods and Services established by the Nice Agreement.[339] The application shall contain the following:

(a) the petition;
(b) a reproduction of the trademark when contains graphic elements, shape, or colour, or a figurative, combined or three-dimensional trademark with or without the use of colour;

338. *See* Andean Court of Justice, Proceeding No. 07-IP-95, 7 Aug. 1995, published in *Gaceta Oficial del Acuerdo de Cartagena*, No. 199, 26 Jan. 1996.
339. *See* Nice Agreement Concerning the International Classification of Goods and Services for the Purposes of the Registration of Marks, under the Nice Agreement Ninth Edition (1957).

(c) power of attorney;
(d) receipt of payment of the official fees;
(e) the authorizations required when applicable;
(f) the certificate of registration in the country of origin issued by the granting authority and the receipt for payment of the official fee, when applicants wish to avail themselves of the right provided for in Article 6 *quinquies* of the Paris Convention. In this regard, Article 142 establishes that said certificate can be submitted within a period of three months after the application filing date.

223. The petition for registration shall be filed in the form established by the Superintendence and shall include the following information: (i) the request for registration of a trademark; (ii) the name and address of the applicant; (iii) the nationality of the applicant and if the applicant is a legal entity, the place of incorporation; (iv) the name and address of the applicant's legal representative, if pertinent; (v) the trademark to be registered when such trademark is denominative only, with-out graphics, shape or colour; (vi) a list of the specific goods or services for which the trademark application is being filed; (vii) the class to which the products or services correspond, and; (viii) the signature of the applicant or applicant's legal representative.[340]

224. Regarding the collective trademarks and certification marks, additional information is required. As to collective trademarks, Article 182 establishes that the application of shall also contain:

(a) a copy of the articles of association of the organization, association, or group of persons applying for registration of the collective trademark;
(b) the membership list; and
(c) a statement of the conditions on and form in which the collective trademark shall be used in connection with the products or services.

As for certification marks, Article 187 indicates the additional information required as follows:

(a) the regulations for use of the certification mark;
(b) a statement of the products or services that may be subject to certification by the owner of the mark;
(c) definition of the characteristics guaranteed by the presence of the mark; and
(d) description of the control to which those characteristics shall be subjected before and after the use of the certification mark.

Madrid Protocol

225. The Madrid Protocol dated 27 June 1989 is a tool that allows the international registration of trademarks. The Madrid Protocol is part of the Madrid System for the international registration of trademarks, which is composed of two separate treaties: The Madrid Agreement Concerning the International Registration of Marks, and the

340. *See* Art. 139 of the Decision.

Protocol Relating to the Madrid Agreement Concerning the International Registration of Marks.[341] Under the scope of the Madrid Protocol, the owner of a trademark can obtain protection for his trademark in 114 countries by submitting one single application subject to the payment of a basic fee, which can be filed in English, French or Spanish, directly at his national trademark office.

Colombia ratified the Madrid Protocol on 29 May 2012 which came into force on 29 August 2012.[342]

SIPI

226. The application for registration can be submitted through an online tool called SIPI.[343] Once the Superintendence receives the hard copy application, it shall, in accordance with Article 140, stamp a date of filing on it, if the applicant provided at least the following information: (i) a statement that the applicant is filing for obtaining a registration of a trademark; (ii) data that allows the identification of the applicant or the person filing the application; (iii) the trademark for which the registration is being applied for, or a reproduction of a trademark in the case of denominative, figurative, combined, or three-dimensional trademarks, whether in colour or not; (iv) a list of specific products or services in respect to which the trademark protection is being applied, and; (v) proof of payment of the official fees. However, if the applicant fails to provide any of those requirements, the Superintendence shall reject the application for processing and no filing date shall be assigned to it.

227. Furthermore, Article 141 mentions that when the sign was used to distinguish products or services at an officially recognized exhibition in any country within six months prior to the filing of the application, the applicant may claim as the filing date the one said exhibition took place. Nevertheless, those acts shall be certified by the competent authority responsible for the exhibition and shall state the date on which the trademark was first used.

228. Another important matter concerning the application is the modifications that can be done at any time during the process. The applicant may request to modify or correct any material mistake of his/her application and the Superintendence may suggest changes to it. Those amendments shall not make important changes in the trademark or add products or services initially specified.[344] In this matter, the Andean Court has stated that the application has two types of elements: substantial and secondary elements. Substantial elements are not susceptible of any modification, that is, they cannot be changed during the process of application. If any modification takes place

341. *See* Art. 1, Madrid Agreement Concerning the International Registration of Marks of 14 Apr. 1891, as revised at Brussels on 14 Dec. 1900, at Washington on 2 Jun. 1911, at The Hague on 6 Nov. 1925, at London on 2 Jun. 1934, at Nice on 15 Jun. 1957, and at Stockholm on 14 Jul. 1967, and as amended on 28 Sep. 1979.

342. *See* Art. 1, Law 1455 of 2011.

343. *See* Art. 3.3.4 Distinguising marks Manual, Code PI01-I01 Superintendence of Industry and Commerce. (2 Aug. 2016).

344. *See* Art. 143 of the Decision.

regarding substantial elements it will be considered a new application. Conversely, secondary elements can be changed without having the mentioned effects.[345]

229. If the application is filed by a national from a country that grants the right of priority to Colombian nationals, he/she shall enjoy said prerogative. Regarding this right, Article 9 of Decision 486 establishes that the first application for the registration of a trademark, that is validly filed in another Member Country or with a national, regional, or international authority to which Colombia is linked by a treaty establishing an analogous right of priority, shall confer the applicant or the applicant's successor the right of priority. The scope and effects of this right are provided for in Article 4 of the Paris Convention. The period of priority is of six months counted from the filing date of the applications where priority is claimed.

In the opinion of the Andean Court, the recognition of the right of priority requires the fulfilment of two conditions: (1) the competent authority must have assigned a date of application for registration in accordance with the Andean provisions, and; (2) the application must be subject of registration.[346] For purposes of right of priority, the applicant must submit a declaration along with the pertinent documents claiming the priority over the previous application. Also, he/she must state its filing date, the office to which it was submitted when it was granted, and the reference number assigned to it. The pertinent documents that shall be submitted are: (i) a copy of the application whose priority is claimed certified by the authority; (ii) a certificate attesting the application filing date issued by the same authority; and (iii) the proof of payment of the official fee, among others. According to Article 15 of Decree 2591 of 2000, the Superintendence will prove that the scope and ownership of the submitted certification and the information of the application coincide.

At this point, all the submissions, both those filed online and those filed as a hard copy, are assigned to an official of the Documentation and Information Centre to digitalize the documents and images, which are uploaded and classified in the SIPI program, making the examiner's work easier and allowing users direct control and monitoring over their submissions.[347]

II. The Formal Examination of the Application

230. Once the application has been filed, Article 144 establishes that the Superintendence shall conduct an examination to determine whether the application complies with the formal conditions. The examination shall be performed within fifteen days following the filing date. In case the application does not comply with all the formal conditions, the Superintendence shall request the applicant to correct those

345. *See* Andean Court of Justice, Proceeding No. 15-IP-97, 21 Nov. 1997, published in *Gaceta Oficial del Acuerdo de Cartagena*, No. 314, 18 Dec. 1997 and Andean Court of Justice, Proceeding No. 65-IP-2001, 17 Oct. 2001, published in *Gaceta Oficial del Acuerdo de Cartagena*, No. 836, 18 Sep. 2002.

346. *See* Andean Court of Justice, Proceeding No. 55-IP-2001, 22 Nov. 2001, published in *Gaceta Oficial del Acuerdo de Cartagena*, No. 741, 6 Dec. 2001.

347. *See* Art. 3.3.14.1 Distinguising marks Manual, Code PI01-I01 Superintendence of Industry and Commerce. (2 Aug. 2016).

defects within a period of sixty days following the notification. If the applicant does not fulfil the requirements by the end of that period, the application will be rejected and will lose its position within the order of priority.

For territorial extension applications filed through the Madrid Protocol, the date of submission at the International Bureau will be deemed to be the date of national designation, except in cases of subsequent designations in which case the date will be designated upon request at the national trademark office.

III. The Publication of the Application

231. Once the exam is performed, and if the application meets the formal conditions, the Superintendence will order its publication in the monthly Intellectual Property Gazette. According to Article 146, anyone having a legitimate interest may oppose the registration within thirty working days following the publication. At the request of any third party, the Superintendence shall grant for once, an additional term of thirty working days for filing the evidence in support of the opposition.[348] Article 146 also establishes that no oppositions based on trademarks having coexisted before with the trademark applied for, may be filed against an application filed within six months following the expiry date of the grace period.

232. If an opposition has been filed, the Superintendence shall notify the applicant who may submit arguments within the following thirty working days in defence of the registration. An additional thirty-working-day term can be granted for once only for filing the evidence in support of the contestation.[349]

As provided in Article 147, the following persons may have legitimate interest to file an opposition in any other of the Member Countries of the ACN: (i) the owner of an identical or similar trademark registered for products and services with respect to which the use of the trademark can induce the public into error; and (ii) the person who has first filed an application to register such trademark. In both cases the opponent must prove a real interest in the market of the Member Country where the opposition is filed. In this sense, the opponent must apply for registration of the trademark at the moment the opposition is filed. Consequently, oppositions to trademarks are allowed regardless of national boundaries within the Andean Community.

It is worth noting that Colombia also accepts oppositions from nationals of Member States of the Inter-American General Convention for Trademark and Commercial Protection (The Washington Convention), which is in force in ten American countries (Colombia, Cuba, El Salvador, Guatemala, Haiti, Nicaragua, Panamá, Paraguay, Peru, and the United States). Opposition for trademarks not registered in Colombia are accepted when: (1) they have been registered in one of the other Member States; (2) the two trademarks in question are so similar that they may cause confusion or error among the relevant public; (3) the opposing party demonstrates that the applicant had knowledge of the existence and use of the opposing trademark in any of the contracting States; and (4) that such trademark covers products in the same class.

348. *See* Art. 1 of Decree 2591 of 2000.

349. *See* Art. 148 of the Decision.

The Superintendence now accepts that, as a result of the broad diffusion of online content throughout the Member States, evidence obtained from the Internet will be adequate to prove use of the opposing trademark.

With regard to the third and fourth requirements, the Superintendence has established that the fact that the signs in conflict are identical (especially those trademarks which are made up) and that the applicant is a direct competitor of the opposing party will be a strong indication towards proving that the applicant had previous knowledge of the use of the trademark. In any case, the analysis for these requirements should be made on a case-by-case basis.

233. In the same sense, when an opposition is filed on basis of the existence of an identical or confusingly similar trademark previously registered in any Member Country of the ACN, the Superintendence has the authority to deny the registration of such trademark. An opposition can also be based on the existence of another application for registration filed in any Member Country of the ACN before the second one. In this case, the second application will be suspended until the registration of the first application is conferred. In that event, the Superintendence may also deny the registration of the second trademark.

234. Pursuant to Article 149, the Superintendence will not consider oppositions that:

(a) do not provide essential information identifying the opponent and the application against which the opposition is being filed;
(b) are filed after the deadlines have lapsed; and
(c) have not paid the prescribed processing fees.

IV. The Final Exam for Registration

235. Pursuant to Article 150, once the term prescribed for oppositions has expired, or if no opposition has been filed, the Superintendence shall proceed to examine the registrability of the trademark. If any opposition has been filed, the Superintendence shall rule on the grant or refusal of the registration. According to the Andean Court, the exam for registration is mandatory and has to be performed even if no oppositions have been filed.[350] The exam must take into account the conditions for registration and the unregistered signs prescribed in Articles 135 and 136. After said exam, the Superintendence shall grant or deny registration by means of a resolution. The exam should be careful and profound in order to determine if two signs may cause confusion to consumers.[351]

236. The confusion as to the identity and similarity of signs can by direct or indirect. The former is characterized by the bond of the identity and similarity of the signs that make consumers acquire specific products and services believing they are buying or hiring others. This is known as the risk of confusion. As for the latter, the

350. *See* Andean Court of Justice, Proceeding No. 16-IP-2003, 1 Mar. 2003, published in *Gaceta Oficial del Acuerdo de Cartagena*, No. 916, 2 Apr. 2003.

351. *See* Andean Court of Justice, Proceeding No. 4-IP-98, 17 Aug. 1998, published in *Gaceta Oficial del Acuerdo de Cartagena*, No. 375, 7 Oct. 1998.

existing bond makes consumers to attribute a common source or origin to two different products or services.[352] This is known as the risk of association.

237. The confusion can be (1) visual; (2) phonetic, and (3) ideological, meaning that the similarities are related to graphics, sounds, and concepts.[353] The Court, relying on scholars, has pointed out three types of similarities that must be taken into account when determining the degree of confusion:[354]

(1) Orthographic similarity: consists of the coincidence of letters, vocal sequence, length, number of syllables, roots, and common endings of the words.
(2) Phonetic similarity: consists of similar sounds between signs when they are pronounced. To determine this similarity the identity of the tonic syllable or their roots and coinciding endings must be taken into account.
(3) Ideological similarity: consists of signs that evoke the same meaning or idea.

238. The exam must be based on comparison rules laid down by scholars, which have been adopted by the case law[355] of the Andean Court. These rules are:

(a) The confusion is the result of the first impression caused by the trademark taken as a unit. Therefore, all the elements forming each mark must be examined without breaking or altering the phonetic and graphic unit. In simpler terms, the elements that compose a trademark must be examined altogether, avoiding the separation of the integrating parts of the mark under comparison.
(b) Trademarks must be examined successively and not simultaneously, as this is the way a common user would act.
(c) Trademarks must be examined taking into account the similarities and not the differences; such similarities derive from the likeness of the elements and the likeness of their location, not from the different elements appearing in the trademark arrangement.
(d) The examiner must take the place of a potential consumer and take into account the nature of the products or services covered by the trademarks being compared.

According to scholars, the first criterion is the most important one and it applies to all kinds of trademarks. This general vision is the impression that an average consumer has about a trademark, which can lead to confusion with respect to other trademarks available in the market. In trademarks, it is crucial to find the feature that penetrates more intensely the consumer's mind and that determines such general vision. For this reason, in order to compare a denominative trademark with a combined trademark, it is essential to determine which element prevails over the other. For instance, if the words are the determining element, the examiner must proceed to examine both

352. *See* Andean Court of Justice, Proceeding No. 58-IP-2001, 19 Sep. 2001, published in *Gaceta Oficial del Acuerdo de Cartagena*, No. 724, 16 Oct. 2001.
353. *See* Andean Court of Justice, Proceeding No. 67-IP-2004, 30 Jun. 2004, published in *Gaceta Oficial del Acuerdo de Cartagena*, No. 1102, 6 Aug. 2004.
354. *Ibid.*
355. *See* Andean Court of Justice, Proceeding No. 8-IP-95, 30 Aug. 1996, published in *Gaceta Oficial del Acuerdo de Cartagena*, No. 231, 17 Oct. 1996.

trademarks accordingly with the comparison rules. However, if the figurative element prevails but the words are similar, it could be understood that both trademarks are not confusing and consequently, they can coexist in the market. Moreover, the comparison must be successive rather than simultaneous since the consumer does not analyse all trademarks at the same time, but in an individualized manner. Trademarks must be compared taken into account the final impression of the consumer after he/she has observed the trademarks.[356]

Moreover, all generic elements must be left aside when evaluating similarities in trademarks. In a recent case from September 2010, the Council of State ruled that generic expressions cannot be considered exclusively to evaluate the risk of confusion; only the distinctive elements of the trademarks must be scrutinized. In the case in hand, the Superintendence rejected the opposition against the trademark 'Condimentos Noe Puro' (Pure Noe Condiments), filed by the company Galletas Noel S.A (Noel Cookies S.A.), as the combination of elements in the first trademark avoided any confusion, which was reaffirmed by the fact that Noe is a biblical character (Noah in Spanish) and Noel is a term to identify Santa Claus in Spanish (Papá Noél). The Council of State determined that the expressions 'Condimentos' and 'Puro' were generic and therefore, the comparison of these signs should not be taken into account as commonly used, generic or descriptive words belong to public domain and therefore cannot be used by an applicant to distinguish goods in the marketplace. Hence, the basis of comparison should be 'Noe' and 'Noel'. The Council of State found these signs to be similar from the phonetic, graphic, visual, orthographic, and auditory point of view, and that the additional 'L' in one of the trademarks was not enough to avoid confusion, especially taking into account that both signs covered goods in Class 30.

239. Furthermore, in order to determine the similarities of the products or services, the exam must take into account the speciality principle, the identity of the products or services, and its classification. For this matter, the exam must be performed according to the criteria set forth by the Court in the proceeding 08-IP-95. In that opportunity, the Court stated that the judge should analyse the degree of competitive connection between the products or services of both trademarks. The following criteria should be used thereto:

(a) the inclusion of the products in the same class;
(b) channels of commercialization;
(c) similar advertising means;
(d) relation between products;
(e) joint or complementary use of products; and
(f) same gender of products.

240. This exam helps to avoid the risk of association that may exist as to the nature of products or services. In this sense, the lack of competitive connection cannot be presumed in any case, not even if the products belong to different classes, or if they belong to the same class.

241. This registrability exam can be illustrated by the one performed by the Superintendence and the Council of State when comparing the *RAFT* trademark with

356. *Ibid.*

the *TAFT* trademark.[357] In this case, the corporation Rhone-Poulenc Agro filed an application for registration of the trademark *RAFT*, to cover herbicides. The Superintendence refused registration, considering that the applied-for mark was confusingly similar to the trademark *TAFT*, previously registered by Hans Schwarzkopf GmbH & Co. for pharmaceutical, hygiene, and veterinary preparations. Rhone-Poulenc Agro filed a nullity action against the Superintendence's Decision, arguing that the marks were not confusable, as herbicides are products totally different from pharmaceutical, hygiene, and veterinarian preparations.

Applying the principles set forth by the Andean Court, the Council of State found that there was an orthographic similarity between the marks in conflict, as they coincided in the letters AFT and they had the same length, number of syllables, and endings. In addition, there was a phonetic similarity between *RAFT* and *TAFT*, as in both marks the emphasis was on the vowel A, one of the three letters that coincided. Furthermore, the Council of State also found that, based on an examination of the products covered by the trademark, there was a competitive connection between the trademarks, given that the marketing channels and advertising means used for all products were the same. The fact that *RAFT* would have been registered only for herbicides and *TAFT* for pharmaceutical was not sufficient to lessen the risk of confusion. Therefore, the Council of State rejected Rhone-Poulenc Agro's claim and confirmed the Superintendence's Decision.

242. Regarding the registrability exam, another illustrative case is the one of a design trademark of *Alpha Shoes S.A.* and *Red Bull GmbH*.[358] *Alpha Shoes S.A* requested that the Council of State annul the resolution of the Superintendence that declared ungrounded its opposition to the registration of the design mark applied for by *Red Bull* consisting of a *wild animal in charging position or bull in fighting attitude*. According to the plaintiff, such trademark was confusingly similar to its prior registration for the design mark *Rhinoceros of four legged beast in walking position*. *Red Bull* countered that there was no visual similarity between the trademarks, as its mark was formed by a shape of a charging fighting bull, which conveyed the idea of strength, defence, and aggressiveness, while the opposing mark was a caricature depicting a walking rhinoceros with shoes. According to *Red Bull*, the graphics of the design made different impressions on consumer's minds. After examining the trademarks as indicated in the comparison rules, the Council of State deemed that their coexistence in the market would not pose a risk of confusion, as an unaware consumer would remember that one of them was formed by a rhinoceros and the other by a bull.

357. *See* Resolution No. 11067 of the Superintendence of Industry and Commerce, 29 May 2000. and *Rhone-Poulenc Agro v. Superintendence of Industry and Commerce*, Council of State, File 7334, 3 Mar. 2005. Other relevant cases include: Sociedad J.P. *Morgan Chase & Co. v. Superintendence of Industry and Commerce*. Council of State. File 1965, 17 Mar. 2005; *Conavi Banco Comercial y de Ahorro S.A. v. Superintendence of Industry and Commerce*. Council of State. File 7268, 14 Apr. 2005; *Parke, Davis & Co. Limited v. Superintendence of Industry and Commerce*. Council of State. File 5214, 2 Mar. 2005; *Ebel S.A. v. Superintendence of Industry and Commerce*. Council of State. File 3449, 22 Apr. 1995; *Kraft Foods Inc. v. Hershey Foods Corp.*, Council of State, File 5449-01, 19 Feb. 2004.

358. *See Alpha Shoes S.A. v. Superintendence of Industry and Commerce*. Council of State. File 7461, 16 Jun. 2005.

243. Once the Superintendence has performed the exam, it shall proceed to grant or deny the registration of the trademark. However, Article 137 establishes that it can deny the registration when it has sufficient reasons to believe that the reason underlying the application was filed to commit an act of unfair competition. Article 21 of Resolution 210 of 2001 indicates that the following are sufficient reasons to refuse the registration of a trademark:

(a) when the Superintendence has opened an investigation for acts deemed to be contrary to the provisions of Law 256 of 1996 (Competition Law) and those amending or supplementing it, based on the same facts; or
(b) when the Superintendence concludes that an investigation for acts assumed to be contrary to the provisions of Law 256 of 1996 (Unfair Competition Law) and those amending or supplementing it, would have been opened based on the same facts submitted to a competent judge as basis of a lawsuit.

§5. Ownership and Transfer

244. The owner of a trademark is the person to whom registration has been granted. This person can be an individual or a legal entity. Decision 486 does not mention who can be the owner of each type of trademark or which requirements he/she shall fulfil. However, a legitimate interest is presumed when a person applies for the registration of a trademark.

245. Regarding collective trademarks, Article 181 establishes that the following legally established associations may apply for its registration: (i) associations of producers; (ii) associations of manufacturers; (iii) associations of service providers; and (iv) legally established organizations or group of persons. As for certification marks, Article 186 indicates that it may be owned by: (i) a public or private business or institution, or (ii) a state, regional, or international organization.

246. As set forth in Article 161, a registration or a pending application of a trademark may be assigned or transferred by an act *inter vivos* or by succession, with or without the business organization to which it belongs, as well as the application for registration. The assignment or transfer shall be registered before the Superintendence, which may deny transfer if it may cause confusion. Any failure to register the assignment renders it unenforceable against third parties. In this regard, the Andean Court has stated that 'the assignment or transfer of trademarks may carry risk of confusion in the market since it generates a crack in its distinctive function, relating the origin of the business organization and the quality of the product or service'. The Decision of the Superintendence denying the assignment or transfer shall be notified to the interested party. In this case, a term shall be granted for purposes of exercising the right of defence, which will start running whenever the notification takes place.[359]

247. Moreover, Article 162 indicates that the owner of a trademark registered or applied for, may grant a licence to one or more parties to use the trademark in question. The licence must be registered before the Superintendence in order to be

359. *See* Andean Court of Justice, Proceeding No. 43-IP-2004, 14 Jul. 2004, published in *Gaceta Oficial del Acuerdo de Cartagena*, No. 1109, 26 Aug. 2004.

opposable to third parties. Furthermore, Article 164 establishes that the owner of the registered trademark shall report to the Superintendence, during the licence period of effectiveness, any change in the name or address of the registered trademark owner. Otherwise, any notification that is made using the data entered in the registration will be considered valid. Furthermore, pursuant to Article 163, the Superintendence shall not register any trademark licensing agreement or assignment or transfers that do not conform to the provisions of the Common Regime for the Treatment of Foreign Capital and for Trademarks, Patents, Licences, and Royalties, or that do not conform to the Andean Community or domestic antitrust. Regarding collective trademarks, Article 183 establishes that they may also be assigned, transferred, or licensed in accordance with the internal by-laws of the association, organization, or group of persons. These acts shall be registered in order to take effect in regard to third parties.

248. The licence grants the licensee the exclusive right of using and exploiting the trademark. However, the licensee's right is limited by the terms and conditions prescribed in the licence agreement. According to Article 594 of the Colombian Code of Commerce, the licence agreement must contain stipulations that assure the quality of the products or services produced or rendered by the licensee. The right holder is in charge of the effective control of such quality and, consequently, has unlimited joint and several liability for damages caused to third parties. Furthermore, said article also establishes that at the request of any person or ex officio, the office in charge of the control of norms and qualities will take the appropriate measures to guarantee the quality[360] and will impose the sanctions, as the case may be.

249. The Andean Court has established the differences between a trademark licence and an assignment or a transfer. In a trademark licence, the owner of the trademark still enjoys his/her exclusive rights and the rights awarded to the licensee are more limited. However, in the assignment or transfer, the owner of the trademark transfers all his/her right to another person.[361]

§6. Scope of Exclusive Rights

250. As mentioned earlier, the only manner of acquiring an exclusive right of a trademark is through the registration. The protection for trademarks is ruled by two important principles: territoriality and speciality. Regarding the former, the exclusive rights of a trademark can only be exercised in the territory where the protection is granted. In this sense, the protection for the trademark is circumscribed to the geographical jurisdiction of the competent authority that grants the registration. Consequently, it is necessary to register trademarks in each one of the Member Countries of the ACN or any other country for ensuring protection. Also, the registration of the trademark applies to specific kinds of products and services, which limits the protection granted by the

360. In Colombia there are several offices in charge of the control of norms and qualities, such as, the Superintendence of Industry and Commerce and The National Institute for the Surveillance of Medicines and Foods (INVIMA).

361. *See* Andean Court of Justice, Proceeding No. 30-IP-97, 8 May 1998, published in *Gaceta Oficial del Acuerdo de Cartagena*, No. 355, 14 Jul. 1998.

trademark. Therefore, identical trademarks may coexist in the name of different owners if they identify different products or services.

251. Regarding registration in other countries, the Supreme Court of Justice stated in the Louis Vuitton case in 2002[362] that the strength of the principle of territoriality of trademarks has been diminished due to treaties such as: (i) the Paris Convention, which contemplates international protection for trademarks through the priority right and the protection of well-known trademarks; and (ii) the Colombian-French Convention of 1901, according to which trademark rights duly obtained in France enjoy protection in Colombia even if it has not been registered in this country, and vice versa.

In this case, the French Company Louis Vuitton requested the cancellation of the registration of the *Louis Vuitton* trademark granted to a Colombian individual. Such trademark goes back to 1854, when Mr Louis Vuitton established a store in Paris bearing his name, with the purpose of manufacturing and selling suitcases and other travel items. The trademark became very successful and well known but it was not registered in Colombia. In 1978, the Superintendence allowed the registration of such trademark given that the application was filed by a Colombian individual. The Supreme Court studied the case and ruled in favour of the original owner of the trademark. It argued that 'in 1901, year in which the Colombian-French Convention was signed, the material possession of the trademark, was what conferred ownership in trademarks and not its registration. Therefore, the Convention had to be interpreted in the sense that the owner of rights in trademarks legitimately acquired in France enjoys protection in Colombia'.

252. Likewise, the Council of State held that trademarks registered in France enjoy protection in Colombia. This was stated in the case of the French corporation Salomon S.A. The plaintiff claimed against the grant of a registered trademark for *Salomon* to a Colombian individual, who had applied on his own behalf for the registration in Colombia of well-known trademarks such as, *Salomon*, *Guess*, and *Benetton*. In this case, the Council of State held that, according to the Colombian-French Convention, a French trademark does not require its registration in Colombia to be protected. However, if there is no registration, protection has to be claimed by the trademark owner through internal mechanisms, that is, through opposition to applications for registration, cancellation actions before the Superintendence against subsequent registrations, or through judicial actions, as the case may be.[363]

Salomon argued that because its mark was well known and famous around the world, the Colombian-French Convention afforded the company protection for its trademark in Colombia even though the mark was not registered there. The Colombian citizen countered that his registration in Colombia was his source of trademark rights, and the Convention had no effect whatsoever. The Council of State adopted the position of the French owner and granted the protection applied for to its trademark *Salomon*, registered in France.

362. *See Louis Vuitton S.A. v. Natalio Isaac Lustgarten Coldman*, Supreme Court of Justice, File 5990, 8 Feb. 2002.

363. *See Salomon S.A. v. Superintendence of Industry and Commerce*, Council of State, File 7894, 24 Feb. 2005.

253. Regarding exclusive rights acquired through registration, the Andean Court has mentioned four specific powers that the owner of a registered trademark may exercise:

(1) to file judicial and administrative actions to prevent third parties to use identical or similar trademarks for identical or related products;
(2) to commercialize the products or services covered by the trademark;
(3) to advertise the trademark; and
(4) to prevent third parties from advertising the trademark.

254. The Court has emphasized that the exclusivity of the right conferred to the trademark owner has a negative and a positive aspect. The former allows the right owner to use, transfer, assign, and license the trademark. As to the latter, the owner of a trademark can prohibit the unauthorized use of such trademark by third parties, which is known as the *ius prohibendi*. The *ius prohibendi* is extended not only to identical signs but also to those confusingly similar, which includes not only the same products and services but also the similar or related ones.[364] In addition, the *ius prohibendi* actions attempt to avoid the double use of identical or similar trademarks, which may create confusion in the market. Accordingly, Article 155 establishes that the owner of a registered trademark has the exclusive right to prevent third parties not having his/her consent from engaging in the following acts:

(a) to use or stamp the mark or a distinctive sign, identical or similar, on products or services for which the trademark was registered; on products related to the services for which it was registered; or on containers, packages, wrappings or crates or arrangements of such products;
(b) to eliminate from or modify the trademark for commercial purposes, after it may have been stamped or placed on products for which it was registered; from or on products related to any services for which it was registered; from or on containers, packages, wrappings crates or arrangements of such products;
(c) to manufacture labels, containers wrappings or crates or other materials reproducing or containing the trademark, as well as to commercialize or retain by force such materials;
(d) to use in trade an identical or similar sign with respect to any products or services different from those for which the trademark has been registered, when use of such sign related to such goods or services could cause confusion or a risk of association with the proprietor of the registration. In the event of utilization of an identical sign for identical products or services, the risk of confusion will be inferred to exist;
(e) use in commerce a sign identical or similar to a famous or well-known trademark with respect to any products or services, when it could cause an unjust economic or commercial damage to the proprietor of the registration due to dilution of the distinctive strength or the commercial or advertising value of the trademark or by reason of an unfair utilization of the prestige of the trademark or its proprietor;

364. *See* Andean Court of Justice, Proceeding No. 4-IP-94, 7 Aug. 1995, published in *Gaceta Oficial del Acuerdo de Cartagena*, No. 189, 15 Sep. 1995.

(f) to utilize publicly a sign identical or similar to a famous or well-known trademark for non-commercial purposes, when it could cause dilution of the distinctive strength or the commercial or advertising value of the trademark or an unfair utilization of its prestige.

255. In this matter, Article 156 indicates the acts that constitute use of a trademark by a third party in the course of commerce:

- to introduce in commerce, sell, offer for sale or distribute products or services under the relevant sign;
- import, export, store or transport products under the related sign; or
- use the sign in advertising, publications, commercial documents or communications written or oral, independently from the mean of communication utilized and without prejudice to any provisions on advertising that may be applicable.

I. Special Protection for Well-Known or Notorious Trademarks

256. Decision 486 establishes a general protection for well-known distinctive signs, which are: (i) trademarks; (ii) advertising slogans; (iii) trade names; (iv) labels or emblems; (v) appellations of origins; and (vi) indications of origin. Article 225 establishes that a well-known sign is protected from non-authorized use or registration, regardless of other Andean provisions that may be applicable and of other provisions of the Member Country in respect of protection against unfair competition.

257. Well-known trademarks enjoy a special protection since it is extended to all kind of products and services and to different territories where their registration was claimed or granted. In accordance with Article 136(h) and Article 155(e) and (f), Article 226 establishes that the use of all or a part of a well-known distinctive sign or the reproduction, imitation, translation, or transliteration, that may create confusion in respect of identical or similar businesses, activities, products or services to those to which it is applied, constitutes unauthorized use of that distinctive sign. Furthermore, it will also constitute unauthorized use, the use of well-known sign or part of it, or the reproduction, imitation, translation, or transliteration, even in respect of businesses, activities, products, or services other that those to which that well-known sign is applied, or its use for non-commercial purposes, when such use could be liable to produce any of the following effects:

(a) the risk of confusion or of association with the owner of the sign, or with the businesses, activities, products, or services belonging to that owner;
(b) unjust economic or commercial injury to the owner of the sign by reason of the dilution of the distinctive force or commercial or advertising value of that sign; or
(c) unfair exploitation of the sign's prestige or fame.

258. The weakening of the distinctive force of a trademark is a phenomenon applicable to well-known or notorious trademarks. The distinctive force of the trademark may fade in the following events: (1) when the trademark is used without authorization to identify products or services different from the ones originally intended to identify, causing the trademark to fail to accomplish its main function of identifying such products, or (2) when the trademark is registered for different products or services that are associated with others of bad quality offered in the market.[365] According to the Andean Court, the weakening of the distinctive force of a well-known trademark is very difficult to prove, unless it is related with trademark confusion. The distinctive force can fade only when the trademark consists of different products.[366]

259. As to the well-known character of a trademark, it is never presumed and thus, it shall be proven by whoever claims such status.[367] In addition, the well-known character must be recognized by the Superintendence by means of a resolution.[368] In this regard, the Andean Court in proceeding 30-IP-2004 applied several criteria established by scholars to decide whether a trademark is well known or not. These are:

(1) wide advertising, which makes the trademark known by a high percentage of the population in general;
(2) extensive use and acceptance by a large number of consumers, depending on the more or less massive nature of the product;
(3) transcendence in the corresponding industrial or commercial field;
(4) its simple mention should elicit in the public a direct association with the product or service identified.

260. Likewise, Article 228 mentions that the following criteria shall be taken into account:

(a) the extent to which it is known in the relevant sector of the public in any Member Country of the ACN;
(b) the age of the distinctive sign and the size of the geographical area where it is used in and outside any Member Country of the ACN;
(c) the age and the size of the geographical area where the distinctive sign is promoted, in or outside any Member Country of the ACN, including its advertising and presentation at fairs, exhibitions, or other events in connection with the products or services, the establishment, or the activity to which it is applied;
(d) the value of all investments made in promoting the distinctive sign or the establishment, activity, products, or services to which it is applied;
(e) sale and income figures of the owner, both at the international level and in the Member Country of the ACN where protection is being sought, in respect of the distinctive sign whose well-known character is alleged;

365. *See* Andean Court of Justice, Proceeding No. 31-IP-96, 3 Dec. 1997, published in *Gaceta Oficial del Acuerdo de Cartagena*, No. 318, 26 Jan. 1998.

366. *Ibid.*

367. *See* Andean Court of Justice, Proceeding No. 08-IP-95, 30 Aug. 1996, published in *Gaceta Oficial del Acuerdo de Cartagena*, No. 231, 17 Oct. 1996.

368. *See* Andean Court of Justice, Proceeding No. 60-IP-2001, 16 Nov. 2001, published in *Gaceta Oficial del Acuerdo de Cartagena*, No. 750, 15 Jan. 2002.

(f) the extent of the inherent or acquired distinctiveness of the sign;
(g) the book value of the sign as a corporate asset;
(h) the volume of orders from persons interested in obtaining a franchise or licence to the sign in a specific territory;
(i) the existence of significant manufacturing, purchasing, or storage activities by the owner of the sign in the Member Country of the ACN where protection is being sought;
(j) the international trade-related aspects; or
(k) the existence or age of any registration or application for registration of the distinctive sign in the Member Country of the ACN concerned or in any other country.

261. According to Article 24 of Resolution 210 of 2001 of the Superintendence, documents reflecting facts, events or figures, submitted to prove the well-known condition of a sign, will only be relevant if they are directly related to the condition of the well-known trademark and are valuated to indicate the conditions that prove said condition. Article 229 establishes that the well-known nature of a sign shall not be denied solely because: (i) it is not registered or in the process of being registered in the Member Country of the ACN concerned or in any other country; (ii) it has not been used nor it is not being used to distinguish products or services or to identify activities or businesses in the Member Country of the ACN concerned; or (iii) it is not well-known abroad.

262. The *HARRODS'* case is illustrative in this matter.[369] In this case, the British firm Harrods Limited requested to the Council of State the annulment of the resolution issued by the Superintendence that allowed the registration of the trademark *HARRODS* in favour of Harrods (Buenos Aires) Limited to cover products of International Class 9. According to the plaintiff, the registration of the trademark *HARRODS* was null because of its prior registration, covering products of Class 28. The plaintiff further claimed the well-known character of trademark *HARRODS*.

In this opportunity, the Council of State concluded that it was not necessary to implement further analyses for establishing that those trademarks were identical. It explained that in the Andean Community the existence of two identical trademarks for identifying different products is possible, except when one of them is a well-known trademark, because this could induce consumers into error in regard to the source of the products. When analysing if *HARRODS* was a well-known trademark, the Council of State studied the history of the expression *HARRODS* as distinctive sign. It found that it appeared in 1849, when a food store with this name had been opened in London,

369. *See Harrods Limited v. Superintendence of Industry and Commerce*, Council of State, File 8303, 22 Oct. 2001. *See also* Andean Court of Justice, Proceeding No. 55-IP-2004, 14 Jul. 2004, published in *Gaceta Oficial del Acuerdo de Cartagena*, No. 1110, 27 Aug. 2004. Other relevant cases include: *Louis Vuitton S.A. v. Natalio Isaac Lustgarten Coldman*, Supreme Court of Justice, File 5990, 8 Feb. 2002; *Laura Ashley Manufacturing B.V. v. Superintendence of Industry and Commerce*, Council of State. File 3426, 15 Nov. 2002; *Warner-Lambert Co. v. Nobel Farmaceútica S.A.*, Council of State, File 05394, 21 Jul. 2004; *Supertex Medical S.A. v. Superintendence of Industry and Commerce*, Council of State. File 6450, 20 Oct. 2006; *Alpina Productos Alminetícios S.A. v. Superintendence of Industry and Commerce*, Council of State. File 627801, 4 Jul. 2003.

UK. In 1889, it became a limited liability company and changed its name into *HARRODS LIMITED*. The store began making sales by catalogue, both at the national and international level. Today it sells a wide variety of products such as cosmetics, jewels, clothing, food, and books. It also found that the trademark is registered in more that forty countries around the world.

The Council of State also explained that *HARRODS* invests approximately GBP 2,300,000 per year in advertising, and its products have been advertised in magazines in Europe and all throughout the American Continent. Finally, the Council of State concluded that the trademark *HARRODS* met the requirements for being considered as a well-known trademark, and that the registration of an identical trademark, even if to cover products of a class different from those in which the well-known trademark had been registered, is not allowed.

263. Another aspect of the *ius prohibendi* is the faculty of the registration owner of taking special action to prevent the use of the trademark by third parties. That owner may also prevent a third party from engaging in the acts established in paragraph 240 (Article 155). However, the right to act against the unauthorized use of such trademark lapses in five years counted form the date on which the owner was informed of that use, except when such use was done in bad faith in which case that right to action would not lapse.[370] For these purposes, Article 234 indicates that when deciding on an action for unauthorized use of a well-known trademark, the national competent authority shall take into account the good or bad faith of the parties in the adoption and use of such trademark. Furthermore, the owner of a well-known trademark may take the previous action and take appropriate measures before the competent authority. Those measures are the provisional and border measures explained in Chapter 12

264. In addition to the special action to prevent the use of well-known trademarks, a regular action for cancellation of the registration may be exercised. The cancellation of the registration takes place when the trademark is confusingly similar or identical to a well-known trademark. (For more information, *see* paragraph 307).

265. Regarding domain names, Article 233 of Decision 486 establishes that when a well-known distinctive sign has been unlawfully registered in a Member Country of the ACN as part of a domain name or electronic mailing address, the lawful right holder of such well-known sign may request to the national competent authority the cancellation or amendment of said registration. The national competent authority shall cancel or amend the registration of domain or electronic mailing address if it is likely to cause confusion or association with the other sign; causes unjust economic or commercial injury to the owner of the sign; and implies an unfair exploitation of the sign's prestige or fame.

266. In Colombia, after the recent transition process between the former administrator *Universidad de los Andes* (the Andes University), the private company. CO Internet S.A.S is the current administrator of the domain. Since 2009, every individual or legal entity that wishes to obtain the registration of a .CO domain can contact any of the accredited registrars, which include the industry's leading companies

370. *See* Arts 131 and 132 of the Decision.

such as Godaddy and Enoms.[371] The applicant must guarantee among other things, that:[372]

(1) The domain name is not identical or confusingly similar to trademarks, trade names, emblems, corporate names or other distinctive signs registered in Colombia in the name of third parties.
(2) The use or registration of a dominion name does not constitute a registered trademark belonging to a third party; consequently, it does not interfere with legitimate rights acquired by any person in Colombia.

If the applicant provides false, incorrect, or inexact information, the registration of the domain name will be suspended. Therefore, if a domain name is identical or similar to a trademark, it will be suspended.

267. The case of *Federación Nacional de Cafeteros* (The National Federation of Coffee Growers)[373] is illustrative in this matter. Colombia and such Federation were successful in an administrative proceeding against a company that had registered colombiancoffeeshop.com, colombiancoffeeshop.info, colombiancoffeeshop.org, and colombiancoffeeshop.ws as domain names on the Internet. The Federation filed a complaint before the Arbitration and Mediation Centre of the WIPO against Mastercafe SL of Spain and its representative in Bogotá, Colombian Coffee Shop S.A., for using the domain name colombiancoffeeshop.co. Colombia alleged that the word 'Colombian' had been registered in the name of Federación Nacional de Cafeteros (the National Federation of Coffee Growers) as a certification trademark in the United States in 1979, to cover the quality of coffee grown in Colombia. The Arbitration and Mediation Centre determined that: (i) the Federation had a legitimate interest, given that Colombian was registered as a certification trademark and any confusion was detrimental to the goodwill and reputation that the mark represented; (ii) the defendants acted in bad faith because, if they were engaged in professional activities relating to Colombian coffee, they must have known about the extended protection and well-known character of this certification mark; and (iii) there was evidence, in the defendant's domain name and associated expressions, of confusability with the trademark owned by the Federation.

Consequently, WIPO recognized the rights that Colombia and *Federación Nacional de Cafeteros* (the National Federation of Coffee Growers) had in the domain names colombiancoffeeshop.com, colombiancoffeeshop.info, colombiancoffeeshop.org, and colombiancoffeeshop.ws.

§7. Limitations of the Scope of Trademark Protection

268. The limitations to the exclusive rights of a registration owner are related to the *ius prohibendi*, which is the right of the trademark's owner to prohibit the

371. *See* <http://www.cointernet.com.co/ > (last visited 17 Jul. 2017).
372. *Ibid.*
373. *See Federación Nacional de Cafeteros de Colombia & República de Colombia v. Colombian Coffee Shop S.A. Edgar Muñoz Camacho, Mastercafe SL*, WIPO, Arbitration and Mediation Centre, Case No. D2004-0677, 21 Oct. 2004.

unauthorized use of such trademark by third parties. The first limitation, established in Article 157 of the Decision, provides that third parties may use the sign registered as a trademark to indicate their names, addresses, or pseudonyms, geographical names, or any other precise indication concerning the kind, quality, amount, purpose, value, place of origin or time of production of their products or of the rendering of their services, or other characteristics thereof, when this is not intended to identify per se their products and services. This use does not require the consent of the right owner when it complies with the following:

(1) it is done in good faith and must not constitute use as a trademark; and
(2) is confined only to identification or information purposes and is not likely to create confusion over the source of the products or services.

269. In the same sense, a trademark registration does not confer the owner, the right to prevent a third party from using the trademark to announce an event in advertising using brand comparisons, offer for sale, or advertise the existence or availability of products or services lawfully marked, when he/she has proceeded in good faith. Furthermore, it does not confer to the owner the right to prevent a third party from advertising the compatibility or suitability of spare parts or accessories that may be used with products bearing the registered trademark, provided that such use is confined to the purpose of informing the public and is unlikely to lead to confusion over the business organization origin or the products or services concerned.

270. The second limitation is established in Article 158 and refers to the exhaustion of the right. The exclusive right over a trademark is exhausted once the product or service has been lawfully put into trade in any country. In this sense, the trademark registration does not confer on the owner the rights to prevent third parties from engaging in trade in a product protected by registration once the owner of the registered trademark or another party with his/her consent or with economic ties to him/her, has introduced that product into the market of any country. In particular, when any of such products, packaging or packing, which has been in direct contact with the product concerned, has not undergone any change, alteration, or deterioration. It is considered to have economic ties when one of the persons is able to exercise a decisive influence over the other, either directly or indirectly, with respect to use of the trademark right or when a third party is able to exert that influence over both persons.

271. Finally, the last limitation refers to agreements between owners of identical or similar trademarks. Article 159 of Decision 486 establishes that when registrations of an identical or similar mark exist in the subregion in the name of different owners and identify the same kind of products or services, the marketing of these in the territory of the Member Country concerned shall be prohibited, except when the owners of said marks enter into an agreement allowing such marketing. Article 159 has provides that the parties must take the necessary precautions to avoid misleading the public as to the origin of the products or services concerned. In this regard, they must include elements relating to the identification of the origin of the products or services in question in appropriate and prominent characters for the proper information of the consuming public. Those agreements shall be registered before the Superintendence and shall conform to the standards governing business practices and the promotion of competition.

Furthermore, the importation of products or services that are identified by identical or similar marks in the name of different owners, will not be prohibited whenever the trademark is not being utilized within the territory of the importer country, except when the owner of such trademark evidences at the Superintendence that the non-utilization of the trademark has been due to justifiable reasons.

272. In sum, trademark coexistence is possible if the following requirements concur:

(1) existence of identical or similar trademarks in the subregion;
(2) agreements between the owners of such trademarks;
(3) adoption of necessary precautions to avoid misleading the public regarding the origin of the products or services concerned, given proper information to the consuming public;
(4) registration of said agreements in the trademark office of each country; and
(5) respect of norms concerning business practices and promotion of competition.

273. Regarding the coexistence prescribed in Article 159, the Court has established that those agreements are important instruments for business organizations that compete in the market, in order to determine that certain identical or similar trademarks may fulfil their functions without any conflict of interest among their owners. However, those agreements will be effective and accepted by the national competent authority, only if they protect the general interest of consumers avoiding the risk of confusion. In this sense, the subscription of agreements between the owners of identical or similar trademarks is not the only requirement for the operation of the trademark coexistence, since the public interest may prevail over individual interests.[374] In this regard, the Council of State's ruling in the case of the trademark *UNIVERSAL* is illustrative.[375] The Superintendence considered that the trademark *UNIVERSAL* in the name of Corn Products International was confusingly similar to the trademark *UNIVERSAL* previously registered by *Navarro Vives e Hijos*, and both trademarks were intended to cover products in the same class. Corn Products International argued that consumers would not be confused because there was an agreement between the owners of the trademark to limit their use: the registered trademark would be used only for coffee and coffee derivatives, while the mark applied for would only cover corn starch and other products.

274. In accordance with the prejudicial interpretation of the Andean Court, the Council of State declared that the coexistence agreement signed by the parties did not exempt the administrative or judicial authorities from their obligation to conduct the registrability exam and protect consumers. Finally, the Council of State ruled that the Superintendence acted validly since the trademarks are identical in phonetic, conceptual, and visual terms, and it will be easy to confuse consumers, as the products in question were related, given the fact that they were all foodstuffs and were sold in the same places.

275. Likewise, the Council of State ruled in favour of the Decision of the Superintendence refusing the registration of the mark *Starbucks Coffee*, regardless of

374. *Ibid.*

375. *See Corn Products International Inc. v. Superintendence of Industry and Commerce*, Council of State, File 7363, 17 Feb. 2005.

the coexistence agreement celebrated between Starbucks Corporation and Mars Incorporated. In this opportunity, Starbucks Corporation applied for the registration of the mark *Starbucks*. The registration was refused since it was orthographically and phonetically similar to *Starburst*, a trademark registered by Mars Incorporated. Starbucks Corporation filed a nullity action against said Decision and requested the Council of State to take into account the worldwide trademark coexistence agreement entered into by the parties. Such agreement had allowed these trademarks to coexist peacefully in the market for several years because Starbucks agrees to refrain from using its trademark with respect to fruit candies and confectionary products, while Mars agrees to refrain from using its mark with respect to coffee, cocoa, espressos, coffee substitutes and coffee beverages, and also, they undertook to respect certain limitations as to the places where these products are sold. The Council of State deemed that the similarity existing between the marks and the consequent risk for consumers were so evident that the companies owning the marks had to enter into an agreement. It considers that the Decision to refuse the registration was valid since the marks lack differentiating capacity, and therefore, its coexistence may lead consumers to error.

276. Conversely, the Council of State declared valid the coexistence agreement signed by Santander Investment Bank Limited and Robert Bosch GmbH.[376] The former, applied to register the word and design mark *BSCH* to cover services in International Class 36. The applicant signed a worldwide agreement with Robert Bosch GmbH, concerning the coexistence of the trademarks *BSCH* and *BOSCH*. The Superintendence refused the registration of *BSCH* as a trademark concluding that it was similar to trademark BOSCH in both orthographic and phonetic terms, and that if they were allowed to coexist in the market they would lead consumers to error. The Santander Investment Bank brought before the Council of State an action of nullity and restoration of rights against said resolution. In this opportunity, the Council of State clarified that coexistence agreements neither make marks registrable per se nor prove that their similarities will not lead consumers to error. However, it held that the trademarks *BSCH* and *BOSCH* could coexist in the market without posing a risk of confusion among consumers. It found that, when the marks were seen as whole units, taking into account their visual, phonetic, and conceptual aspects, there were more differences than similarities between them. Indeed, the Council stated, as *BSCH* was the acronym of the corporate name of the bank, it was graphically representable and different from *BOSCH*. In addition, each of the letters in *BSCH* had to be pronounced separately, while *BOSCH* was pronounced as one word.

§8. Use Requirements

277. According to the Andean legislation, trademarks shall be used. In this regard, Article 165 of Decision 486 establishes that a trademark registration may be cancelled after an uninterrupted period of non-use, without valid reasons, in any Member Country of the ACN. The period of non-use must be of at least three years immediately before starting any the cancellation proceedings. As set forth in Article

376. *See Santander Investment Bank Limited v. Superintendence of Industry and Commerce*, Council of State, File 7319, 11 Aug. 2005.

166, the use of a trademark in a form different from that in which it was registered only with respect to details or features that do not alter its distinctive character, does not constitute grounds for cancellation of registration for non-use, or lessen the protection afforded to the trademark. The non-use of a trademark may only affect one or several products and services in respect to which it was registered. In this case, the Superintendence shall order to shorten or limit the list of products or services originally included in the trademark application, in order to remove those products and services in respect of which the trademark has not been used. For these purposes, the identity, and similarity of products and services must be taken into consideration.

278. Regarding the use of a trademark, the Andean Court has stated that the Andean legislation not only grants the right of the exclusive use to the trademark owner, but also establishes a duty to use such trademark. The fulfilment of said obligation mandates the real and effective use of the trademark. For these purposes, it must be taken into account the type, scope, duration of the use, and other circumstances of the specific case. In this sense, 'the relevant factor is the determination if the use is purely apparent, that is, if the user lacks of an authentic economic interest in the production and marketing of the products or services identified by the trademark'. It could be understood that the duty of use has not been fulfilled when it is proven by the weakness of the use, that the right holder is just interested in keeping the ownership of the trademark but is not at all interested in an effective use of it in the market.[377]

279. Pursuant to Article 166, a trademark is considered in use when:

(a) the products or services distinguished by the mark have been placed in circulation in any Member Country of the ACN or are available in the market under that trademark, in the form and amounts that are normal, taken into account the nature of the products or services and the methods used for their marketing; or
(b) it exclusively distinguishes products intended for exportation from any of the Member Countries as prescribed in item (a).

280. In this regard, the Andean Court has established that 'the use of a trademark shall be real and effective. Therefore, the intention of using or advertising the product or service is not enough; the use shall be shown in an external and public way'. The Andean regime considers the distinctiveness as the main function of the trademark. For this reason, the use of a trademark must be materialized by means of real acts of commerce, which will be subject to a fee, such as the sale or disposition of the products or services.[378]

281. Moreover, the Court has mentioned that 'the provisions of the Andean regime do not establish minimum conditions regarding the quantity or volume of marketed products in relation to the use of a trademark'. Scholars and case law have pointed out for these purposes the following guidelines: the use must be serious, in good faith, normal, and unequivocal.

377. *See* Andean Court of Justice, Proceeding No. 17-IP-95, 9 Nov. 1995, published in *Gaceta Oficial del Acuerdo de Cartagena*, No. 199, 26 Jan. 1996.

378. *See* Andean Court of Justice, Proceeding No. 17-IP-95, 9 Nov. 1995, published in *Gaceta Oficial del Acuerdo de Cartagena*, No. 199, 26 Jan. 1996.

The quantitative element is relative and cannot be established in absolute terms for determining the use of a trademark. The use must be determined in relation with the kind of products or services identified by the trademark and with the characteristics of the business organization that uses such trademark. Therefore, if the trademark is related to capital assets, it could be enough to demonstrate two or three sales per year, given its nature, complexity and high price. However, if the trademark relates to products such as corn, it could not be understood as real marketing the sale of three corn bundles per year.[379]

Likewise, a trademark use will not be considered unreal or ineffective, if the trademark is used only in a specific geographical zone and not in all the national territory or in all Member Countries of the ACN. As mentioned earlier, all the circumstances of the specific case must be taken into account to determine the real and effective use.

282. The burden of proof of trademark use rests in the head of the owner of the registration. For these purposes, Article 167 indicates that to prove trademark use, the owner may employ commercial invoices, accounting documents, or auditing certificates, among others, that demonstrate the regular nature and amount of trade that exists in the product identified by the trademark.

§9. Duration of Protection; Renewal; Termination

283. The registration of a trademark is limited in time. Article 152 establishes that it lasts for ten years counted from the date in which registration was granted and may be renewed for successive ten-year periods. For these purposes, the owner of a registered trademark or any party with a legitimate interest must apply before the Superintendence its renewal within six months before the expiration date of the registration. Said person shall attach the payment receipt of the prescribed fees in the application.

284. Pursuant to Article 153, the owner of the registered trademark, or anyone having legitimate interest, enjoys a period of grace of six months following the date of expiration of the registration. These persons shall also attach the payment receipt of the prescribed fees and shall, at the same time, pay the surcharge prescribed by domestic legislation. The trademark renewal as all the procedures now can be done through a simple online payment procedure with the SIPI website. I must be noted that during the whole period, the registered trademark retains its full validity.

285. It is also pointed out that for the renewal, it is not required to prove the use of trademark and it is granted automatically on the same terms as the original registration. However, the owner of the registered trademark may reduce or limit the products or services listed in the original registration.

286. The protection for trademarks terminates in four events: (1) the abandonment of the rights of registration; (2) the lapsing of registration; (3) the nullity of the registration; and (4) the cancellation of the registration.

379. *See* Andean Court of Justice, Proceeding No. 17-IP-95, 9 Nov. 1995, published in *Gaceta Oficial del Acuerdo de Cartagena*, No. 199, 26 Jan. 1996.

I. Abandonment of the Rights of Registration

287. As set forth in Article 171 of the Decision, the owner of a registration may, at any time, resign to his/her registration rights. Such abandonment may be total or partial. If it is partial, the cancellation of the registration shall relate only to those products or services that the owner has resigned. It is also pointed out, that abandonment is not permitted when there are encumbrances or securities over real property registered in the Superintendence. However, abandonment is permitted when the owners of those rights have given their express consent to such registration. The abandonment of a trademark becomes effective only when it is recorded in the Superintendence.

II. Lapsing of Registration

288. The registration of a trademark is limited in time but can be renewed indefinitely. According to Article 174 of Decision 486, when the owner or the person having legitimate interest does not request renewal within the legal time limit, including the period of grace, the registration of the trademark shall lapse. Likewise, the registration shall lapse when the owner or the person having legitimate interest does not pay the prescribed fees.

III. Nullity of the Registration

289. The nullity of the registration of a trademark can be absolute and relative. Regarding the former, Article 172 of the Decision establishes that the Council of State shall, either ex officio or at the request of a party, and at any time, declare the registration of a trademark absolutely null and void when it has been granted in contravention of the provisions of Articles 134.1[380] and 135.[381]

290. As for the relative nullity, the Council of State shall either ex officio or at the request of a party declare the relative invalidation of a trademark registration when it has been granted in contravention of the provisions of Article 136[382] or obtained in bad faith. The legal action of relative nullity will lapse five years following the granting date of the contested registration.[383]

291. Several cases have been decided under Colombian law regarding the absolute and relative nullity action established in Article 172. Hereby a sample of cases that are noteworthy.

380. Article 134.1 mentions the conditions that a sign must meet to be registered as trademark (perceptibility, distinctiveness, and possibility of graphic representation).
381. Article 135 establishes a list of three categories of unregistered signs: not capable of distinguishing products or services, liable to mislead or confuse consumers, and contrary to law, morality, public order, or good manners.
382. Article 136 establishes a list of signs that constitute an impediment to the right of third parties.
383. *See* R. Metke Méndez, *Lecciones de Propiedad Industrial* (First Edition, Medellín-Colombia, Editorial Diké, 2001), 102.

The Corporation Tecnas S.A. producer of the *EL FORTIN* liquid firewood smoke sauces, filed before the Council of State and action for declaration of nullity and restoration of rights against the resolution by which the Superintendence granted the registration of the trademark *HUMO DE LEÑA LIQUIDO* (liquid firewood smoke) in the name of Mr León Sardi Herrera to cover all products in International Class 30.[384] According to the plaintiff, said registration was absolutely null and void since the mark was not sufficiently distinctive since it just indicated to consumers the characteristics of the products. In this case, the product was a firewood smoke-flavoured sauce used to give meat a smoky taste. The Council of State concluded that the plaintiff was correct in arguing that the phrase HUMO DE LEÑA LIQUIDO was not registrable, as the expression was the very definition of the product and described its own characteristics.

Regarding the relative invalidation of a trademark registration obtained in bad faith, the Council of State declared null the registration of the trademark *TAPA ROJA* granted to Mr Carlos Castro, covering products in International Class 33 (alcoholic beverages).[385] In this case, *Fábrica de Licores del Tolima Ltda.* (FLT) had used the *TAPA ROJA* mark since 1965 and its registration was granted in 1983. However, in 1993, FLT lost its right because the company failed to renew the trademark registration. Mr Castro applied for the registration of said trademark, which he obtained in 1998. FLT filed a nullity action before the Council of State based on a so-called preferential right derived from a FLT's prior registration and a permanent health registration for the production of *aguardiente* (an aniseed-derived spirit) covered by this trademark. In addition, FLT stated that *TAPA ROJA* was a well-known trademark that did not need a registration in order to be deemed as such. The Council of State rejected those theories. Notwithstanding, it declared null the registration granted to Mr Castro establishing that he had acted in bad faith. According to the Council of State, Mr Castro was well aware of the relationship between FLT and the trademark *TAPA ROJA*, since he personally rendered services to the distillery and had participated in the placement and consolidation of the mark in the national market. Therefore, the only thing Mr Castro could be expecting from the registration was to benefit from an eventual payment by the distillery for using the trademark, given that the Colombian Constitution provides that only the State may participate in the production of wines, liquors, and spirits.

Another illustrative case regarding relative invalidation of a trademark is the FITNES case.[386] Nestlé S.A. applied in Colombia for registration of the graphic-mixed trademark FITNES for products in Class 29. The legal owner of the word trademark FINESSE (Alpina Productos Alimenticios S.A.), filed an opposition against registration of the mark FITNES, but finally the Superintendence granted the registration of such mark. The opposer strongly disagreed with the Decision and resorted to the Council of State by applying for the nullity of FITNES registration owned by Nestlé. The

384. *See* Class 30: (Staple foods) Coffee, tea, cocoa, sugar, rice, tapioca, sago, artificial coffee; flour and preparations made from cereals, bread, pastry and confectionery, ices; honey, treacle; yeast, baking-powder; salt, mustard; vinegar, sauces (condiments); spices; ice.

385. *See Fábrica de Licores del Tolima Ttda. v. Superintendence of Industry and Commerce*, Council of State, File 6370, 3 Mar. 2005.

386. *See Alpina Productos Alimenticios S.A. v. Superintendence of Industry and Commerce*, Council of State, File 5393, 30 Mar. 2000.

Council of State requested the compulsory prejudicial interpretation form the Andean Court,[387] which stated that when comparing two trademarks in their phonetic aspects, the following rules must be followed. If the compared denominations contain identical vowels and are located in the same order, it can be concluded that the denominations are similar, because that order of distribution of vowels generated the impression that the denomination causes impact on the consumers. If the tonic syllable of the compared denominations is coincident, both for identical or very similar and because they occupy the same position, the denominations are similar. If the tonic syllable and the syllable located in the first position in the mark analysed are equal, then their resemblance is more similar. If, on the contrary, when comparing the marks the tonic syllable is different and the one located in the first position is coincident, then the probability of similarity between both will be lower.

The Council of State based on the previous rules, decided that it was evident that the trademark FITNES for Class 29 was in close resemblance, both in regard to spelling (visual comparison) and phonetics, with the registered trademark FINESSE, which covers products in the same class, and this did not make the existing graphical differences sufficient for considering the marks to be different from each other. Consequently, the likelihood of confusion between the marks was so high that their coexistence in the market could be expected to induce consumers to error. Therefore, the Council of State cancelled the registration of the trademark FITNES, since it was confusingly similar with the trademark FINESSE.

292. Article 172 also establishes that both nullity actions shall not affect the actions that may be brought for compensation of damages. Moreover, it was pointed out that a registered trademark could not be declared null and void on grounds that have ceased to be applicable at the time of the proceeding for invalidation.

293. The invalidation can be total or partial. It is partial when it is applicable only to one or some products or services for which the trademark as registered. In this case, such invalidation shall be pronounced only in respect of those products or services. Consequently, they shall be removed from the trademark registration.

294. The nullity of a trademark registration is declared by means of the ordinary procedure of the Administrative law. If the lawsuit complies with all the requirements of the admissibility test, the judge will proceed to notify the public entity, the public ministry and third parties with direct interest in the process. In addition, the judge proceeds to fix in a list the order of admission of the lawsuit for a term of ten days, so the defendant can file a counter memorial and submit the proofs he/she deem advisable. Once the previous term has expired, the submitted proofs are studied for a period of thirty days. Thereafter, the Council of State grants a term of ten days to both parties to present the final arguments and the Andean Court will proceed to perform the prejudicial interpretation. Finally, the Council of State rules on the trademark's invalidation and informs the parties of its Decision.[388]

295. The declaration of nullity bears the effect of making the null and void act to disappear from the legal life as from the time when the nullity took place. Acts performed under the authority of an act which turned out to be null and void, are acts

387. *See* Andean Court of Justice, Proceeding No. 8-IP-2000, 4 Feb. 2000, published in *Gaceta Oficial del Acuerdo de Cartagena*, No. 539, 28 Feb. 2000.

388. *See* Art. 78 of the Decision.

which bear no juridical effects and which give rise to the right to claim either compensation for damages or that the circumstance concerned be carried back in time to the moment when nullity occurred.[389]

IV. Cancellation of the Registration

296. The cancellation of the registration of a trademark takes place in three different events: (1) when the trademark has not been used within a period of at least three years; (2) when the trademark has become a common or generic name to identify or denote goods or services for which it was registered; and (3) when the trademark is identical or similar to a well-known trademark. The cancellation of the registration in those events takes place by different procedures, as follows.

297. Article 165 of Decision 486 establishes that the national competent authority shall, at the request of an interest party, cancel a trademark registration after an uninterrupted period of non-use in any Member Country of the ACN, without valid reasons, by the owner, a licensee, or any other person authorized by the owner. For these purposes, according to Article 15 of Decree 2153 of 1992, the national competent authority is the Superintendence of Industry and Commerce. Regarding the interested party who files the cancellation petition, the Andean Court has established that 'it is extended to holders of subjective rights and legitimate interested parties that can be the individual or legal entity that intends to use an unused registered trademark, as well as the person who intends to register an identical or similar sign that can be confusing with the unused trademark'.[390] The period of non-use must be of at least three years immediately before the filing of the cancellation proceedings. This cancellation of a registration may be requested as a defence in an opposition proceeding lodged on the basis of the unused trademark. It is also pointed out that no cancellation proceeding may be initiated until three years after the date of the granting of the registration.

298. It is important to note that when the trademark has been used by the licensee and not by the owner of the registration, the fact that the licence agreement has not been registered before the Superintendence does not rebut the factual statement of the use of the trademark in the market.[391]

299. Article 168 of Decision 486 mentions that the person who obtains a favourable ruling, has the preferential right to registration. This right may be invoked at the filing time of the request for cancellation or within three months following the effective date of the Decision that ended the Administrative procedure for trademark cancellation.

300. According to Decision 486, the owner of a trademark registration that has been challenged with a cancellation action for non-use has two possible defences: (1) to file evidence of use of the trademark; and (2) to evidence that the lack of use of the

389. *See* G. Cavelier, *Cancellation and Nullity of Trademarks in Colombia* (Second Edition, Bogotá, Cavelier Abogados, 1988), 10.

390. *See* Andean Court of Justice, Proceeding No. 15-IP-99, 27 Oct. 1999, published in *Gaceta Oficial del Acuerdo de Cartagena*, No. 528, 26 Jan. 2000.

391. *See* Legal Opinion (*Concepto*) 04045240. Superintendence of Industry and Commerce, 31 May 2004.

trademark was due to force majeure or *acts of God*; and the third one has been accepted by Jurisprudence of the Andean Court of Justice.

301. It is important to note that the Andean Court of Justice has stated that the demonstration of the well-known character of the challenged trademark is also a possible defence in a cancellation action. However, this defence is not contemplated by Decision 486 of the Andean Community and has not been accepted by the Colombian Trademark Office.

A. Evidence of Use of the Trademark

302. The Decision understands that a trademark is being used whenever the products or services identified with the trademark are available in the market in any country of the Andean Community, in the amounts and in the manner that normally occurs, taking into account the nature of the products or services and the normal manner in which they are commercialized in the market. Also, the Decision understands that the trademark is being used when it distinguishes products intended exclusively for export from any Member Countries of the Andean Community. For purposes of cancelling a trademark, the Superintendence shall take into account the concept of real and effective use established by the Court. Moreover, it shall analyse the criteria established in Article 166 regarding the use of a trademark accordingly with the proofs of the trademark use given by the owner (for more information, *see* Section 8).

B. 'Force Majeure' or Acts of God

303. The owner of the trademark registration has the burden of proving that the lack of use of the trademark was due to *force majeure or acts of God*, situation that the Superintendence shall analyse on a case-by-case basis. In this matter, the Court has stated that if a *force majeure* or an *act of God* takes place, the term of three years will be suspended. However, it will continue when the just cause of non-use disappears.[392]

C. Well-Known Character of the Trademark

304. Even though the Decision does not contemplate the demonstration of the well-known character of the challenged trademark as a valid defence in a cancellation proceeding, case law from the Andean Court has done so. Indeed, the Court has stated that the institution of the cancellation action for non-use shall have a different treatment when the challenged trademark is a well-known trademark. In this case, it is necessary that the Superintendence makes a completely different analysis from the one it makes with a trademark that is not well known, in order to avoid unfair competition that allows third parties to profit from the reputation of a trademark through the filing of a cancellation action.[393] Using these arguments, the Andean Court states that, in its

392. *See* Andean Court of Justice, Proceeding No. 15-IP-99, 27 Oct. 1999, published in *Gaceta Oficial del Acuerdo de Cartagena*, No. 528, 26 Jan. 2000.

393. *See* Andean Court of Justice, Proceeding No. 46-IP-2006, 23 Aug. 2006, published in *Gaceta Oficial del Acuerdo de Cartagena*, No. 1415, 18 Oct. 2006.

criteria, a well-known trademark should not be cancelled even if it has not been used in the market.

305. The second event in which a trademark can be cancelled is when its owner has caused or allowed that it becomes a common or generic sign to identify or denote the goods or services for which it was registered. According to Article 169, in this event, the Superintendence shall order, ex officio or at the request of any party, the cancellation of the trademark or the limitation of its scope of protection. A trademark is considered to have become a common or generic sign if, in commercial circles and for the public, it has lost its distinctive character as an indication of the corporate source of the product or service to which it is applied. Said article also pointed out the elements that must exist in relation to the trademark for this to occur:

(a) the need of competitors to use the sign to carry out their business activities, given the absence of any other appropriate name or sign to designate or identify in their trade, the good or services in question;
(b) widespread use of the trademark by the general public and among commercial circles as the common or generic indication of the good or service in question; and
(c) ignorance or limited knowledge by the public that the trademark denotes a specific corporate origin.

306. An illustrative case regarding this event of cancellation is the case of the word trademark PANETTONE.[394] The company Bimbo de Colombia S.A. requested the cancellation of the trademark PANETTONE in the name of Mamipan de Colombia S.A. According to Bimbo de Colombia, the trademark lost its distinctive character and became a common and generic sign to design one kind of bread. In this opportunity, the Superintendence considered underground the arguments of the plaintiff and therefore, denied the cancellation by means of Resolution 24010 of 28 August of 2003. However, Bimbo de Colombia S.A. filed legal remedies against said Decision based on the following arguments:

- The term PANETTONE is used to designate a sweet bread with fruit specially made for Christmas.
- Competitors need to use said term to identify that kind of product in the market, since there are no equivalent terms.
- The owner of the trademark PANETTONE did not protect his/her exclusive right over the term by the effective means.

The owner of the trademark submitted a number of proofs that were not able to convince the Superintendence of the distinctive character of the term PANETTONE. Conversely, the Superintendence considered that the term PANETTONE evoked in consumer's minds a special Christmas bread, which is neither a cake nor a muffin given the lower density of its mass and its size. Therefore, the Superintendence proceeded to cancel the registration of the trademark PANETTONE.

394. *See* Resolution 032915 of 12 Dec. of 2005 of the Superintendence of Industry and Commerce.

307. The last event in which a trademark can be cancelled, consists when it is identical or similar to a well-known trademark. Article 235 of Decision 486 establishes that the Superintendence shall cancel the registration of a trademark at the petition of the legitimate owner of the well-known trademark. In this regard, it is convenient to analyse the Decision of the Superintendence concerning the cancellation of the trademark NAUTICA.[395] In this case, Nautica Apparel, Inc. requested the cancellation of the trademark NAUTICA in the name of a Colombian Company, Piedrahita Velez Ltda, given that it was identical to their well-known trademark NAUTICA. The trademark NAUTICA is a well-known trademark that was first registered in the United States in the name of Nautica Apparel, Inc. The Superintendence established the requirements that shall be met for the cancellation of the identical or similar trademarks:

(1) Request of the legitimate owner of the well-known trademark: the cancellation is never ordered ex officio by the Superintendence.
(2) Similarity or identity between the trademarks: the registered trademark has to be identical or similar enough that it could be confused with the well-known trademark.
(3) Notoriety when applying the registration: the trademark shall be well known at the time when the similar or the identical trademark was applied for registration. The trademark shall be considered well known according to the concept of notorious mark contained in the legislation applicable by the time the similar or identical trademark applies for registration.

The Superintendence based its analysis on the previous requirements and concluded that the trademark NAUTICA was well known by the time the registration was granted in the name of Piedrahita Velez Ltda. The Superintendence held that NAUTICA of Nautica Apparel, Inc. enjoyed of great diffusion among consumers given the advertising campaigns in the United States and other countries. Moreover, the sales of the products under said trademark permit the general knowledge among consumers around the world. Therefore, the trademark in the name of Piedrahita Velez Ltda was cancelled.

308. The procedure for all the events of cancellation of trademarks is the same. Pursuant to Article 170 of the Decision, once the Superintendence has received the petition to cancel a registration, it shall request the owner of the trademark in question to submit his/her arguments, along with the necessary evidence, within sixty working days counted from the date of the notification. At the expiration of the previous period, the Superintendence shall proceed to decide whether or not to cancel the trademark registration and shall inform the parties of its Decision thought a reasoned resolution.

309. The cancellation only has effects in the future and from the time when the Decision was taken. The use, exploitation, and other acts, carried out by the owner of the trademark between the registration date and the date of the cancellation do not constitute base for requesting compensation for damages, whatever their nature may be.[396]

---

395. *See* Resolution 00777, 25 Jan. 1995, of the Superintendence of Industry and Commerce.

396. *See* G. Cavelier, *Cancellation and Nullity of Trademarks in Colombia* (Second Edition, Bogotá, Cavelier Abogados, 1988), 16.

§10. Infringements and Remedies

310. For a complete explanation on infringements, *see* Chapter 12.

Chapter 5. Trade Names

§1. Sources and Legislation

311. Trade names in Colombia are protected by means of international and national provisions. Regarding international law, Colombia has ratified two important conventions that provide trade names protection: the General Inter-American Convention on Protection on Marks and Trade Names of 1929 (the Washington Convention)[397] and the Paris Convention for the protection of Industrial Property of 1883 (the Paris Convention).[398] Besides the mentioned conventions, Colombia is part of the ACN, which establishes the common intellectual property regime to all Member Countries by means of Decision 486 of 2000 (Decision 486).

312. Regarding national provisions, the Colombian Code of Commerce establishes a set of norms applicable to trade names, which were not replaced by Decision 486, and therefore, are still in force. In addition to the Code of Commerce, Colombia has enacted other laws and decrees applicable to trade names:

(1) Decree 2153 of 30 December 1992, which establishes the functions of the Superintendence of Industry and Commerce (the Superintendence).
(2) Decree 2591 of 13 December 2000, which regulates some important aspects of trade names contained in Decision 486.
(3) Resolution 210 of 15 January 2001 and Unique Circular No. 10 of 2001, which provide some general formalities for the protection of trade names.
(4) Decree 138 of 25 January 2005, which regulates Law 875 of 2004 concerning the use of the Red Cross emblem and other emblems protected by the Geneva Convention of 1949 and its additional protocols.

§2. Subject Matter of Protection

313. The existence of different provisions applicable to trade names in Colombia has generated some difficulties regarding its understanding and scope of protection. The concept of trade name was first defined in Article 583.4 of the Colombian Code of Commerce as the sign that identifies the entrepreneur as such. In the same sense, Article 15 of the Washington Convention establishes that 'trade names are understood as the names and surnames used by manufactures, industrialists, merchants or agriculturists to denote their trade or calling, as well as the firm's name, the name or title legally adopted and used by associations, corporations, companies or manufacturing, industrial, commercial or agricultural entities'. However, the definition established in

397. *See* General Inter-American Convention on Protection on Marks and Trade Names, approved by Law 59 of 25 Mar. 1936.

398. *See* Paris Convention for the protection of Industrial Property, approved by Law 178 of 28 Dec. 1994.

Decision 486 is slightly different. Pursuant to Article 190, a trade name is understood as any sign that identifies an economic activity, a company, or a commercial establishment. In regards to this definition, it is important to clarify that although the Code of Commerce establishes that a trade name is the sign that identifies the entrepreneur as such and that a trade emblem is the sign that identifies commercial establishment, the Decision 486 blends those two definitions into one.

314. The difficulties to fully identify trade names in Colombian legislation need a clarification regarding the differences between trade names and corporate names.[399] Trade names and corporate names serve different purposes and are regulated by two different mechanisms. While commercial provisions rule corporate names, intellectual property provisions regulate trade names. In addition, whereas trade names are distinctive signs with which the company operates and carries on business, corporate names are legal names that identify a legal entity as subject of rights and duties. This difference implies important consequences:

(1) Exclusive rights of trade names are acquired through their use by an individual or a legal entity for the first time in commercial activities, while exclusive rights of corporate names are acquired through the registration in the commercial registry.
(2) The deposit or registration of trade names before the Superintendence is optional, while the registration of corporate names before the Chamber of Commerce is mandatory in accordance with Article 19 of the Code of Commerce.[400]
(3) A business or establishment may have more than one trade name, while corporate names are unique, meaning that a legal entity can only have one legal name.

315. Trade names may match firm names, corporate names, or any other names entered in the corporation registries or registries carried for commercial purposes. Moreover, trade names can be identical to trademarks that identify certain products or services of such company. For instance, corporate name – *PROLINAL Ltda.*, trade name – *PROLINAL*, trademark – *PROLINAL*.

316. Therefore, corporate names are legal names that serve for identification of legal entities, while trade names are subject of intellectual property rights that consist of signs that distinguish a company in the course of trade from similar ones. The latter is the subject matter of this monograph.

399. The name (for legal entities or individuals) are part of a legal institution of Civil Law known as 'attribute of the personality'. The attributes of the personality are the following properties of an individual or a legal entity: (a) name; (b) capacity; (c) residence; (d) nationality; (e) equity; and (f) civil status (just for individuals).

400. Article 19 Code of Commerce: Obligations of the businessmen: (a) Must be registered in the commerce registry.

§3. Conditions of Protection

317. Decision 486 does not mention the conditions that shall be fulfilled by trade names to be protected as such. However, the Andean Court has accepted two conditions: novelty and lawfulness.[401]

Regarding novelty, the Court stated that it has two aspects: first, it must be capable of distinguishing the company, and second, it must be distinguished from other signs.

As to the second requirement, trade names shall not consist of signs that: (1) are contrary to law, public morals, public order, or good manners; (2) can mislead or confuse consumers; (3) imply a risk of confusion, association, or dilution of other distinctive signs; and (4) may constitute an impediment to the right of third parties.

318. Trade names protection is not subject to any formalities. However, it is advisable to register the trade name before the Superintendence for proving purposes. In other words, its registration or deposit is based on a declarative system. Article 603 of the Code of Commerce indicates that if the application complies with the formal requirements established for registration of trademarks, the registration of trade names must be granted and published. However, according to the Andean Court,[402] the requirements established for trademarks apply differently regarding trade names:

(a) Perceptibility: the sign shall be capable of being apprehended through the senses. As trade names consist of a word or a phrase, they must be able to be visually perceived.[403]
(b) Distinctiveness: it consists of the ability of a trade name to identify the economic activity of a company or a commercial establishment from similar ones in the market.[404]
(c) Possibility of graphic representation: this requirement allows the sign to be represented by images or in writing. Scholars have established that trade names are only composed of one or several pronounceable words presented in a written form. In this sense, trade names that consist of drawings or graphical expressions cannot be registered.[405]

§4. Scope of Exclusive Rights

319. According to Article 191 of Decision 486 and Article 603 of the Code of Commerce, exclusive rights of trade names are acquired through their use by an individual or a legal entity for the first time in commercial activities, without the need

401. *See* Andean Court of Justice, Proceeding No. 8-IP-97, 9 Mar. 1998, published in *Gaceta Oficial del Acuerdo de Cartagena*, No. 349, 19 Jun. 1998.
402. *See* Andean Court of Justice, Proceeding No. 111-IP-2002, 19 Mar. 2003, published in *Gaceta Oficial del Acuerdo de Cartagena*, No. 917, 10 Apr. 2003.
403. *Ibid.*
404. *Ibid.*
405. *Ibid.*

for registration. The Andean Court[406] has established that the use of a trade name must be:

(a) Personal: the right holder must be the individual or legal entity that directly develops the economic activity identified by the trade name.
(b) Public: it must be publicly known.
(c) Sufficient: the use must be enough to be recognized by consumers.
(d) Continuous: it must be uninterrupted since the right over a trade name is granted by its use and ends when the use of such name cease or when the activities of the business or establishment using that trade name cease to exist.

320. The use of the trade name must also be real and effective regarding the economic activity it intends to identify.[407] In this sense, according to the Andean Court, the burden of proof of trade names is set on the person who claim its existence and protection.[408] The required evidence is specified in the Colombian Code of Civil Procedure (Decrees 1400 and 2019 of 1970).

321. To illustrate a manner in which the use of a trade name can be proved, it is worth mentioning the case of the trade name *TECNIPAN*.[409] In this case, *Tecnipan Ltda.* filed a nullity action before the Council of State against the resolution by which the Superintendence allowed the registration of the trademark *TECNIPAN* in the name of *Central Impulsora S.A. de C.V.* The plaintiff argued that the trade name *TECNIPAN* had been effectively used since 1987 and the application for the registration of the trademark was filed in 1999. Therefore, the trade name was protected and the trademark was not eligible for registration. For purposes of proving the effective and real use, *Tecnipan Ltda.* submitted the following:

(a) the register of the Company *Tecnipan Ltda.* before the Chamber of Commerce of Barranquilla in the year 1992;
(b) sales and income figures of *Tecnipan Ltda.* from 1993 to 2001;
(c) certification of orders to different suppliers of raw materials;
(d) copy of an article in a newspaper (*El Heraldo*) promoting the trade name *TECNIPAN*.

The Council of State deemed that the use of the trade name had been adequately proven and hence, the registration of the trademark *TECNIPAN* was declared null and void.

322. Article 193 of Decision 486 establishes that the owner of a trade name may register or deposit it before the Superintendence. However, as mentioned before, the registration is based in a declaratory system. According to Article 605 of the Code of Commerce, it is assumed that the date on which the application for registration was filed, was the date in which the owner began using the trade name. It is also assumed

406. *See* Andean Court of Justice, Proceeding No. 8-IP-97, 9 Mar. 1998, published in *Gaceta Oficial del Acuerdo de Cartagena*, No. 349, 19 Jun. 1998.
407. For further information, *see* Ch. 4, s. 8.
408. *See* Andean Court of Justice, Proceeding No. 8-IP-97, 9 Mar. 1998, published in *Gaceta Oficial del Acuerdo de Cartagena*, No. 349, 19 Jun. 1998.
409. *See Tecnipan Ltda. v. Superintendence of Industry and Commerce*, Council of State. File 8610, 3 Aug. 2006.

that the publication of said registration will be taken as the date in which third parties acknowledge the use of the name.[410] Regarding this provision, the Superintendence has affirmed that the deposit of the trade name implies an assumption about the date in which it was first used. In any case, it is required to submit additional evidence of use of the trade name.[411]

323. The owner of a trade name that has not been registered before the Superintendence has the opportunity to protect his/her exclusive right against confusingly similar distinctive signs by filing an opposition. He/she must file an opposition when the application of a similar or identical trademark is published in the Intellectual Property Gazette. Nonetheless, when the trade name has been registered, the owner can protect his/her exclusive right by opposing the registration of a trademark or filing a nullity action against the registration (*see* paragraph 324). In this matter, it is illustrative the case of the trade name *RIOFLEX*.

324. In this case, Floriberto Ríos Vasquez filed a nullity action against the resolution that granted the registration of the trademark *RIOFLEX* in the name of Mr Mendez Segura.[412] The plaintiff indicated that an identical trade name was being used to identify his company since its registration in the commercial registry in August 1995. However, once the application for the registration of the trademark was filed, the Superintendence proceeded to publish it in the Intellectual Property Gazette, and no oppositions were filed. The Council of State recognized that the trade name *RIOFLEX* was used before the registration of the trademark, but it was established that the owner did not file the opposition when the application of the trademark was published, losing the opportunity of protecting his right. According to the Council of State, if the trade name is not registered, the only way of protecting it is by means of an opposition because the Superintendence has no instruments to conclude that the trademark is identical or confusingly similar to the trade name. Therefore, the Council of State ruled in favour of the Superintendence.

325. For registration purposes, the Superintendence must perform an examination to determine if the trade name is eligible for registration taking into account Article 194, which indicates that in the following cases trade names are not registrable:

(a) when they consist totally or in part of a sign that is contrary to public morals or public order;
(b) when their use can cause confusion in commercial circles or in the public as to the identity, nature, activities, line of business, or any other aspect of the company or establishment that is designated by that name;
(c) when their use can cause confusion in commercial circles or in the public as to the corporate source, origin, or other characteristics of the goods or services produced or marketed by the company; or
(d) when a prior application or registration of the trade name already exists.

410. *See also* Art. 17 Decree 2591 of 2000.

411. *See* Legal Opinion (*Concepto*) 01099622. Superintendence of Industry and Commerce, 29 Nov. 2001.

412. *See Floriberto Rios Vasquez. v. Superintendence of Industry and Commerce*, Council of State. File 4128, 27 May 1999.

326. The registration of a trade name is limited in time. Article 196 establishes that it lasts for ten years counted from the day registration was granted and may be renewed for successive ten-year periods. For these purposes, the owner of a registered trade name must apply before the Superintendence its renewal within six months before the expiration date of the registration. The Superintendence may demand evidence of use of the trade name. According to Article 198, the owner of the registered trade name enjoys a period of grace of six months following the date of the expiration of the registration. The owner must attach the payment receipt of the applicable fees and must, at the same time, pay the surcharge provided for in domestic legislation. During the whole period, the registered trade name remains fully valid.

327. Before Decision 486, the legislation was silent regarding the renewal of the registration of trade names and emblems. This is the reason they were never renewed. Nowadays, it is understood that trade names and emblems registered after Decision 486 should be renewed.

328. A trade name is an intangible good that can be subject to contracts, such as assignments and licences. According to Article 199 of Decision 486 and Article 608 of Code of Commerce, the assignment shall be registered before the Superintendence in accordance with the procedure applicable to the assignment of trademarks and a fee shall be payable.[413] However, contrary to trademarks, trade names may only be assigned together with the business or establishment with which it is being used. This was first established in Decision 486, since the previous legislation was silent regarding this matter. As for the licences, it is provided that it may be registered before the Superintendence.

329. Moreover, Article 192 of Decision 486 establishes that the owner of a trade name may prevent the use by third parties of an identical or similar distinctive sign in commercial activities, when such use would cause confusion or a risk of association with his/her company or its products or services.[414] In these cases, the Superintendence must perform the comparison examination applying the rules established by the Andean Court.[415]

330. In the case of well-known trade names, the owner may also prevent the use of identical or similar distinctive signs, when such use could produce unjust economic or commercial injury to the owner or involve taking unfair advantages of the prestige of the owner's name or company. For these purposes, the owner of the trade name must prove its notoriety in accordance with the Andean legislation[416] and the Superintendence must recognize it by means of a resolution.

331. In this matter, there are two illustrative cases. The first concerns the trade name *MANUELITA*.[417] The company *Manuelita S.A.* filed a nullity action before the Council of State against the resolution by which the Superintendence allowed the registration of the trademark *MANOLITA* in the name of Pedro Samaniego Cely. According to the plaintiff, the trademark was confusingly similar to the trade name

413. *See* Ch. 4.
414. *See also* Ch. 4, s. 6 (Arts 155 and 156 of the Decision).
415. *See* Ch. 4, s. 4.
416. *See* Ch. 4, s. 6.
417. *See Sociedad Manuelita S.A. v. Superintendence of Industry and Commerce*, Council of State. File 3971, 7 May 1998.

MANUELITA, which was registered before the Superintendence on July 1987, prior the registration of said trademark. It was also argued that the trade name *MANUELITA* was well known, and therefore, the registration infringed the protected trade name. The Council of State stated that the trade name was effectively used and registered before the application for the registration of the trademark was filed. It established that between the trademark and the trade name existed, orthographic, phonetic, and ideological similarities could confuse consumers. Consequently, the Council of State declared null and void the registration of the trademark *MANOLITA*.

The second case is the conflict between the trademark *EAN International* and the trade name *Escuela de Administracion de Negocios – EAN*.[418] The latter, opposed to the registration of the trademark EAN International based on its trade name and emblem *EAN*, which refers to educational services of International Class 41. The Superintendence granted the registration and the school brought a nullity action against this Decision before the Council of State. It was established that if a sign to be registered as a trademark was similar to or identical to a protected trade name, to the extent that it would cause consumer confusion as to the products or services to be covered by the sign and the economic activity performed by the owner of the trade name, the sign in question would not be sufficiently distinctive, and, therefore, not eligible for registration. The Council of State reminded that the trade name of the plaintiff was *Escuela de Administración de Negocios – EAN* and not just *EAN*, which was relevant in comparing the signs, given that the comparison must be made without dividing the signs, as the case law of the Andean Court has taught. The Council of State concluded that the trade name was generic, descriptive or evocative of the services rendered, characteristics which would not be eliminated by the inclusion of EAN, because this is just an abbreviation of the name of the school. Likewise, the Council deemed that there was no likelihood of confusion between these names given that there were more differences than similarities, the only similarity being the part 'EAN' that, moreover, appeared in different grammatical and conceptual concepts.

332. Regarding the limitations to the exclusive rights over a trade name, Article 192 refers us to Article 157 and Article 158 of Decision 486. (For further information, *see* Chapter 4, Section 7.)

333. The owner of a registered trade name may renounce the rights granted by that registration. The abandonment shall come into effect only when it has been registered before the Superintendence. The abandonment does not imply a termination of the trade name protection, since it only ends when the use of such name ceases or when the activities of the business or establishment using that trade name cease to exist. In the same sense, if the use of a trade name ceases, its protection terminates even if its registration has not expired yet.

§5. Infringements and Remedies

334. For a complete explanation on infringements, *see* Chapter 12.

418. *See Escuela de Administración de Negocios – EAN v. Superintendence of Industry and Commerce*, Council of State. File 5307, 4 Jul. 2003.

Chapter 6. Industrial Designs

§1. Sources and Legislation

335. The legislation regarding industrial designs is the same that governs patents of invention. Accordingly, the regime for industrial designs is comprised in Decision 486 of 2000 of the Andean Community (the Decision), which suspended the provisions in the Commercial Code in the matter. As to international instruments, the Paris Convention is also applicable to industrial designs and so is the TRIPS Agreement.[419] Similarly, the Locarno Agreement Establishing an International Classification for Industrial Designs of 1968 (the Locarno Agreement) is applied when it comes to the classification of industrial designs.[420]

336. Apart from these instruments, the prejudicial interpretations of the Court of Justice of the Andean Community (the Andean Court) are a relevant legal source for industrial designs as they provide important concepts to develop and apply the matter. Moreover, the resolutions of the Superintendence of Industry and Commerce (the Superintendence) are to be taken into account as they resolve specific domestic queries.

§2. Subject Matter of Protection

337. According to Article 113 of the Decision, an industrial design is the 'particular appearance of a product that results from any arrangement of lines or combination of colours, or any two-dimensional or three-dimensional outward shape, line, outline, form, texture, or material, without the intended use or purpose of said product being thereby changed'. This definition leads us to the following conclusions.

First, that the subject matter of protection regarding industrial designs is outside the aspect of the product created by the designer that does not modify the intrinsic characteristics of the product or its usefulness. Therefore, the design has to be visually perceivable, meaning that any design that cannot be seen while normally using the product will not be worthy of protection.[421]Even though the definition provided in the Decision contemplates materials and textures as components of industrial designs, this does not mean that protection will be granted to the texture itself; it will only be

419. Both instruments only establish that industrial designs should be protected in Member Countries. They do not specify the conditions of protection nor the requirements for it. Said instruments provide just the framework, which has to be expanded by Members in further negotiations in other fora.

420. Colombia is not part of the Locarno Agreement. Nevertheless, the Superintendence of Industry and Commerce applies the classification provided thereto, as provided for in the Decision.

421. *See* J.M. Otero, *Los Diseños Industriales en la Decisión 486 del Acuerdo de Cartagena*, in R. Metke, *Lecciones de Propiedad Industrial (II)* (Bogota Raisbeck, Lara, Rodríguez y Rueda (Baker & McKenzie, 2002), 160.

protected as long as it provides a different aspect to the design. This element differentiates the protection given to industrial designs from the one granted to utility models. As to the former, the protection is only granted to the outside of the product while the latter also protects inner aspects of it.[422]

Second, Article 113 prescribes that the design must provide the product a particular appearance, which implies that the design must be distinguishable from other designs given its unique characteristics. But that appearance cannot be related to a technical effect; in that case, the creation would be protected as a utility model. The other characteristic that must be met by an industrial design to be protected according to the Andean legislation is that the appeal must be perceived visually by the consumer, therefore it has to be present on the outside of the product since the purpose of an industrial design is to differentiate products of the same nature and quality so that the customer is inclined by those that are more aesthetically appealing.[423]

338. It is also important to differentiate industrial designs from other forms of intellectual property. As to works of art applied to the industry, Article 3.14 of Decision 351 of 1993 defines them as 'an artistic creation with utilitarian functions or incorporated in a useful article, whether a work of handicraft or one produced on an industrial scale'. In other words, works of applied art add aesthetic value to an article that has certain technical characteristics that permit it to solve a technical need. These works are protected by means of the copyright regime, as established in Decision 351, given the elevated artistic merit that they contain. Also, the artistic component of the creation can be intellectually separated from the material support of the work, which is not possible with industrial designs because they are integrating elements of the product and therefore cannot be conceived independently from it.[424]

339. As to the difference with three-dimensional marks, they are signs consisting of a three-dimensional shape formed in a three-dimensional space; it is a body with volume. The Andean Court has established that a three-dimensional trademark 'must show characteristics that would differentiate it from the usual or required form of the product. It must have a distinctive shape through the alteration of ordinary or common features or lines'.[425] Henceforth, the three-dimensional mark must be perceivable both

422. *See* M. Pachón and Z. Sánchez, *El Régimen Andino de Propiedad Industrial* (Bogota, Ediciones Jurídicas Gustavo Ibáñez, 1995), 160.

423. *See* Court of Justice of the Andean Court, Proceeding 71-IP-2005, 6 Jul. 2005, published in *Gaceta Oficial del Acuerdo de Cartagena*, No. 1235, 23 Aug. 2005.

424. *See* J.M. Otero, 'Los Diseños Industriales en la Decisión 486 del Acuerdo de Cartagena', in R. Metke, *Lecciones de Propiedad Industrial (II)* (Bogota Raisbeck, Lara, Rodríguez y Rueda (Baker & McKenzie) 2002), 169.

425. *See* Court of Justice of the Andean Community, Proceeding No. 82-IP-2000, 2 Mar. 2001, published in *Gaceta Oficial del Acuerdo de Cartagena*, No. 651, 20 Mar. 2001.

by the sight and touch,[426] which is different to what is required for industrial designs. As explained at the beginning of this section, the protection granted to industrial designs is determined by what is visually perceivable. In addition, the function of trademarks is to identify the product or service from others that are offered in the market. On the contrary, the function of industrial designs is to attract customers with the outside aspect of the product. However, the difference between the two concepts is not always clear in practice. That is why the Superintendence has established that the protection granted under industrial designs is compatible with that granted under trademarks. Therefore, the applicant may choose which form of protection he/she prefers or choose simultaneous protection under both systems,[427] bearing in mind that if, simultaneous protection is chosen, the sign should be registered as a design and then as a trademark so that the novelty is not affected.

§3. Conditions of Protection

340. Article 115 sets forth the conditions of protection of industrial designs but, basically, it only requires that the design be deemed new. According to said provision, a design shall not be considered new when it only embodies secondary differences in relation to earlier creations, or that it refers to a category of products different from that to which said creations belong to. In the same sense, it considers that a design will not be new if it was disclosed to the public by any means or in any place before the date the application was filed or the priority was validly claimed.

341. According to the Superintendence, the concept of novelty adopted in the Decision is that of universal novelty. More specifically, the Superintendence considers that a design will be new if the design contains a substantial contribution from the designer; Article 115 requires that the modifications added by the designer cannot be minimal or secondary with respect to another creation that is already disclosed. To establish whether an industrial design is novel, the Andean Court believes that the whole composition of the design must be analysed, along with other designs that are in the state of the art. The result of such comparison will show that the design is new when: (i) it is not identical to a previous design; (ii) it is not substantially similar to a previous one; and (iii) it differs from a previous design in more than secondary characteristics. Such secondary differences can only be determined when the general impression of the design in interested public (the usual customers of that product) differs from the one produced by another design previously available to them. Likewise, the new design must confer an added value to the product, expressed on the aesthetic

426. In this point, the Andean Court in the Process 23-IP-98 has specified that if the mark has been incorporated in a three-dimensional support, but the mark itself is represented only in two dimensions, this cannot be considered as three-dimensional. It gives the example of a mark representing an orange; if the orange is merely drawn on the object, it will be two-dimensional, but if it is the representation of the orange itself, it will be three-dimensional. Accordingly, three-dimensional marks have to be perceived by the touch and they include wrappings, bottles, etc. *See* Court of Justice of the Andean Community, Proceeding No. 23-IP-98, 25 Sep. 1998, published in *Gaceta Oficial del Acuerdo de Cartagena*, No. 379, 27 Oct. 1998.

427. *See* Superintendence of Industry and Commerce, Legal Opinion 03029044 of 26 May 2003.

appearance of it. In the Court's opinion, since the purpose of a design is to give the product an appealing appearance, the criterion to establish the existence of substantial differences is determined by the choices made by the medium customer; if for him/her it is indifferent to purchase any of the products that are being compared, the differences would be irrelevant and therefore not substantial.[428]

342. Furthermore, the design will lack novelty if it is: (i) a common form, (ii) it is already a trademark,[429] or (iii) it is publicly known or registered in another country.[430] The novelty is affected by any type of disclosure in any place or time, regardless of the medium used for such purpose. By explicit mandate of Article 133 of the Decision, Article 17 is applicable concerning the disclosure made by the applicant or his/her assignees during the year before filing the application.[431]

343. If the Superintendence considers the design to be new, it can proceed with the registration process unless the following prohibitions contained in Article 116 are applicable to that particular design:

(a) industrial designs whose prohibition of commercial exploitation within the territory of a Member Country where registration is being applied for is necessary to protect morality or public order. To those ends, commercial exploitation of an industrial design shall not be considered contrary to morals and public order merely when such exploitation has been prohibited or regulated by a legal or administrative provision;
(b) industrial designs whose appearance were dictated entirely by technical considerations or by the performance of technical functions, that fail to incorporate any arbitrary contribution from the designer; and
(c) industrial designs that consist only in a form whose exact reproduction were necessary to allow that the product incorporating the design is mechanically assembled or connected to another product of which it is a part of. This prohibition shall not be applicable to products in which the design consists on a way to allow the assembly or multiple connections of the product or of its connection within a modular system.

---

428. *See* Court of Justice of the Andean Court, proceeding 71-IP-2005, 6 Jul. 2005, published in *Gaceta Oficial del Acuerdo de Cartagena*, No. 1235, 23 Aug. 2005.

429. As stated in the previous section, the protection granted to three-dimensional marks and to industrial designs can coexist. Hence, the prohibition for industrial designs that are already marks shall be understood as a prohibition regarding the time of the registration. In short, if a design is protected by means of the industrial design regime, the designer could request protection under the trademark regime, but he/she could not ask for protection under industrial designs when the design in question is already a registered mark.

430. Superintendence of Industry and Commerce, *¿Qué documentos se necesitan para Solicitar un Registro de Diseño Industrial?*, in < http://www.sic.gov.co/disenos-industriales > (last visited 1 Dec. 2017).

431. *See* Ch. 2.

§4. Formalities: Procedure for Obtaining Protection

344. The protection granted to industrial designs is not free of formalities as what happens under copyright law. In the opinion of Andean Court, the registration of the design is the necessary condition for protecting such creation. Once the registration process is completed, the right holder is granted exclusive exploitation over the design. That process is contemplated in the Decision and will be explained next.

345. As per Article 117 of the Decision, the Superintendence is the competent authority to receive and study applications to register industrial designs. It also provides that the following are the elements the application must contain:

(a) the petition can be filed online through SIPI, or a hard copy filed in the Unique Form for Industrial Designs, which is distributed freely at the Superintendence or can be downloaded from its website. According to Article 118 the form must contain: (i) the request for registration of the industrial design; (ii) the name and address of the applicant; (iii) the nationality address of the applicant and, if the applicant is a legal entity, the place of incorporation; (iv) an indication of the kind or type of product to which the design shall be applied and the category and subcategory of such products; (v) the name and address of the designer, if other than the applicant; (vi) the date, number, and identification of the office where any applications for registration or other protection of an industrial design were filed or obtained abroad by the applicant or assignee in respect of the same design claimed in the application being filed in the respective Member Country, if applicable; (vii) the name and address of the applicant's legal representative, if pertinent; and (viii) the signature of the applicant or the applicant's legal representative;[432]

(b) a graphic or photographic representation of the industrial design. This representation, in the case of two-dimensional designs incorporated onto a flat material, may be replaced by a sample of the product incorporating the design. In the case of three-dimensional designs, the graphic representation must show all three dimensions of the design. According to the Superintendence, (i) the drawings must be presented without any measurements or technical specifications; (ii) it cannot refer to or represent a mark; (iii) it cannot have frames or indicators; and (iv) each drawing must be individually numbered;[433]

(c) powers of attorney as the case may be. The application can be filed by a natural person or through attorney, case in which a power is needed. If a legal person files the application, it must also include the certificate of existence and representation of the company or corporation;[434]

(d) proof of payment of the filing fees;

(e) a copy of the document recording the assignment or transfer to the applicant of the right to register the industrial design, if applicable; and

---

432. *See* Superintendence of Industry and Commerce, *¿Qué documentos se necesitan para Solicitar un Registro de Diseño Industrial?* in < http://www.sic.gov.co/disenos-industriales > (last visited 1 Dec. 2017).

433. *See* Art. 9 Superintendence of Industry and Commerce's Resolution 46528 of 2017.

434. *See* Ch. 2.

(f) copies of any applications for registration or other protection of an industrial design filed abroad by the applicant or assignee in respect of the same design for which a registration application or claim is being filed in the respective Member Country.

346. The day the Superintendence formally receives the application shall be considered as the filing date, if it verifies that the application contains at least the elements mentioned in Article 119. These elements are: (i) a statement that the applicant is filing for the registration of an industrial design; (ii) data identifying the applicant or person filing the application that will enable the competent national office to communicate with that person; (iii) a graphic or photographic representation of the industrial design (this representation, in the case of two-dimensional designs incorporated onto a flat material, may be replaced by a sample of the product incorporating the design); and (iv) a proof of payment of the prescribed fees. Failure to comply with any of these requirements causes the rejection of the application and it will not be stamped with a filing date.

347. Once the Superintendence verifies the presence of the latter requirements, it has fifteen days to decide whether it meets the terms and conditions of form specified in Articles 117 and 118. If said requirements are not present in the application, Article 120 instructs the Superintendence to notify the applicant to complete those requirements within a period of thirty days following the date of notification. This period may be extended once, upon request, for an equal period. If the applicant does not submit all the requirements within the time period for such purpose, the application shall be considered abandoned and shall lose its priority. In any case, the Superintendence can keep confidentiality over the information contained in the application.

348. If, on the contrary, the application fulfils the requirements, the Superintendence will order its publication in accordance with Article 121 of the Decision. Before this date, no one may consult the contents of the application unless written consent from the applicant is given thereto.[435] Starting from that moment, and for the next following thirty days, Article 122 gives any person with a legitimate interest the opportunity to present valid reasons for opposing the registration of the industrial design. That period may be extended for an equal one upon request of the party. At the end of said period the applicant will have thirty days to present arguments against the oppositions. As per Article 123, this period can be extended for an equal one.

349. When the period for the objections is terminated, or none have been raised, the Superintendence will examine if the design complies with the novelty requirement established in Article 113, and is not comprised in any of the cases of non-registrability of Article 116. Despite this, Article 124 provides that the Superintendence will not examine ex officio the novelty of the design unless an objection regarding this point was raised. It will only do so if the lack of novelty is utterly obvious. If the application fulfils the requirements, the Superintendence will grant the registration of the industrial design.[436] Article 127 orders the Superintendence to classify designs in accordance

435. Article 125 also provides that any party that proves that the applicant is attempting to use against him/her the rights derived from the application, may consult the file before its publication without the consent of the applicant.

436. *See* Art. 126 of the Decision.

with the Locarno Agreement, despite the fact that neither Colombia nor any of the other Members of the Andean Community are contracting parties of such treaty.[437] Notwithstanding, the Superintendence uses the Locarno classification when it registers an industrial design[438]The product's classification must be provided by the applicant in the submission and will be verified by an officer of the Superintendence as part of the reviewing process of the application.[439]

350. Once the design is registered, the right owner acquires exclusive rights in regards to the design for a period of ten years, counted from the filing of the application before the Superintendence. Nevertheless, in the terms of Article 580 of the Code of Commerce,[440] the Superintendence, the public ministry or any interested party may request the Council of State to declare null and void the registration of the industrial design when:[441]

(a) the subject matter of the registration is not an industrial design according to the requirements established in Article 113;
(b) the industrial design fails to comply with the requirement of novelty set forth in Article 115;
(c) the registration was granted for subject matter that is excluded from protection by the stipulations of Article 116; or
(d) there are grounds for declaring the registration null and void according to domestic legislation covering administrative acts.[442]

§5. Scope of Exclusive Rights

351. The owner of the rights regarding industrial designs is, in the first place, the designer or designers when several people made the design in question. However, it can also be a legal entity or any individual to whom the designer has assigned his/

437. *See* World Intellectual Property Organization, 'Contracting Parties to the Locarno Agreement', in http://www.wipo.int/treaties/en/ShowResults.jsp?lang=en&treaty_id=14 (last visited 1 Dec. 2017).
438. Superintendence of Industry and Commerce, 'Industrial Designs: International Classification', in <http://serviciospub.sic.gov.co/~oparra/serv_57/externas/disenos/CInternacionalDeLocarno.pdf> (last visited 1 Dec. 2017).
439. *See* Art. 9 Superintendence of Industry and Commerce's Resolution 46528 of 2017.
440. This is the only article of the Code of Commerce that is still in force today as to industrial designs.
441. *See* Art. 132 of the Decision.
442. Article 84 of the Contentious Administrative Code provides the cases in which an administrative provision can be declared null and void. Said article establishes that the Council of State will declare null and void a provision when: (i) it infringes the norm in which it is established on; (ii) it was promulgated by a person or entity lacking competence; (iii) it was promulgated without following the procedure; (iv) it disregards the right of defence; (v) it was falsely motivated; or (vi) it was promulgated by someone that deviated from the powers originally granted to him/her by the law.

her rights.[443] When several people independently make the same design, the first one that files for registration or that claims priority shall be the one entitled to protection.[444]

352. According to Article 129 of the Decision, after registration the right holder can prevent third parties from using the design and can proceed against any third party who manufactures, imports, offers for sale, markets, or makes commercial use of products that incorporate or reproduce the industrial design when this is done without his/her consent. In the same sense, Article 129 also authorizes the right owner to proceed against any party that produces and markets an article whose design presents only minor differences with respect of the protected design. In sum, the essence of the rights over an industrial design is the faculty to use it in an exclusive way and prevent others from any attempt to use the design.[445]

353. It is important to remember that, as the registration of the industrial design only protects the outside aspect of an item, it cannot protect elements or characteristics dictated by technical or functional considerations or that fail to incorporate an arbitrary contribution of the designer. In that sense, Article 130 of the Decision establishes that the system does not grant protection to elements whose reproduction is necessary for the assembly of the product incorporating the design to another product to which it is a part of. However, the preceding restriction is not applicable when the design consists precisely in a new form of assembling the products together.[446]

354. Moreover, Article 131 provides cases in which rights-owners cannot oppose commercial use of the product incorporating the design or reproduction of it. Namely, when products incorporating the design have been introduced into the country by the rights-holder or by any other person authorized by him or with economic ties to that rights-holder, the rights conferred by the registration would be considered exhausted and therefore any legal action is pointless. For this purpose, two persons shall be considered to have economic ties when one is able to exercise a decisive influence over the other, either directly or indirectly, with respect to the exploitation of the industrial design, or when a third party is able to exert that influence over both persons.

§6. Infringements and Remedies

355. For a complete explanation on infringements, *see* Chapter 12.

443. The assignment has to be registered before the Superintendence.

444. *See* Art. 128 of the Decision.

445. *See* Court of Justice of the Andean Court, Proceeding 55-IP-2002, 17 Jul. 2002, published in *Gaceta Oficial del Acuerdo de Cartagena*, No. 82, 1 Aug. 2002.

446. *See* Superintendence of Industry and Commerce, Art. 3.2 Industrial design Manual, in <http://www.sic.gov.co/recursos_user/documentos/publicaciones/Manual_Dise%C3%B1o_indutrial_FINAL%20IMPRESION.pdf> (last visited 1 Dec. 2017).

Chapter 7. Plant Variety Protection

§1. Sources and Legislation

356. Protection of Plant Varieties in Colombia is the result of the country's involvement in international law and international organizations, more specifically of the accession to the WTO and the International Convention for the Protection of New Varieties of Plants (the Convention).[447] Regarding the WTO, Colombia is obliged to follow the provisions established in the TRIPS Agreement, which mandates Member Countries to adopt a system of protection of new plant varieties. This can be done by means of: (i) a patent system, (ii) a sui generis protection, or (iii) a combination of both systems.[448] Regarding the Convention, it developed said sui generis protection in the form of the so-called plant breeder's rights protection. Colombia by means of the law 243 of 1995 ratified the International Union for the Protection of New Varieties of Plants (UPOV) Act of 1978, which contains the basics provisions applicable in Colombia.

357. Besides the above-mentioned set of norms, Colombia is part of the ACN, which, by means of Decision 345 of 1993 (the Decision), establishes the common provisions for the protection of plant breeder's rights within ACN Member Countries. This Decision is the most important regulation applicable in Colombia regarding plant varieties' protection. Furthermore, Colombia has recently negotiated a PTA with the United States,[449] which mandates that both parties ratify the UPOV Act of 1991. Article 16.1(3) of the PTA establishes that each party shall ratify the UPOV Act of 1991 by 1 January 2008 should the PTA enter into force by that date. In case the PTA enters into force after 1 January 2008, both parties shall ratify it by the date of entry into force of the treaty in question. In any case, Colombian legislation in the matter is not very different from what is established in the UPOV Act of 1991 since Decision 345 was mainly inspired in it. Therefore, the protection awarded in Colombia to plant varieties is similar to what is required under UPOV, except in terms of duration of the protection.

358. In the national sphere, the Colombian Government has enacted several decrees and resolutions, which contain the guidelines for an effective protection. Regarding the decrees, the Colombian Government by means of the Ministry of Agriculture enacted Decree 533 of 1994, which was then modified by Decrees 2468 of 1994 and 2687 of 2002. As to resolutions, the Colombian Government by means of the Colombian Institute of Agriculture and Livestock (ICA), enacted Resolutions 1974 of 1994, 1893 of 1995, 3123 of 1995, and 2046 of 2003, and Circulars 000005 of 2006. These regulations: (1) modify the penalties included in the Criminal Code

447. *See* International Convention for the Protection on New Varieties of Plants (1961, as reviewed in 1972, 1978, and 1991).

448. *See* Art. 27.3(b) TRIPS Agreement.

449. At the moment, the Preferential Trade Agreement is fulfilling the previous constitutional procedures to the ratification in both countries.

about intellectual property; (2) designate ICA as the national competent authority and grant it specific functions in this matter; (3) instruct the opening of the National Registry of Protected Plants Varieties at ICA; (4) establish procedures for obtaining the certificate of plant breeder; and (5) set forth the different fees that shall be paid within the protection process.

§2. Subject Matter of Protection

359. A variety is defined in Article 3 of the Decision as a set of cultivated botanical individuals, which are distinguishable by specific morphological, physiological, cytological, chemical characteristics, and that can be perpetuated by reproduction, multiplication or propagation. In addition, Article 1 of ICA's Resolution 1893 adds an important element to the previous definition in order to clarify the variety that is subject matter of registration and protection: a set of botanical units that have been cultivated and improved by human effort.

360. The scope of applicability of protection is similarly established in the different versions of UPOV Acts, Decision 345, and Decree 533. As provided for in Article 4 of UPOV Act of 1978, the Convention may be applied to all botanical genera and species. Accordingly, Article 2 of the Decision indicates that the protection is extended to all botanical genera and species insofar as the growing, possession, or use thereof are not prohibited for reasons of human, animal, or plant health. Furthermore, Decree 533 also establishes that this protection shall not apply to wild species, meaning those plant species that have not been planted or improved by human activity.

361. With reference to the limitation of applicability, UPOV Act of 1978, Decision 345 and Decree 533 establish contrary provisions. On the one hand, Article 2(2) of the UPOV Act of 1978 mentions that each Member State of the Union may limit the application of this Convention within a genera or species to varieties with a particular form of reproduction or multiplication, or a certain end-use. On the other hand, the Decision and Decree 533 establish that a whole genera or species can be excluded from protection. Therefore, while in the UPOV Act of 1978 the exclusion or limitation must refer expressly to varieties of a certain genera or species, Decision 345 and Decree 533 establish the possibility of exclusion for all variety belonging to a genera or species, that their cultivation, possession, or use are not prohibited for reasons of human, animal, or plant health.[450]

§3. Conditions of Protection

362. Regarding the conditions required for the protection, UPOV Act of 1978, the Decision, Decree 533, and ICA's Resolution 1893 should be read together to conclude that those conditions are: (1) novelty, (2) distinctiveness, (3) uniformity, (4) stability, and (5) variety denomination. These conditions are explained as follows.

450. *See* P.F. Robledo del Castillo, *Los Derechos del Obtentor de Variedades Vegetales en Colombia* (Bogota-Colombia, *Universidad Externado de Colombia*, 2006), 125.

I. Novelty

363. According to Article 8 of the Decision of 1993, a variety shall be deemed novel if reproductive or multiplication material or harvested material thereof has not been lawfully sold or disposed of to others in another form. The sale or disposal must be made by or with the consent of the breeder or his/her successor for purposes of commercial exploitation of the variety. Therefore, a variety shall be deemed novel when:

(1) The exploitation begun up to one year before the filing date of the application for a plant breeder's certificate or of the claimed priority, if the sale or delivery was made within the territory of any ACN Member Country.
(2) The exploitation begun up to four years prior to, or in the event of trees and vines, at least six years prior to the filing date of the application for the granting of a plant breeder's certificate or of the priority claimed, if the sale or delivery has been made in a territory other than that of an ACN Member Country.

364. Article 9 of the Decision establishes the different acts in which novelty is not lost when a sale or a disposal of the variety to others occur. These acts are the following:

(a) when they are the result of an abuse to the detriment of the plant breeder or his/her successor;
(b) when they are part of an agreement to transfer the right over the variety, always provided that this shall have not been physically delivered to a third party;
(c) when they are part of an agreement pursuant in accordance to which a third party shall have increased, on behalf of the plant breeder, the stock of reproduction or multiplication;
(d) when they are part of an agreement pursuant which a third party shall have carried out field or laboratory tests, or processing tests at a small scale for the purpose of evaluating the variety;
(e) when they involve harvested material that has been obtained as a secondary product or a surplus of the variety or of the activities mentioned under (c) and (d) above; or
(f) when they are performed in any other unlawful manner.

II. Distinctiveness

365. Distinctiveness is an essential condition for the protection of plant breeders' rights. In this matter, Article 6 of UPOV Act 1978 and Article 10 of the Decision establish that a variety shall be deemed to be distinct if it is clearly distinguishable from any other variety whose existence is a matter of common knowledge at the time of the filing of the application or the date of any priority claimed. A variety is a matter of common knowledge from the date of the filing of an application for the granting of a plant breeder's certificate or for the entry of the variety in an official register of cultivars in any Member Country of UPOV or ACN.

Article 37 of the Decision created an Andean Subregional Committee for the Protection of Plant Varieties, which formulates technical criteria for distinctiveness in relation to the state of art, among other functions.[451] The work of the Committee is crucial to determine the minimum number of characteristics that have to differ from one variety to another.

III. Uniformity

366. As provided for in Article 11 of the Decision, a variety shall be deemed to be uniform if it is sufficiently homogeneous in its essential characteristics, despite the variations that may be expected from its way of reproduction, multiplication, or propagation. The condition of uniformity is fulfilled when the common variations expected after its propagation, still allow its precise description, especially in terms of the element of distinctiveness.

IV. Stability

367. Stability is another condition that has to be met by a plant variety in order to be granted protection. Article 12 of the Decision establishes that a variety shall be deemed to be stable if its essential characteristics remain unchanged from generation to generation and at the end of each particular cycle of reproduction, multiplication, or propagation.

V. Variety Denomination

368. According to Article 34 of ICA's Resolution 1893, a suitable denomination shall be given to each new plant variety and it shall be taken as its generic designation. The breeder shall submit the proposed denomination to ICA. Such submission must not constitute an impediment for its free use even after protection has expired. Moreover, Article 35 of said resolution establishes that the denomination may not consist solely of figures; it may be: (i) from one to three words, (ii) of a combination of letters and figures, (iii) of a combination of words and letters, or (iv) of a combination of words and figures. These figures shall have a meaning in connection to the words.

369. Article 36 of Resolution 1893 indicates that a denomination cannot be used as a variety when it:

(a) does not allow to identify the plant variety;
(b) is susceptible to mislead or to cause confusion concerning the origin, characteristics, value, or identity of the variety or the breeder;

451. *See* Art. 38(c) Decision 345 of 1993.

(c) is identical or can be confused with another denomination that designates a previously existing variety of the same botanical species or of a closely related species in Colombia or in another country. Nevertheless, this denomination will be acceptable if the other variety has not been registered or it has not been cultivated during a sufficient period of time;
(d) is identical or can be confused with another denomination on which a third person has a prior right that prohibit the use of the variety denomination;
(e) is contrary to the public order;
(f) only refers to common attributes of other varieties of the same species;
(g) consists of a botanical or common name of a genera or species, or includes that name, being this situation susceptible to be confusing;
(h) suggests that the variety comes from another variety or it is related with it, when in fact it is not true; or
(i) includes terms such as 'variety', 'cultivated', 'form', 'hybrid', or any translation of them.

370. The same denomination must be applicable in all ACN and UPOV Member Countries. If the variety is already protected, or if an application of protection for that variety has been filed in another ACN Member Country, ICA shall register that same denomination. Nonetheless, it can reject the applied for denomination if it considers it unsuitable for Colombia because of linguistic reasons or because it falls within any of the scenarios mentioned in the preceding paragraph. In such case, the breeder can submit a different denomination for the variety.[452] Also, any person that offers for sale or markets propagating material of a protected variety within the territory shall be obliged to use that same denomination, even after the plant breeder's right has expired, except when prior rights prevent such use.[453]

371. A plant variety can be identified in the market by a trademark or other similar indication easily recognizable. Nevertheless, such distinctive sign shall not be its generic denomination.[454] In other words, excluding the generic denomination of the variety, any distinguishing sign can be registered as a trademark, whenever the requirements established in the industrial property legislation are complied with. In this matter, the trademark related to a plant variety must be registered in Inter-national Class 31. This class includes agricultural, horticultural, and forestry products, and grains not included in other classes; fresh fruits and vegetables; seeds, natural plants, and flowers.[455]

372. In reference to the variety denomination, ICA shall publish the Protected Plant Varieties Gazette. This Gazette is published annually and it includes the denominations of varieties that have been proposed, registered or annulled.[456]

373. Regarding the nullity of a variety denomination, Article 41 of ICA's Resolution 1893 indicates that a denomination will be annulled when:

452. *See* Art. 37 ICA's Resolution 1893 of 1995.
453. *See* Art. 39, *ibid.*
454. *See* Art. 13, Decision 345 and Art. 43, ICA Resolution 1893 of 1995.
455. *See* Nice Agreement Concerning the International Classification of Goods and Services for the Purposes of the Registration of Marks, under the Nice Agreement Ninth Edition (1957).
456. *See* Art. 38 ICA Resolution 1893 of 1995.

(a) The petition of any person or ex officio, whenever the denomination has not been registered, or when there are circumstances that justify the refusal of the applied denomination.
(b) The petition of the holder of the plant breeder's right or by a third party, if the competent authority decides on the annulment of the denomination of the variety, or if it is determined that a right of a third party exists in connection with the denomination, and the holder of the plant breeder's right agrees upon the nullity.
(c) The petition of a person who is obliged to use the denomination of the variety if there is a final Decision of a competent authority that prohibits this person to use the denomination. In this case, the holder of the plant breeder's right should have participated or should have the possibility of participating in the respective legal action.

374. Whenever a variety denomination is declared null and void, a term of three months shall be granted by ICA to the plant breeder so that he/she submits a proposal for a new denomination. If the new denomination is accepted, it will be registered. Nonetheless, if it is rejected or if the plant breeder does not submit a new denomination, ICA may establish a provisional or a permanent denomination ex officio or by the request of the right holder or by an interested third party.[457]

§4. Formalities: Procedure for Obtaining Protection

375. Decrees 533 of 1994, 2468 of 1994, and 2687 of 2002, and ICA's Resolutions 1974 of 1994, 1893 of 1995, 3123 of 1995, and 2046 of 2003 contain the procedural provisions to be followed in order to obtain protection. For the sake of clarity, this section is divided in four main procedural steps: (1) application; (2) examination; (3) granting of certificate; and (4) registration.

I. The Application for Plant Variety Protection

376. Article 1 of Resolution 1974 establishes that the Sub-Management of Agricultural Protection and Prevention by the Group of Rights of Plant Breeders and Seed Producers will be in charge of executing the functions designated to ICA in connection to the plant variety protection. Therefore, the application for the granting of a plant breeder's certificate shall be presented in the Group of Rights of Plant Breeders and Seed Producers.[458]

377. According to the Decision and Decree 533, the plant breeder's certificate will be granted to an individual or a legal entity, which has created plant varieties. Article 7 of ICA's Resolution 1893 establishes that when several persons have jointly obtained a plant variety, they will have the right to apply together for the granting of a plant breeder's certificate. In spite of this, if several persons have separately obtained a plant variety, the application for the granting of a plant breeder's certificate will

457. *See* Art. 42 ICA Resolution 1893 of 1995.
458. *See* Art. 28 ICA Resolution 1893 of 1995.

belong to the one who has filed the application first. Article 9 of Resolution 1893 also provides that the person who is not a permanent resident in Colombia will have to designate an agent in the country. This agent will be able to initiate the proceedings for obtaining the plant breeder's certificate.

378. The breeder may defend his/her rights before ICA in case the application has been filed or the plant breeder's certificate has been granted to a person different than the breeder. As for the application, the breeder may claim to ICA to have the application assigned to him/her. And as for the plant breeder's certificate, the breeder may request ICA to transfer him/her the ownership of the rights granted with the protection. In case the plant breeder's right is granted while an assignment petition is pending, ICA will consider said petition as a transference petition.[459]

379. The application shall be filed in accordance with all the requirements established by the Group of Rights of Plant Breeders and Seed Producers of ICA. Such requirements are as follows: (1) the application shall be filed with a technical questionnaire, which is supplied by ICA, paying the respective fees and filing the pertinent information in an original version and two copies; (2) the application shall be filed in Spanish. As for foreign documents, they must be duly legalized through a Colombian consular certification in the country of origin or through Apostille, and must be accompanied by an official translation. ICA will determine which kind of documents can be waived from the previous requirements.[460]

380. Article 10 of Decree 533, provides that the application for the granting of a plant breeder's certificate shall contain the following:

(a) name, address, and nationality of the applicant and of the breeder when the latter is acting through an agent;
(b) common and scientific names of the species;
(c) proposed generic denomination;
(d) identification of the breeder and place where the variety was bred, specifying the country of origin;
(e) most noteworthy morphological, physiological, health, phonological, and physicochemical aspects and industrial or technological properties that permit a description of the variety;
(f) genetic origin of the variety;
(g) the claim of the right of priority, when appropriate;
(h) geographical origin of the plant material constituting the raw material of the new variety to be protected;
(i) the application for the breeder's certificate for a variety protected abroad shall specify all the countries in which the said certificate is registered, including the date of such registration.

In accordance with the application, the date of its filing will be the day in which the application form, the technical questionnaire, and the respective payment receipt are filed before ICA.[461]

459. *See* Art. 8 ICA Resolution 1893 of 1995.
460. *See* Art. 29 ICA Resolution 1893 of 1995.
461. *See* Art. 44 ICA Resolution 1893 of 1995.

381. When the application is filed, ICA has to follow some procedures to recognize the plant breeder's rights. First, it shall have a term of fifteen working days to indicate whether the application has been accepted or rejected for formal issues.[462] If the applicant has not fulfilled an essential requirement for performing the test, ICA will grant a term of sixty days in order to meet that requirement. If the applicant does not furnish all the requirements in that period of time and does not declare a valid justification, the application will be rejected.[463] Second, ICA shall indicate the quantity, date, and place where the breeder will have to deposit the live sample for the accomplishment of tests.[464] Said live sample is defined in the Decision and ICA Resolution 1893 as a sample of the variety supplied by the applicant for a breeder's certificate, which shall be used for the testing of novelty, distinctiveness, uniformity, and stability.[465] Finally, Article 3 of Decree 533 of 1994 provides that ICA will publish the Protected Plant Varieties Gazette, which is an annual publication that informs on the filing of applications, including the identification of applicants, the varieties filed for protection, the denominations given them, the acceptance or rejection of applications, the grant of breeders' certificates, declarations of lapse or invalidation of breeders' certificates and all legal acts subject to registration.[466]

382. Once the Gazette is published, Resolution 1893 allows the filing of oppositions against the application or the concession of the plant breeder's right. As provided for in Article 52, any person will be able to file an opposition within the three months following the date in which the application or the concession is published in the Protected Plant Varieties Gazette. The oppositions will be examined by ICA when the respective fee has been paid and must be based on:

(a) the allegation according to which the applicant or the holder of the right is not the proprietor of the variety;
(b) the allegation according to which the variety was not new or different in the pertinent dates, or that is not uniform or stable; and
(c) the allegation according which the denomination of the variety is inadmissible. In this case, ICA will revoke the grant of the plant breeder right. Afterwards, it will reopen the concession procedure requesting the applicant to propose another denomination. If the applicant fails to propose a suitable denomination, the application for the plant variety will be rejected.[467]

383. The person, who has filed an application for the granting of a plant breeder's certificate in a country that grants Colombia reciprocal treatment, shall enjoy a right of priority, whereby the applicant could file for protection for the same variety in any of the other ACN or UPOV Member Country. The right of priority is granted for a

462. *See* Art. 45 ICA Resolution 1893 of 1995.
463. *See* Art. 46, *ibid.*
464. *See* Art. 30, *ibid.*
465. *See* Art. 3 Decision 345 and ICA's Resolution 1893 of 1995.
466. *See* Art. 31 ICA Resolution 1893 of 1995.
467. *See* Art. 53 ICA Resolution 1893 of 1995.

period of twelve months counted as from the filing date of the first application.[468] The importance of this right is that it allows a plant variety to continue being considered as new despite exceeding the maximum terms of sale or delivery already mentioned in Section 3, Chapter 7.

384. According to the Decision and ICA Resolution 1893, the breeder shall claim the priority of the first application in the subsequent application, in order to benefit from the right of priority. The competent national authority of the ACN or UPOV Member Country in which the subsequent application has been filed, may require the applicant to supply a copy of the documents of the first application. These documents shall be supplied within a period of not less than three months from the date of said filing. The authority shall certify that those documents are authentic and shall verify that the sample or other evidence given is from the same variety.

II. The Examination of a Plant Variety

385. Once the applicant deposits the live sample, the test of distinctiveness, uniformity and stability is performed directly by ICA or by a foreign entity. ICA can also validate foreign test results as long as they are certified by a national competent authority of a foreign country, and as long the applicant pay the respective fee.

386. The UPOV designed a technical evaluation, known as DUS test[469] that shall be followed to determine whether the conditions of distinctiveness, uniformity, and stability are met. The basic principles are included in a document named 'Guidelines for the Conduct Test for Distinctiveness, Uniformity and Stability',[470] also known as 'Test Guidelines'. Regarding the DUS test, every UPOV Member Country shall follow the Test Guidelines, since they are provided to harmonize the examination of new plant varieties in all Member Countries.

387. As provided for in Article 19 of Decision 345 and Article 16 of ICA's Resolution 1893, ICA shall issue a technical report on novelty, distinctiveness, uniformity, and stability. This report shall be made within a period of three years for short-cycle varieties and ten years for medium and long-cycle varieties, both periods being calculated as from the filing date of the application for protection. If the report is favourable and the application complies with all other requirements, the plant breeder's certificate shall be granted and registration with the corresponding denomination shall be ordered.

468. *See* Art. 12(1) UPOV Act of 78, 18 Decision 345 of 1993 and 32 of ICA Resolution 1893 of 1995.

469. *See* the name given to the test. It stands for Distinctiveness, Uniformity, and Stability. *See General Introduction to the Examination of Distinctness, Uniformity and Stability and the Development of Harmonized Descriptions of New Varieties of Plants*, available online at <upov.int/en/publications/tg-rom/tg001/tg_1_3.pdf> (last visited 1 Dec. 2017).

470. *See Test Guidelines*, available online at <upov.int/en/publications/tg-rom/index.html> (last visited 1 Dec. 2017).

III. The Plant Breeder's Certificate

388. The period of protection of plant breeder's rights starts on the date on which the Decision granting the plant breeder's certificate comes into effect.[471] That date shall be the date the certificate is granted. In case of plant breeder's certificates granted abroad, ICA has a period of thirty calendar days, following the filing date of the application for protection to issue a Decision.

389. Article 17 of ICA's Resolution 1893 indicates that a plant breeder's certificate shall contain:

(i) the individual or legal entity, to which the protection of the plant breeder's rights of new plant variety is granted;

(ii) the number of records of the plant breeder's rights in the National Register of Protected Plant Varieties;

(iii) the expiration date of the protection;

(iv) the name, genera, and species;

(v) the denomination of the protected variety.

390. First the plant breeder's certificate is granted, a specific procedure follows. In the first place, ICA shall notify the Board of the ACN that a certificate was granted. The notification shall take place within a period not exceeding 48 hours following the date of publication in the Protected Plant Varieties Gazette.[472] Second, the plant breeder must pay the respective fee. In this matter, the Decision establishes that in order to keep the plant breeder's certificate in force, the appropriate fees shall be paid in accordance with the provisions laid down in the domestic legislation of the ACN Member Countries. In Colombia's case, ICA has enacted Resolution 00020827 of December 2016, which established the fees that the plant breeder shall pay. For said payment, Decision 345 indicates a grace period, which consists of six months following the expiration of the initial period but a surcharge applies. Throughout this grace period, the plant breeder's certificate remains valid.[473]

IV. National Register of Protected Plant Varieties

391. Once the plant breeder's certificate is granted, the next step will be the registration of the plant variety in the National Register of Protected Varieties. A plant variety is registered when it fulfils the conditions of novelty, distinctiveness, uniformity, stability, and a proper denomination.[474] This register, shall contain: (i) a phonotypical description of the protected variety; (ii) the number of the plant breeder's certificate; (iii) the denomination of the variety; (iv) the particulars of the breeder and his/her representative, if any; (v) the identity of the owner of the protection right when is not the same person as the breeder; and (vi) any other legal acts that affect the plant breeder rights.[475]

471. *See* Art. 13 Decree 533 of 1994.

472. *See* Art. 18 ICA's Resolution 1893 of 1995.

473. *See* Art. 34 Decision 345 of 1993.

474. *See* Art. 5 ICA's Resolution 1893 of 1995.

475. *See* Art. 6 Decree 533 of 1994, and 4 of ICA's Resolution 1893 of 1995.

392. When the variety is registered, the plant breeder's right holder acquires certain obligations, which refer to either the maintenance of the registry or to the maintenance of the protection. Regarding the former, he/she shall pay a renewal fee between 5 January and 31 March each year, in accordance to the fees established by the ICA's Agreement.[476] If the plant breeder does not pay the renewal fee during that period of time, it will be understood as if he/she resigns to the protection.[477] Regarding the maintenance of the protection, the holder of the plant breeder rights acquires the following obligations:

(a) maintain and reconstitute the plant variety as necessary throughout the term of the plant breeder's certificate;[478]
(b) guarantee that he/she will be able to supply to ICA all the vegetative propagating material during the term of protection. This material must be able to reproduce plants that contain the specific characteristics of the variety at the moment of the granting of the protection;[479]
(c) supply to ICA all the information and assistance needed in order to confirm that he/she has accomplished the obligations mentioned in paragraph (b);[480] and
(d) report the procedures for maintaining the purity of the variety and inform to ICA when such purity has been discontinued.[481]

393. Pursuant to Article 23 of ICA's Resolution 1893, the protection of the plant breeder's right will terminate in the following three events:

(1) The abandonment of the protection by the holder of the right. The plant breeder can resign to the right of the protection by means of a written declaration before ICA.
(2) The expiration of the protection. The protection is limited in time. For further details, refer to Section 8 referring to the duration of the protection.
(3) The nullity of the plant breeder's right.

394. Pursuant to the Decision and ICA's Resolution 1895, ICA may declare the plant breeder's certificate null and void, either ex officio or at the request of a party. This request shall be filed in writing, after the respective fee has been paid. This request cannot be filed when it is possible to file a legal action against the act that granted the plant breeder's right or while it is pending an ICA's Resolution concerning a legal remedy related to the granting of the certificate.[482]

395. ICA will declare the plant breeder's certificate null or void in two cases. First, when it is established that the variety did not fulfil the conditions of novelty,

476. *See* ICA's Latest Provision, Resolution 00020827 of December 2016.
477. *See* Art. 22 ICA's Resolution 1893 of 1995.
478. *See* Art. 22 Decision 345 of 1993.
479. *See* Art. 19 ICA's Resolution 1893 of 1993.
480. *Ibid.*
481. *Ibid.*
482. *See* Art. 25 ICA Resolution 1893 of 1995.

distinctiveness, uniformity, and stability when the certificate was granted; and second, when the certificate was granted to a person who was not entitled thereto.[483]

V. The Cancellation of the Plant Breeder's Right

396. As provided for in Article 35 of the Decision and Article 26 of ICA's Resolution, ICA shall cancel the certificate in the following cases:

(a) where it is established that the protected variety has ceased to meet the conditions of uniformity and stability;
(b) where the breeder does not supply the information, documents, or material necessary for testing the maintenance or reconstitution of the variety;
(c) where the breeder does not propose a new variety denomination within the prescribed period, after the first denomination was rejected; and
(d) where the payment of the fee does not take place by the expired period of grace.

397. ICA shall notify to the Board of the ACN, any nullity, cancellation, cessation, or loss of plant breeder's rights. This notification shall be done within twenty-four hours of the issuing of the Decision, and shall be duly published in the Member Country, whereupon the variety shall become of public domain.[484]

§5. Ownership and Transfer: Assignment and Licences

398. A plant breeder's certificate shall be granted to the plant breeder of the variety or to whom it has been lawfully transferred.[485] The plant breeder is considered to be the person, whether an individual or a legal entity,[486] who has created a plant variety. In addition, a plant breeder may be the creator's employer and the successor of the employer or of the creator.[487] According to Article 4 of the Decision, creation must be understood as the production of new varieties through the application of scientific knowledge to the inheritable improvement of plants.

399. The application for the granting of plant breeder's rights, as well as the right itself can be assigned or transferred. For this, two main requirements shall be fulfilled. First, the assignment shall be done in writing and must be duly signed by the contracting parties. Second, it shall be registered in the National Register of Protected Plant Varieties once the respective fee is paid.[488]

400. When the contracting parties do not agree on the terms of the assignment, the co-applicants or co-owners of the plant breeder's rights may assign or transfer their rights separately and may exclude third parties from exploiting the variety.

483. *See* Art. 33 Decision 345 of 1993 and Art. 24 ICA Resolution 1893 of 1995.
484. *See* Art. 36 Decision 345 of 1993, and 27 ICA Resolution 1893 of 1995.
485. *See* Art. 14 Decision 345 of 1993.
486. *See* Art. 14 Decision 345 of 1993, and Decree 533 of 1994.
487. *See* Art. 1 ICA Resolution 1893 of 1995.
488. *See* Art. 10 ICA Resolution 1893 of 1995.

However, they are not able to grant licences solely to exploit the variety without the consent of the other applicants or owners.[489]

401. Regarding licences, Article 29 of the Decision and Article 55 of ICA's Resolution 1893, establish that the applicant or the owner of a plant breeder's rights may grant the right to exploit the protected variety to a third party. A licence of plant varieties can be defined as a contract where the plant breeder or his/her successor authorizes the exploitation of the plant variety, in exchange of certain fee. The authorization given may be subject to different terms and conditions that have to be specified in the agreement, that is, duration of the licence, scope, payment of fees, and cancellation clauses, among others.

§6. Scope of Exclusive Rights

402. Regarding the exclusive rights of a plant breeder, it is important to clarify that they do not define what right holders are entitled to do, but what third parties must refrain from doing.[490]

403. According to Article 5 of UPOV Act of 1978, the effect of the right granted to the plant breeder is that his/her prior authorization shall be required for: (i) production for purposes of commercial marketing, (ii) the offering for sale, and (iii) the marketing of the reproductive or vegetative propagating material of the variety. The vegetative propagating material includes whole plants. It is also pointed out that the plant breeder right shall be extended to ornamental plants or parts thereof normally marketed for purposes other than propagation when they are used commercially as propagating material in the production of ornamental plants or cut flowers. In addition, it is established that any UPOV Member State may grant more extensive rights to plant breeders by means of its own law or a special agreement. Therefore, UPOV Act of 1978 indicates a minimum protection that shall be conceded in all Member Countries.

404. Colombia grants an extensive right by means of the Decision and ICA's Resolution 1893. It is established that the granting of a plant breeder's certificate confers the owner the right to prevent third parties from engaging in the following acts in respect of reproductive, propagating, or multiplication material of the protected variety without his/her:

(a) production, reproduction, multiplication, or propagation;
(b) preparation for the purposes of reproduction, multiplication, or propagation;
(c) offering for sale;
(d) sale or any other act that entails placing reproductive, propagating, or multiplication material on the market for commercial purposes;
(e) export;
(f) import;
(g) possession for any of the purposes mentioned in the foregoing subparagraphs;

489. *See* Art. 11 ICA Resolution 1893 of 1995.
490. *See* P.F. Robledo del Castillo, *Los Derechos del Obtentor de Variedades Vegetales en Colombia* (Bogota-Colombia, Universidad Externado de Colombia, 2006), 173.

(h) commercial use of ornamental plants or parts of plants as multiplication material for the production of ornamental and fruit plants, or parts thereof or cut flowers; or
(i) the performance of the acts mentioned in the foregoing subparagraphs in respect of harvested material.

405. The extension of the plant breeders rights established in Colombia refers to paragraph (i) above, since the harvested material of the plant variety is included in the scope of protection. For this reason, the harvested material must be obtained through the unauthorized use of reproductive or multiplication material of the protected variety, unless the owner has had reasonable opportunity to exercise his/her exclusive right.

406. Moreover, the plant breeder's certificate entitles the owner thereof to exercise all the previous rights in respect to other varieties. More specifically, in respect to those that: (i) are not clearly distinguishable from the protected variety;[491] (ii) which production calls for repeated use of the protected variety;[492] and finally, (iii) are essentially delivered from the protected variety, except where the variety is itself an essentially derived variety.[493] Regarding the latter, Article 3 of the Decision establishes that a variety shall be deemed to be essentially derived from another variety when:

(a) it is predominantly derived from the initial variety, or from a variety that is itself predominantly derived from the initial variety. Such variety shall retain the expression of the essential characteristics that result from the genotype or combination of genotypes of the initial variety;
(b) it is clearly distinguishable from the initial variety; and
(c) except for the differences which result from the act of derivation, it conforms to the initial variety in the expression of the essential characteristics that result from the genotype or combination of genotypes of the initial variety.

407. In addition, Article 17 of the Decision grants provisional protection to the applicant during the period between the filing of the application and the grant of the certificate. It is also provided that no action for damages may be brought until the plant breeder's certificate is granted, but such action may cover damages caused from the publication of the application. Therefore, the provisional protection confers to the plant breeder the power to protect it against infringements while the granting of the certificate is still pending.

§7. Limitations of the Scope of Protection

408. The Decision and ICA's Resolution 1893 contemplate certain exceptions to the plant breeder's rights. Accordingly, Articles 25, 26, and 27 establish limitations to the exclusive rights conferred to the plant breeder by means of the certificate.

491. *See* Art. 24(2) Decision 345 of 1993.
492. *Ibid.*
493. *See* Art. 24(3) Decision 345 of 1993 and, 8 Decree 533 of 1994.

409. Regarding Article 25, the certificate does not confer to the owner thereof the right to prevent third parties from using the protected variety where such use takes place:

(1) in a private circle, for non-commercial purposes;
(2) for experimental purposes; and
(3) for the breeding and exploitation of a new variety, except in case of a variety essentially derived from a protected variety.[494] This is known as the phyto-improver privilege. The phyto-improver is defined as the person who, applying improvement techniques to plants, obtains new harvest.[495] This exception is important in the development of new plant varieties, since genetic improvement can be obtained only if the produced material in any stage of the development can be used as the basis for a new obtaining. However, the importance of this exception to the industry does not waive the phyto-improver from the obligation to request the plant breeder's authorization when the production of the new variety calls for repeated use of the protected variety.[496]

410. As to Article 26, it established that anyone who stores and sows for personal use, or sells as raw material or food, the product of his/her cultivation of the protected variety shall not be thereby infringing the plant breeder's right. This is also contemplated in ICA's Resolution 1893, and it is known as the farmer's privilege. This privilege shall not apply to the commercial use of multiplication, reproductive or propagating material, including whole plants and parts of plants of fruit, ornamental, and forest species. Furthermore, and in accordance with ICA's Resolution, when a farmer wants to reserve seeds of a protected variety, product of his/her own exploitation for sowing it for his/her own use, he/she shall have to communicate it to ICA indicating where he/she will make the preparation of the respective seed. The sowing is only possible for farmers with an equal or smaller agricultural exploitation area of five harvested hectares. Nonetheless, the right of the plant breeder shall be exercised reasonably with respect to the first sowing. Moreover, ICA's Resolution provides two more exceptions: (i) by no reason the seed could be sold to third parties, and (ii) for biosafety reasons, varieties obtained by methods of genetic engineering are not included. In conclusion, ICA's Resolution provides a much limited farmer privilege since it only allows the sowing of seed and does not mention the sale of the product of the cultivation of the protected variety as a raw material or as food.

411. As to the final exception, Article 27 of the Decision establishes that the acts mentioned in Article 24 (exclusive rights of the plant breeder) cannot be exercised when the material of the protected variety has been sold or otherwise marketed by the owner of said right, or with his/her consent.[497] In other words, the sale or marketing of the material of the protected plant variety to a third party by the owner of the plant breeder right exhausts his/her right, since he/she will not be able to restrict the acts

494. *See* Art. 25 Decision 345 of 1993 and Art. 13 ICA's Resolution 1893 of 1995.
495. *See* Art. 2 Decision 193 of 1983.
496. *See* Art. 24(2) Decision 345 of 1993.
497. *See* Art. 27 Decision 345 of 1993 and Art. 15 CA's Resolution 1893 of 1995.

done by the third party.[498] In spite of this, there are two exceptions to such limitation. The first one is applied when the acts of the third party involve further reproduction, multiplication, or propagation of the protected variety, subject to the free available limitation. The second one refers to the acts of third parties that involve export of the material of the protected variety that allows its reproduction thereof, to a country that does not grant protection to the plant varieties to which the export variety belongs. The latter is permitted where said material is for human, animal, or industrial consumption purposes.[499]

412. As an interpretative matter, Article 16(2) of UPOV Act of 1991 establishes what should be understood as material of protected plant variety. In this sense, material means:

(a) propagating material of any kind;
(b) harvested material, including entire plants and part of plants; and
(c) any product made directly from the harvested material.

413. Further limitations to the exclusive right granted to the breeder may only be exercised for public interest reasons.[500] The Ministry of Agriculture may declare the free availability of the variety, assuring an equitable compensation to the plant breeder. This declaration can take place only when it is necessary to protect national security and public interest, with the purpose of assuring the suitable exploitation of the protected variety.[501] ICA will determine the amount of the compensation, once the ministry issues the declaration. For that matter, it will hear the parties (right holder and licensee) and an expert, and then determine the compensation on the basis of the scale of exploitation of the protected variety.[502] The free availability declaration shall remain in force for as long as the circumstances that brought it up remain, and for a maximum period of two years, which may be renewed once for a similar period.[503] During this time, ICA shall allow exploitation of the variety by means of a compulsory licence to interested persons who fulfil the following requirements:[504]

(a) offer sufficient technical guarantees;
(b) apply to ICA for such licence; and
(c) pay the respective fee established in the ICA Circular 000005 of 2006.

498. *See* P.F. Robledo del Castillo, *Los Derechos del Obtentor de Variedades Vegetales en Colombia* (Bogota-Colombia, Universidad Externado de Colombia, 2006), 194.
499. *See* Art. 27 Decision 345 of 1993 and Art. 15 ICA's Resolution 1893 of 1995.
500. *See* Art. 9 UPOV Act of 1978.
501. *See* Art. 30 Decision 345 of 1993 and Art. 56 ICA's Resolution 1893 of 1995.
502. *Ibid.*
503. *See* Art. 32 Decision 345 of 1993 and Art. 58 ICA's Resolution 1893 of 1995.
504. *See* Art. 31 Decision 345 of 1993 and Art. 57 ICA's Resolution 1893 of 1995.

§8. Duration of Protection

414. The protection granted to the plant breeder is limited in time. The UPOV Act of 1978 establishes that it may not be less than fifteen years, counted as from the date of issuing of the certificate of protection. For vines, forest trees, fruit trees, and ornamental trees, including, in each case, their rootstocks, the period of protection may not be less than eighteen years, calculated as from the date of issuing of the certificate of protection.[505] Nevertheless, the UPOV Act of 1991 provides for a longer period of protection. Article 19 establishes that the period shall not be shorter than twenty years from the date of the grant of the plant breeder's right. For trees and vines, said period shall not be shorter than twenty-five years. In this matter, Colombian legislation indicates that the term of protection shall be twenty years in the case of vines, forest trees and fruit trees, including the rootstocks thereof, and fifteen years for all other species, both terms being counted from the date of grant of protection.[506] Therefore, Colombian legislation agrees with UPOV Act of 1978 and disregards UPOV Act of 1991.

§9. Infringements and Remedies

415. Article 62 of Resolution 1893 provides that ICA may sanction whoever offers for sale or commercializes multiplying material of a protected variety in the country, without using the registered denomination of the variety. Moreover, ICA will sanction whoever uses the registered denomination of a protected variety in the country, or a denomination that is susceptible of confusion, for another of the same botanical species or of another resemblance.[507] For this matter, ICA shall apply the sanctions in accordance with Decree 1840 of 1994.[508]

416. Regarding the infringements, the holder of a plant breeder right whose rights have been threatened or infringed will be able to bring administrative or judicial actions before the competent authority. The actions will be brought for two main purposes: (1) to prevent or restrain any act that constitute an infringement or violation of the plant breeder's rights; and (2) to secure the appropriate forms of compensation or indemnification.[509] For these purposes, the regulations and procedures contained in the Code of Commerce ought to be applied regarding infringements of industrial property rights, without prejudice to the criminal actions that may be available.[510]

For further explanation on infringements, *see* Chapter 12.

505. *See* Art. 8 UPOV Act of 1978.
506. *See* Art. 21 Decision 345 of 1993, Art. 7 Decree 533 of 1994, and Art. 21 ICA's Resolution 1893 of 1995.
507. *See* Art. 62 ICA's Resolution 1893 of 1995.
508. *See* Art. 63, *ibid.*
509. *See* Art. 60 ICA Resolution 1893 of 1995 and Art. 23 Decision 345 of 1993.
510. *See* Art. 15 Decree 533 of 1994.

§10. OVERLAPPING AND RELATIONS TO OTHER INTELLECTUAL PROPERTY LAWS

417. Plant variety protection is similar to patents since the effect of the right granted to the owner is that his/her authorization shall be required for purposes of use, commercial marketing, and offering for sale. Therefore, the protection itself is not considered to be different. Nevertheless, the conditions required for the protection differ from one to another.

The sui generis protection (plant variety protection), was created for many important reasons. First of all, the plant breeders found it impossible to fulfil the conditions required for patent protection, especially those regarding to the inventive step and the industrial application.[511] Moreover, a patent was not the appropriate protection for a plant, whose essential characteristics remain just for one generation. Therefore, stability was required so that such characteristics remain unchanged from generation to generation. Finally, since the matter of protection is new varieties, not just a botanical individual, they needed the requirement of uniformity in its reproduction, multiplication, and propagation.[512]

Other differences between plant variety protection and patent protection can be established regarding their national competent authority and the procedures followed. As for the former, ICA is the national competent authority regarding plant variety and the Superintendence of Industry and Commerce is in charge of patent system. Regarding the latter, procedures followed in patents and in plant variety differ from one another (*See* Chapter 2, Section 4 and Chapter 7, Section 4).

511. *See* A.M. Hernández Salgar, *Biodiversidad y Variedades Vegetales* (Bogota-Colombia, Instituto Alexander von Humboldt, 2000), 30.

512. *Ibid.*, XI.

Chapter 8. Layout-Designs of Integrated Circuits

§1. Sources and Legislation

418. The issue of layout-designs of integrated circuits in Colombia has very little development. It was not originally contemplated in the title in the Code of Commerce dedicated to industrial property and it has not been subject to further legal development at the domestic level. Consequently, the only norms applicable are those contained in the TRIPS Agreement and the Decision 486 of 2000 (the Decision). However, by explicit reference of Article 35 of the TRIPS Agreement, Colombia has to comply with Articles 2 through 7,[513] 12,[514] and 16.3[515] of the Washington Treaty of Intellectual Property in Respect of Integrated Circuits,[516] even though it did not sign such treaty.

419. In the current state of affairs, integrated circuits are not as relevant as other forms of intellectual property in Colombia. The Superintendence of Industry and Trade (the Superintendence) has not received yet the first application for a layout-design. Nonetheless, the Decision, regulated by Decree 2591 of 2000 and the Unique Circular No. 10 of the Superintendence (*Circular única No. 10 de la Superintendencia de Industria y Comercio*), provide the legal framework in which an application for the protection of the layout-design of an integrated circuit has to be filed.

§2. Subject Matter of Protection

420. The subject matter of protection is the layout-design of an integrated circuit. To give further meaning to this idea, first we must define the term 'integrated circuit', which, according to Article 86 of the Decision, is 'a product, in final or intermediate form, of which at least one element is an active element and some or all of whose interconnections are an integral part of the body or surface of a piece of material that is intended to be used electronically';. In simpler terms, integrated circuits are 'small

513. Article 2 contains a series of definitions including that of a circuit, layout-designs, protected layout-design, among others. Article 3 specifies the subject matter of the treaty, while Art. 4 mentions the legal for of protection. Article 5 contains provisions regarding the obligation to respect the principle of national treatment in regards to integrated circuits and Art. 6 specifies the scope of the protection. Finally, Art. 7 contains provisions regarding the exploitation, registration and disclosure.

514. Article 12 establishes a safeguard concerning the Paris and Berne Convention, specifying that the Washington treaty shall respect obligations acquired under any of those conventions.

515. Article 16 contains instructions as to the entry into force of the treaty. Paragraph 3 further specifies that parties may not apply the treaty to layout-designs existing at the entry into force of it, unless this affects the protection already accorded to that design.

516. It is very important to clarify that this treaty never entered into force given that it did not reach a sufficient number of ratifications by the signing countries. Despite this fact, the treaty is still alive thanks to the specific reference made in the TRIPS Agreement.

microchips containing a large number of electrical connections that perform the same function as a larger circuit made of separate parts'.[517]

Still, integrated circuits would be worthless if they could not be mass-produced to spread the benefits achieved through them; they need an established plan to determine the order of the different elements within the circuit. That arrangement involves an intellectual effort that requires not only a team of experts but also considerable investment. Consequently, 'the object of protection via Intellectual Property in the arena of the integrated circuit development industry is precisely that plan of arrangements of elements, i.e., layout-designs that constitute the integrated circuit as such'.[518] Article 86 of the Decision defines layout-designs as 'the three-dimensional arrangement of the elements, regardless of the form, of which at least one is an active element, and their interconnection into an integrated circuit, as well as that three-dimensional arrangement prepared for use in an integrated circuit to be manufactured'.

421. As in other areas of intellectual property, the subject matter of protection of layout-designs is limited to the design itself. It is 'not extended to ideas, processes, systems, techniques or data encoded or incorporated into the layout-design'.[519]

§3. Conditions of Protection

422. According to the wording in Article 87 of the Decision, layout-designs are only protected if they are an original design. They are considered as original when they are the 'result of its creator's intellectual efforts and [are] not in common use in the integrated circuit industry. Where composed of two or more elements in common use in the integrated circuit industry, a layout-design shall be considered original only if the combination of elements, as an assembly, meets this requirement.'[520]

423. If these requirements are met, the design is worthy of receiving protection. Article 88 provides that the designer would be the owner of the rights, but if two or more persons prepared the layout-design, they shall share the right to protect it. Likewise, it sets forth that 'the right to protect a layout-design created under a project or service contract entered into for this purpose or within the framework of an employment relationship in which the designer has such function, shall correspond to the person who contracted for the project or service, or the employer, unless otherwise stipulated under a contract'.

517. Taken from Advanced Learner's Dictionary, Oxford University Press, Sixth Edition, 2000.

518. Unofficial translation made by the author. Wilson Rafael Ríos Ruiz, *Propiedad Intelectual respecto de los Circuitos Integrados (Chips), in Revista de la Propiedad Intelectual No 2, Universidad Externado de Colombia* 2001, at <http://revistas.uexternado.edu.co/index.php/propin/article/view/1197/1135> (last visited 1 Dec. 2017).

519. Article 99 of the Decision.

520. Article 87 of the Decision, but said originality does not imply that the layout-design has to be unique. Article 103 of the Decision provides that the right owner of a registered layout-design cannot prevent a third party from using or commercializing the design when it was created by a third party, even if it is identical to the layout-design in question. This is different to what happens under patent legislation where the subject matter of the patent must be unique, that is, it cannot be present in the state of the art.

§4. Formalities: Procedure for Obtaining Protection

424. If the designer considers that the layout-design complies with the aforementioned requirements, he/she may register the design. The application shall be filed before the Superintendence and include the elements set forth in Article 89 of the Decision which are:

(a) the petition: the designer can submit the petition online or can fill out a special form made by the Superintendence which must contain the necessary data to identify the applicant or his/her attorney, if that is the case. The applicant or the attorney must sign the petition;[521]
(b) a copy of the drawing of the layout-design and, if commercially exploited, a sample of that integrated circuit;
(c) if pertinent, a statement of the date of first commercial exploitation of the integrated circuit anywhere in the world;
(d) if pertinent, the statement of the year in which the integrated circuit was created;
(e) a description of the electronic operation to be performed by the integrated circuit in the layout-design. The description must describe in a clear way all of the electronic functions that will be performed by the circuit;[522]
(f) copies of any applications for registration or other protection filed for or obtained abroad by the applicants or their assignees, referring to all or part of the layout-design for which a registration application is being filed before the Superintendence;
(g) powers of attorney as may be needed; and
(h) a proof of payment of the filing fee.

425. Once the application is ready, the designer must file it before the Superintendence where it will be stamped with a date. This date will only be assigned if the petition includes all the requirements; otherwise, it will not be admitted. According to the Superintendence, the stamping of this date is one of the most important steps in the registration process because it allows determining the existence of a right of priority. It is also the element upon which the protection time will be fixed.[523] For this matter, the Superintendence will examine that the petition contains the petitioner's information, which would allow it to contact the applicant, a graphic representation of the layout-design, and will also assure that the filing fees were paid.[524]

426. After the application is admitted, the Superintendence will examine if the subject matter of the application constitutes a layout-design in the sense of Article 86 of the Decision, and if it contains all the information required. The originality of the design will only be addressed if an opposition was raised in that sense. In any case,

521. Superintendence of Industry and Trade, *Cómo solicitar un registro de esquemas de trazado de circuitos integrados: Documentación necesaria*, in < http://www.sic.gov.co/recursos_user/documentos/propiedad_industrial/Formatos/PI02-F03.pdf> (last visited 1 Dec. 2017).

522. *Ibid.*

523. Superintendence of Industry and Trade, 'Cómo solicitar un registro de esquemas de trazado de circuitos integrados: Documentación necesaria', in <www.sic.gov.co/propiedad/Nuevas_Creaciones/Esquemas/Como/Documentacion.php>, (last visited on 28 Aug. 2007).

524. Article 92 of the Decision.

the Superintendence can examine if there are any mistakes in the application and will give the designer a three-month period to correct such mistakes. If the mistakes are not corrected, the Superintendence will consider that the designer abandoned the application.

427. Once the application has been corrected, the Superintendence, in accordance with Article 94, will publish the application of the layout-design so that third parties can oppose the registration in the terms of Article 95. If the opposition was not successful or if none were filed, the Superintendence shall 'register the layout-design and issue a registration certificate containing the date included in the corresponding registry'.[525]

428. The registration granted is not absolute; the Superintendence can declare it or null and void at any time either ex officio or at the request of a party. Article 108 establishes that this can be done if:

(a) the subject matter of the registration is not a layout-design according to the requirements stipulated in Article 86;
(b) the registration fails to comply with the requirements for protection set forth in Article 87;
(c) the registration was granted for a layout-design applied for after the expiration of one of the periods established in Article 97; or
(d) there are grounds for declaring the registration null and void according to domestic legislation covering administrative acts.

429. Likewise, the Council of State can annul a registration if it finds that it was granted to someone that was not entitled to such right. As per Article 110 of the Decision, only the person that was rightfully entitled to obtain registration may raise issues regarding the invalidation of the registration. 'That right of action shall lapse five years from the date the registration was granted or two years following the date on which the person to whom that right belongs found out about the marketing ... of the product incorporating that layout-design, whichever period expires first.'[526] The holder of the register has two months to present his/her arguments and submit proof. In the terms of Article 111, this period can be extended for two additional months at the request of the party. When this period ends, the Council of State will decide if it declares null the registration or not.

§5. Duration of Protection

430. The protection for layout-designs is for ten years, counted from the last day of the year the layout-design was first commercially exploited anywhere in the world or the filing date of an application for registration in Colombia, whichever took place first. As per Article 97, if the layout-design has been commercially exploited anywhere in the world, the application must be filed within two years counted from the first exploitation. Failure to comply with this requirement would cause the registration to be denied. If, on the contrary, the layout-design has never been commercially

525. Article 96 of the Decision.
526. Article 110 of the Decision.

exploited, the application must be filed no later than fifteen years counted from the creation of the design.

§6. Scope of Exclusive Rights

431. Article 99 sets forth the exclusive rights conferred to right holders upon registration of the layout-design. This provision allows right holders to impede third parties from any of the following acts:

(a) reproducing, through incorporation into an integrated circuit or in any other way, all or part of the protected layout-design that complies with the requirements for originality stipulated in Article 87;
(b) marketing, importing, offering for sale, selling, or otherwise distributing a protected layout-design or an integrated circuit in which a protected layout-design is incorporated; or
(c) marketing, importing, offering for sale, selling, or otherwise distributing an article incorporating such a protected integrated circuit, only insofar as it continues to contain an unlawfully reproduced layout-design.

432. According to Article 100 of the Decision, the owner of the registration can only oppose the preceding activities if these have commercial or industrial purposes. Thus, he/she cannot oppose: (i) acts carried out in a private circle not having commercial purposes; (ii) acts carried out for experimental purposes; and (iii) acts carried out for teaching or scientific purposes. Furthermore, Article 101 provides that right holders cannot oppose acts of commerce when the layout-design in question has been introduced into the commerce of any country by the right holder or any other person with the consent of or having economic ties to that right holder.[527]

§7. Licences

433. The right holder of a layout-design registration can choose not to exploit the design and grant a licence instead so a third party can exploit it. Article 106 of Decision 486 establishes that in order for this procedure to be adequate, the licence has to be registered before the Superintendence. The absence of this registration shall render the licence invalid with regard to third parties. Alternatively, if the Superintendence finds that there is a lack of exploitation of the design, or if public interest reasons so require, it can grant a compulsory licence of the layout-design. Article 107 of the Decision empowers the Superintendence to order at any time the following:

527. Article 101 of the decision states that for the purposes of this provision, 'two persons shall be considered to have economic ties when one of the persons is able to exercise a decisive influence over the other, either directly or indirectly, with respect to exploitation of the layout-design, or when a third party is able to exert that influence over both persons'.

(a) that layout-designs that are registered or for which registration has been filed shall be used or exploited industrially or commercially by a governmental institution or by one or more public or private legal entities that have been expressly appointed to do so; or

(b) that the said layout-design shall be subject to the granting of one or more compulsory licences, in which case the competent authority may grant a licence to any person who applies for it, subject to the conditions that have been stipulated for that purpose.

434. The conditions stipulated for compulsory licences with respect to invention patents are also applicable to compulsory licences in regard to layout-designs of integrated circuits.

§8. Infringement and Remedies

435. For a complete explanation on infringements, *see* Chapter 12.

Chapter 9. Trade Secrets and Confidential Information

§1. Sources and Legislation

436. The WTO brought, at the international level, the first body of provisions for the protection of confidential information. This was achieved through Article 39 of the TRIPS Agreement, which obliges WTO Member Countries to protect confidential information against unfair competition practices. In fulfilment of such obligation, the ACN included norms for the protection of confidential information in Decision 486 of 2000 (the Decision), which establishes the intellectual property regime for the regional group.

437. Although there is no specific domestic law in Colombia regulating trade secrets and confidential information, the following statutes and regulations have included mechanisms to protect them. These are:

(1) Articles 61 and 62 of the Code of Commerce, regarding the reserve of commercial books and documents.
(2) Article 583 of Decree 624 of 1989 establishes the reserve for tax declarations.
(3) Articles 58(2) and 62(8) of the Labour Code provide obligations to employees regarding confidential information.
(4) Articles 23(4) and 48 of Law 222 of 1995, which indicates the obligation of managers referring industrial reserve and the partner's right to inspect commercial documents of the company.
(5) Article 85 of Law 489 of 1998 provides the protection of trade secrets in an industrial and commercial enterprise of the State.
(6) Articles 16 and 20 of Law 256 of 1996 (Unfair Competition Law), regarding violation of trade secrets.
(7) Articles 192, 194, 195, and 308 of Criminal Code (Law 599 of 2000) include provisions on criminal penalties directly or indirectly related to trade secrets.
(8) Decree 2085 of 2002 regarding the protection of pharmaceutical test data.
(9) Decree 502 of 2003 regarding the protection of agricultural test data.
(10) Decision 632 of 2006 of ACN regarding undisclosed test or other data of pharmaceutical or of agricultural chemical products.

438. The enactment of the Colombian Political Constitution of 1991, which included the right of private property, more specifically, the right of intellectual property, and the right of privacy as constitutional provisions in Articles 15,[528] 58,[529] and 61,[530] influenced all the above-mentioned laws and regulations enacted after 1991. According to the right of privacy, any person has the right to its personal privacy. Besides, it provides that all constitutional guaranties must be respected when data is compiled. Moreover, the correspondence and all other forms of private communications cannot be violated. The government may order the presentation of accounting books and confidential commercial documents for purposes of judicial taxation and inspection, monitoring, or intervention. This right allows the development of several provisions for the protection of trade secrets and confidential information.

Provisions related to the protection of reserved documents which may be connected to trade secrets are included in constitutional, commercial, administrative, criminal, labour, and tax laws. They are explained in Section 3.

§2. Subject Matter of Protection

439. Colombian legislation uses different terminology to refer to secrets related to business organizations. Terms, such as trade secrets, industrial secrets, and business secrets are used indistinctively, regardless of the differences that may exist from one to another. Although scholars[531] establish some distinctions from a theoretical point of view, all these concepts are equally protected and therefore we do not make any distinction for the purposes of this review. Taking into account the generic term used by most of international legislation, for purposes of this review we will refer to trade secrets only.

440. Another important point that must be clarified is the distinction between a trade secret and the 'know-how' of a company. On the one hand, some scholars insist that the concepts of trade secrets and know-how are exactly alike.[532] It is considered that the know-how is a term used to identify those industrial secrets that refer to the techniques applied for the production of goods and services. In simpler terms, the know-how refers to all the ideas, products, and industrial proceedings that should

528. Although the protection to the right of intimacy is more sophisticated and has been more developed in the current constitution, the former Constitution (1886) also established this right in its Arts 23 and 28.

529. *See* Art. 58 Right of Private Property. Colombian State guarantees the private property and other rights acquired by civil laws. These rights cannot be violated by subsequent laws.

530. *See* Art. 61 Right of Intellectual Property. Colombian State protects intellectual property according to the formalities provided in municipal laws.

531. *See* J.A. Gómez Segade, *El secreto Industrial (Know How) Concepto y protección* (Madrid, Tecnos, 1974), 51, 57, and 65.

532. *See* J.F. Creed, and R.B. Bangs, *Know How Licensing and Capital Gains*, cited by G. Cabanellas de las Cuevas, *Régimen Jurídico de los Conocimientos Técnicos* (Buenos Aires, Heliasta, 1984), p. 27; and D.R. Mac Donald, *Know How Licensing and the Antitrust Laws*, cited by Aura E. Rincón Peña, *El Secreto Empresarial en el Marco de las Relaciones Laborales*, XIII (2007) (unpublished dissertation, Universidad Externado de Colombia), on file at the library of *Universidad Externado de Colombia*, p. 21.

remain secret given its competitive value.[533] Article 1 of Decree 2123 of 1975 defines know-how as the secret experience of the way of doing something, related to an art or a technique and that can be subject of an assignment and transfer. In this sense, the confidentiality is essential to the know-how. On the other hand, scholars like Herbert Stumph consider that know-how is the knowledge and experience related to the technical, commercial, and economical aspects of the company that permits the production and sale of goods, as well as its organization and its management.[534] Stumph affirms that the know-how normally consists of a secret, but when it becomes public, it does not lose its value. We do agree with the latter concept and therefore, for purposes of this review, know-how is taken as a broad concept that may include secrets as well as public knowledge.

441. Trade secrets consist of an intangible good that can be materialized into graphs, figures, designs, drawings, models, and documents, among others, and that can be the subject to many types of contracts, e.g., assignment and technology transfer.[535] Article 260 of the Decision defines trade secrets as any undisclosed information within the lawful control of an individual or legal entity that may be used for any productive, industrial, or commercial activity and that is capable of being transmitted to a third party. The subject matter of a trade secret may be related to the nature, characteristics, or purpose of the products, production methods or processes, or the means or forms of distribution or marketing of goods or rendering of services. The information shall meet the following characteristics to be considered as a trade secret:

(a) is secret in the sense that it is not generally known among or easily accessible to persons within circles that normally deal with that kind of information;
(b) has commercial value because it is secret; and
(c) has been subject of reasonable measures to keep it secret, by the person lawfully in control of the information.

442. Article 261 of the Decision establishes that the information whose disclosure is the result of a legal provision or a Court order is not considered a trade secret. In addition, information provided to any authority or disclosed by legal provisions by a person in lawful possession of it, is not considered public property if such information is supplied for the purpose of obtaining licences, permits, authorizations, registrations, or any other legal acts.

443. Trade secrets are an alternative to protect inventions as long as they meet the characteristics mentioned above.[536] Therefore, regarding inventions, trade secrets can be divided into two main categories: (i) inventions or production methods that do

533. *See* A. Gómez Segade, *El secreto Industrial (Know How) Concepto y protección* (Madrid, Tecnos, 1974), 66.
534. *See* author cited in Legal Opinion (*Concepto*) 01096187. Superintendence of Industry and Commerce, 28 Jan. 2002.
535. *See* Aura E. Rincón Peña, *El Secreto Empresarial en el Marco de las Relaciones Laborales*, XIII (2007), (unpublished dissertation, Universidad Externado de Colombia), on file at the library of *Universidad Externado de Colombia*.
536. *See* Legal Opinion (*Concepto*) 02100353, Superintendence of Industry and Commerce, 27 Nov. 2002.

not meet the patentability requirements and therefore can only be protected as trade secrets; and (ii) inventions or production methods that fulfil the patentability requirements and can therefore also receive patent protection.[537] The latter indicates that a person can choose whether to protect his/her invention by means of a trade secret or a patent. However, the fundamental nature of the protection by trade secrets and patents is different. While protection of trade secrets requires that the subject of protection remains confidential, patent protection requires the disclosure of said information.

444. In any case, choosing protection under one form of intellectual property or the other, has certain advantages and disadvantages, as has been recognized by the WIPO. Regarding the advantages, protection of trade secrets is: (i) not limited in time; (ii) involves no registration cost; (iii) has immediate effect; and (iv) does not require formalities for its protection.[538] As for the disadvantages, (i) protection of an invention by means of a trade secret does not provide the exclusive right to exclude third parties from making commercial use of it, only patents and utility models can provide this type of protection; (ii) the protection lasts as long as the information is kept secret; and, (iii) a trade secret may be patented by someone else who developed the relevant information by legitimate means.[539]

§3. The Protection of Trade Secrets and of Confidential Information

445. Recent developments on protection of trade secrets and confidential information are the result of Articles 15 and 61 of the Colombian Constitution that establish the right of privacy and the right of intellectual property. As announced earlier, provisions related to the protection of reserved documents which may be connected to trade secrets are included in constitutional, commercial, health, administrative, criminal, labour, and tax laws. Those provisions are examined in the following subsections.

I. Protection by Means of Commercial Law

446. The protection by means of Commercial Law is divided into three subsections: Corporate Law, Competition Law, and Contract Law. Corporate Law establishes a specific protection regarding manager's obligations and partner's right of inspection within companies. As for Competition Law, an important protection is given to trade secrets and confidential information by means of two legal actions. Finally, Contract Law provides a relevant protection to trade secrets by different contractual clauses. These three subdivisions are developed as follows.

537. *See* <wipo.int/sme/en/ip_business/trade_secrets/patent_trade.htm> (last visited November 2017).

538. *See* <www.wipo.int/sme/en/ip_business/trade_secrets/patent_trade.htm> (last visited November 2017).

539. *Ibid.*

A. Corporate Law

447. Regarding Corporate Law, Article 23(4) of Law 222 of 1995 includes an obligation for managers regarding commercial and industrial reserve of the company. According to said article, managers shall hold and protect the trade and industrial reserve.[540]

448. Article 200 of the Code of Commerce establishes that managers have unlimited joint and several liability when they harm the partners, the company, or third parties intentionally or unintentionally. However, managers who do not know or vote against the actions or omissions that harm the company will not be liable. Moreover, managers will be presumed liable in any case of breach or abuse of their functions, violation of law, or violation of the corporate by-laws. If the manager is a legal entity, it will be liable along with its legal representative.

449. When managers breach the obligation of protecting the commercial or industrial reserve, they are presumed liable and two different actions may be exercised: (1) individual liability action, and (2) legal corporate liability action. The former is derived from the substantial norm contained in Article 200 of the Code of Commerce and may be exercised by anyone who has been harmed by an act of a company's administrator. This possibility is confirmed by the last paragraph of Article 25 of Law 222 of 1995. This action does not recognize any indemnification to the company but the restoration of rights and indemnification to those individuals that follow this civil liability action.[541]

450. As per the legal corporate liability action, Article 25 of Law 222 of 1995 establishes that the company may file a legal action against the managers prior the Decision of the board of partners or of the general meeting of shareholders. Nevertheless, when the Decision is taken and the legal action is not filed within three months, it may be filed by the controller of the company, by any other manager, or by any partner. Note that this action protects the company itself and is not aimed to protect an individual.

451. In addition, although Article 48 of Law 222 of 1995 establishes that partners have the right to inspect commercial books and documents of their company, this right is not extended to trade secrets or to other data which disclosure may harm the company. In this matter, the Superintendence of Corporations has stated that the inspection cannot be related to activities, businesses, and the know-how of the company.[542] Likewise, Article 61 of the Code of Commerce provides for the reserve of commercial books and documents. Such article establishes that commercial documents and accounting books can only be inspected by their owner or other specific persons authorized by the constitution.

540. Article 22 of Law 222 of 1995 establishes that the following individuals are managers in a company: (i) legal representative; (ii) liquidator; (iii) factor; (iv) members of the board of directors; and (v) whoever has any of those functions according to the corporate by-laws.

541. *See* F. Reyes Villamizar, *Derecho Societario* (Second Edition, Bogotá, Temis, 2006), pp. 605 and 606.

542. *See* Legal Opinion (*Concepto*) 220–3036, Superintendence of Corporations, *Derecho de inspección y derecho de información*, 21 Jan. 2000.

B. Competition Law

452. Pursuant to Article 262 of the Decision, persons who are lawfully in control of a trade secret, have the possibility of preventing it from being disclosed, acquired, or used by third parties in a contrary manner to fair trade practices. The following acts are considered unfair competition in respect of a trade secret:

(a) using, without the authorization of the person lawfully in control of that information, a trade secret to which the third party has access under a confidentiality obligation resulting from a contractual or labour trade practice;
(b) communicating or disclosing, without the consent of the personal lawfully in control of that information, the trade secret referred in paragraph (a) with the intent of obtaining advantages for oneself or another party or of causing injury to the person in control of that information;
(c) acquiring a trade secret by unlawful means or contrary to fair practice;
(d) using, communicating, or disclosing a trade secret acquired in the way described in paragraph (c);
(e) using a trade secret obtained from another person, knowing, or negligently failing to know, that the party who communicated the secret has acquired it by use of the means cited under paragraph (c), or did not have consent to communicate it from the person lawfully in control of that information; and
(f) communicating or disclosing a trade secret obtained in the way described under paragraph (e), for the benefit of oneself or a third party or the inure the person lawfully in control of that trade secret.

453. For this purpose, a trade secret is considered to have been acquired by contrary means to fair trade practices when such acquisition is the result of industrial espionage, breach of contract or other obligations, breach of trust, breach of duty of secrecy, or inducement to breach.

454. Regarding the breach of secrecy, Article 16 of Colombian Competition Law (Law 256 of 1996) establishes that said breach will come as an unlawful disclosure or use without authorization of the owner when the information disclosed was lawfully accessed to but was confidential, or unlawfully obtained through espionage activities or analogous procedures, or under violation of laws. It is also provided that the breach of secrecy applies even if it is not done within the market or for competitive purposes.

455. Regarding the breach of contract, Article 264 of the Decision indicates that any person lawfully in control of a trade secret may transfer it to a third party or authorize its use by a third party who will not be able to disclose the secret by any means, unless it is agreed to with the person having transferred or authorized the use of that secret. Additionally, agreements for the transfer of technological know-how, technical assistance, or the provision of basic or detailed engineering may include confidentiality clauses to protect the trade secrets contained therein, provided that such clauses are not contrary to Competition Law.

456. The acts of unfair competition are protected by means of two legal actions: (i) declaratory and condemnation action, and (ii) preventive and restraining action. Regarding the former, the affected party is entitled to request that a Court declares the unlawfulness of the acts performed and, consequently, that the infringing party is ordered to withdraw the effects of such acts and compensate damages. Therefore, in case the secret is disclosed, the only obligation of the infringer is to compensate damages to the plaintiff since the secret is already public. However, in case the secret is used and has not been disclosed yet, the infringer shall: (i) stop using the secret; (ii) keep the information secret; and (iii) compensate the damages to the plaintiff.

457. As for the preventive and restraining action, the person who believes to be affected by unfair competition, is entitled to request from a Court a restraining order against the performance of such conduct, or to prohibit it, although the damages may have not been caused yet. This legal action is applicable against unlawful violation of trade secrets, which have not been disclosed yet. The infringer would not be able to use or disclose those secrets.

458. These legal actions may be filed before the Superintendence or before a circuit civil judge. According to Article 23 of Law 256, these actions lapse two years after the infringer has been identified by the affected person, or three years following the occurrence of the last unfair act.

459. In order to issue a Decision in a case, four elements shall be analysed: (1) the existence of a trade secret; (2) the disclosure or use of said secret by a third party who has unlawfully accessed or otherwise lawfully accessed to but with confidential duty; and (3) if the disclosure or use was done without the authorization of the person lawfully in control of the secret. It is very complex to determine the first element regarding the existence of a trade secret. Consequently, the Superintendence and civil judges follow a method, which consist in identifying five conditions:

(1) the existence of knowledge based on products, procedures, facts, activities, among others;
(2) the knowledge must be confidential;
(3) the secret must be based on trade-related procedures and experiences;
(4) the lawfully holder of the secret must have taken measures to keep it unknown; and
(5) the information must have a competitive value.

460. As mentioned earlier, Article 16 of Law 256 of 1996 establishes that the breach of secrecy applies even if it is not done within the market or for competitive purposes, as was confirmed by Superintendence in a case where an employee moved from one company to another one in the same industrial sector, to further share trade secrets related to the manufacturing process used by his previous employer. The Superintendence considered that the disclosure of information does not have to represent adverse effects within the market, because the mere act of disclosure fulfils the unlawful conduct.[543]However. If an unfair competition action does not proceed, other Civil Law provisions on torts or breach of contracts may apply for the protection of trade secrets and the affected party may file an ordinary action before the civil jurisdiction to relief damages. Those actions may be filed by means of Contract Law or tort law as the case may be. The applicability of this alternative has to be analysed on a case-by-case basis.

543. *See* Decision 1647, Superintendence of Industry and Commerce, 30 Dec. 2011.

C. Contract Law

461. The main protection given to trade secrets refers to different clauses stipulated in contracts, especially those of commercial and employment nature. The most common clause is the confidentiality clause that establishes the duty of secrecy regarding specific information.

462. Contract Law establishes that the breach of not to do obligations may result in a compensation of damages (indemnification).[544] However, according to Article 1592 of Civil Code, another way of assuring the fulfilment of the confidentiality obligation is related to penalty clauses, which may be considered as an anticipated estimation of the prejudice that may result from a breach by the parties. Such provision attempts to quantify the probable amount of damages, reason why this clause is common in commercial and employment contracts.

II. Protection by Means of Administrative Law

463. The protection of trade secrets is also extended to industrial and commercial enterprises of the State. Article 85 of Law 489 of 1998 defines an industrial and commercial enterprise of the State as a public entity created or authorized by law that develops activities of industrial and commercial nature in conformity with civil and commercial provisions. In addition, this article indicates that those provisions that protect trade secrets and other commercial information are applicable to industrial and commercial enterprises of the Colombian State. Thus, for cases in which a citizen exercises his/her right of information through a formal petition,[545] any information that falls within the definition of trade secret shall be reserved.[546]

III. Protection by Means of Taxation Law

464. Article 583 of Decree 624 of 1989 (Taxation Code) establishes the reserve in tax declarations. The tax information in respect to the taxable base and the private tax assessment is considered confidential information. Consequently, public servants of the National Tax Bureau (DIAN) can only use such information for the controlling, gathering, determining, discussing, and managing of taxes and are prevented by disciplinary rules of releasing such information to third parties. In accordance with the regime of duties, misconducts, and sanctions provided for in the Disciplinary Code of Public Servants (Law 734 of 2002), officers shall be sanctioned with destitution, suspension, fine, or written reprimand when they breach their duties.

465. Articles 34.4 and 34.5 of the Disciplinary Code will be breached by DIAN officers should they release confidential information. The former article, establishes that public servants shall only use the reserved information that they have access to

544. *See* Art. 1612 Civil Code.
545. Article 74 of Colombian Constitution establishes that every individual has the right to access to public documents, except in those cases duly specified in laws (e.g., reserved documents).
546. *See* Legal Opinion (*Concepto*) 811, Superintendence of Public Utilities (1998).

for purposes of fulfilling their functions. Article 34.5 indicates that public servants shall protect the documents or information they have access to due to their functions against misappropriation, destruction, concealment or misuse.

466. In 1993, the Constitutional Court issued an important Decision in the matter in the case of *Bavaria S.A. v. Ministry of Finance – DIAN*. The plaintiff, the Colombian brewery Bavaria S.A., filed an action for protection of fundamental rights (*tutela*) against DIAN since this Bureau ordered the disclosing of a standard chart of raw material of several beers and malts produced by the company, as well as a list of their suppliers for 1991. The plaintiff considered that the documents used in an investigation performed by the DIAN were reserved. The Constitutional Court, in accordance with Article 15 of the Constitution, held that 'The Government may demand accounting books and confidential commercial documents for purposes of judicial taxation and inspection, monitoring, or intervention', in such a way that 'the activities performed by the State to determine and charge taxes limit the right of property in several ways; however, those limitations are based in the Constitution, where the public interest prevails over the particular interest. Limiting the activities performed by the State to protect trade secrets will result contrary to the nature and the goals of the State.'[547] Thus, the Court found that Bavaria's fundamental rights were not at stake and therefore did not grant any protection to the company.

IV. Protection by Means of Criminal Law

467. Colombian legislation includes several Criminal Law provisions that protect directly or indirectly trade secrets and confidential information. In this matter, five kinds of crimes are punished: (1) violation of industrial reserve; (2) unlawful use of privilege information; (3) unlawful violation to communications; (4) use and disclosure of reserved documents; and (5) abusive access to information technology.

468. Regarding the direct protection, Article 308 of the Criminal Code (Law 599 of 2000) establishes the violation of industrial reserve as a crime as follows: whoever uses, discloses, or reveals a discovery, scientific invention, process, or industrial application that he/she has known for reason of his/her job, profession or labour, and that should be kept secret, incurs in prison from thirty-two to ninety months and a fine from 26.66 to 3,000 minimum monthly wages (approximately USD 6,500 to USD 734,000).[548] In the same penalty incurs whoever unduly knows, copies, or obtains secret related to a discovery, scientific invention, processes, or industrial applications. If a profit is obtained for him/her or for a third party, the penalty will be of 48 to 126 months in prison and the fine will increase from to 133.33 to 4,500 minimum monthly wages (approximately USD 32,600 to USD 1,101,000).[549]

The profit obtained must imply a real economic increase in the offender's personal worth. The most common case consists in receiving a payment in exchange of the disclosure of the industrial reserve. It is relevant to clarify that these provisions refer only to industrial aspects of a business organization. Therefore, violation of reserve

547. *See* Constitutional Court, Judgment T-381, file T-10813, 14 Sep. 1993.
548. Calculated on 20 Nov. 2017 using <xe.com/ucc/> COP 3,015.33= USD 1.
549. *Ibid.*

regarding to trade aspects, such as sale, distribution, client list, and supplier list, among others are not sanctioned by this crime.

469. As for the indirect protection, the Criminal Code establishes four different types of crimes regarding confidential information in Articles 258, 192, 194, and 195. According to Article 74 of the Criminal Procedure Code (Law 906 of 2004) these are the kind of crimes that can only be denounced by the affected party only (*querellables*). These crimes are explained in the following paragraphs.

470. First, Article 258 of the Criminal Code establishes the unlawful use of privileged information as follows: the employer or member of the management board that unlawfully uses privileged information for its own or third-party profit, that he/she has known for reason of his/her job or profession, and that should be kept secret, will incur a fine.

471. According to the Superintendence of Corporations,[550] privileged information is considered unlawfully used when whoever lawfully controls the reserved information, performs any of these conducts:

(a) discloses it to a person who does not have the right to know it;
(b) uses it for his/her own or third-party profit;
(c) maliciously hides it, harming the company or obtaining profit for himself/herself or for a third party;
(d) makes public such information in an inappropriate time; or
(e) keeps the information secret or discloses it just to a specific group, when there is duty of making it public.

472. Second, Article 192 mentions the unlawful violation to communications in the following way: whoever unlawfully misappropriates, hides, loses, destroys, intercepts, controls, or prevents a private communication addressed to another person, or unduly knows its contents, incurs prison from sixteen to fifty-four months. If the author reveals its contents or uses it for its own or for third-party profit, the penalty is increased to prison from thirty-two to seventy-two months. This provision applies to any type of confidential information including trade secrets.

473. Third, Article 194 establishes the use and disclosure of reserved documents: whoever uses or discloses the contents of a document that should be kept secret, and does it for its own or third-party profit, or if it harms another person, incurs in a fine. This provision shall be read in conjunction with Article 62 of Commerce Code, which establishes that if the accountant or the holder of accounting books violates its reserve, they shall be sanctioned for the use or disclosure of reserved documents.

474. Finally, Article 195 establishes the abusive access to information technology in the following way: whoever unlawfully enters into an information technology system which is protected by safety measures or remains logged, against the will of who has the right to exclude him/her from the use of that system, incurs in a fine. This provision has a severe limitation for the protection of trade secrets, since it only applies for secrets included in an information technology system. Nevertheless, technological advances allow the creation of registers and data bases that may be related to trade

550. *See* Circular No. 20 of 1997, Superintendence of Corporations.

secrets or confidential information. Consequently, this provision may be applied to protect trade secrets or confidential information.

475. The competence to decide criminal offences rests in criminal judges, with a previous indictment by the prosecutor. The competent judge depends on the kind of crime. Regarding the violation of industrial reserve, the competent judge is the circuit criminal judge. As for the unlawful violation to communications, the use and disclosure of reserved documents, and the abusive access to information technology, the competent judge is the municipal criminal judge. The affected party should denounce the crime before any prosecutor with jurisdiction in his/her domicile. The prosecutor will initiate the investigation, obtain the necessary evidence, and if he/she finds that such felony was committed, will turn the results of the investigation to the criminal judge.

V. Protection by Means of Labour Law

476. In harmony with Article 265 of Decision the 486, Article 58.2 of the Colombian Labour Code establishes special obligations for employees. Accordingly, employees shall not disclose without the consent of the right holder, the information he/she has access to by reason of his/her work, employment, job, or professional performance, especially the information related to confidential or private information, which disclosure may harm the employer. If this occurs, the employer may declare the employee's breach of employment agreement and may declare a crime regarding the violation of industrial reserve (*see* paragraph 463.

The obligations in Article 58 are of general nature given that they apply to every employment relationship. However, it is convenient to specify in writing this particular obligation, as well as the information that the employer intends to remain confidential.

477. Pursuant to Article 62(8) of the Labour Code, the revelation of trade secrets or the disclosure of confidential information by the employee is considered a mayor offence and a just cause of termination of the employment agreement. In this sense, the employer may dismiss the employee due to the obligation of loyalty that is implied in a labour contract. This does not prevent the employer to seek relief through other actions such as the criminal and civil or commercial actions explained in the sections above. Case law has stated in different occasions that employers shall communicate the specific reasons for the termination of the contract to employees[551] and that employees have the right of defence prior to the termination of the employment agreement, and, of course, have the right to be heard in their claims before the labour jurisdiction.[552]

551. Constitutional Court, Judgment C-594, file D-1999, 21 Oct. 1998.
552. Constitutional Court, Judgment C-299, file D-1904, 17 Jun. 1998.

Chapter 10. Data Exclusivity

478. Article 266 of the Decision provides special protection against unfair commercial use and against disclosure of tests made for the approval of marketing of pharmaceutical or of agricultural chemical products, which are composed of new chemical entities. This protection is generally known as 'Data Exclusivity'.

With respect to this special protection, the main justification to grant protection to clinical data and the creation of this category of information, are the human and economic efforts made by laboratories in the process of obtaining the information. In this regard the WHO, the WIPO and the WTO have pointed out that this protection works as a form of compensation for the Research and Development made the laboratories in order to guarantee the safety and efficacy in new drugs.[553]

In this matter, the Colombian Government enacted Decree 2085 of 2002 and Decree 502 of 2003, which made possible the effectiveness of the current protection of this kind of data. In 2004, the Andean Court of Justice decided that Decree 2085 violated the Andean legislation because it established time periods for protecting the undisclosed information.[554] Nevertheless, Decision 632 of 2006 of ACN was enacted afterwards allowing Member Countries to select, adopt, and implement the measures they deem advisable to guarantee the protection of the test data.

479. According to Article 1 of Decree 2085 and Article 5 (paragraph) of Decree 502, a new chemical entity is defined as the moiety that has not been included in the Colombian pharmacological norms (the list of approved chemical entities for human use pharmaceuticals). Article 2 of Decree 2085 and Article 5 of Decree 502, establish that when the marketing of a pharmaceutical or agricultural chemical products containing new chemical entities has been approved, a third party cannot directly or indirectly use in a subsequent application the undisclosed information that was originally submitted for the approval of the first product. This protection is granted for certain periods of time:

(a) three years calculated from the approval to market the products in Colombia, for those applications filed within the first year in which the decree was enforced (2002–2003);
(b) four years calculated from the approval to market the products in Colombia, for those applications filed within the second year in which the decree was enforced (2003–2004); and
(c) five years calculated from the approval to market the products in Colombia, for those applications filed within the third year in which the decree was enforced (2005 onwards).

553. *See* World Health Organization, World Intellectual Property Organization and World Trade Organization. Promoting Access to Medical Technologies and Innovation. Geneva, 2013.
554. *See* Andean Court of Justice, Proceeding No. 114 AI-2004, 8 Dec. 2005, published in *Gaceta Oficial del Acuerdo de Cartagena*, No. 1295, 9 Feb. 2006.

480. According to Article 4 of Decree 2085 and Article 6 of Decree 502, such undisclosed information may be used when either one of the following conditions takes place:

(a) the holder of the health registration for the new chemical entity authorizes its use in a subsequent application;
(b) the Ministry of Health establishes that it is necessary to use such information when public interest prevails, and;
(c) the new chemical entity has not been commercialized in Colombia within one year after the health registration is granted.

Decree 2085 provides an additional exception to the protection that is not included in Decree 502: the undisclosed information may be used when the new chemical entity subject of the application for the approval of marketing is similar to a chemical entity already included in the health register and whose protection has expired.

481. The National Institute for the Surveillance of Medicines and Foods (the INVIMA) enacted Circular 005 of 2003 instructing the proper application of Decree 2085. According to said provision, the application for such protection shall contain the following:

(a) express mention of the new chemical entity used in the pharmaceutical product;
(b) declaration under oath establishing that the information, subject of protection, has not been disclosed; and
(c) proof of the effort made by the laboratory in the process of obtaining the undisclosed information.

482. The Revision Commission of the INVIMA shall conduct a pharmacological test to determine the novelty of the chemical entity. Afterwards, the new chemical entity can be registered in the Colombian pharmacological regulations. The protection starts from the date the authorization of commercialization is granted, that is, from the day of the notification of the administrative act that grants the health registration.[555]

555. *See* Circular DG 005 of 15 Jan. 2003, National Institute for the Vigilance of Medicines and Foods (INVIMA).

Chapter 11. GIs and Appellations of Origin

§1. Sources and Legislation

483. Colombian legislation regarding GIs has its foundation in international instruments, especially in: (1) the Convention concerning Industrial Property with France[556] (the Colombian-French Convention); (2) the Paris Convention for the Protection of Industrial Property;[557] (3) the General Inter-American Convention on Protection on Marks and Trade Names;[558] and (4) the Colombian accession to the WTO. Regarding the Colombian-French Convention, the appellations of origin duly obtained in France enjoy protection in Colombia, even if the national competent authority has not awarded the protection to such appellations. Concerning the Paris Convention, it constitutes the broader multilateral instrument for the repression of products bearing false indications about their sources. As for the Inter-American Convention, Colombia is obliged to follow international rules on defence against unfair competition and false indications of geographical origin. Regarding the WTO, Colombia is obliged to follow the provisions established in the TRIPS Agreement. The latter is the more universal agreement concerning GIs.

484. To implement these international obligations at the domestic level, Colombia has developed comprehensive regulations for GIs. This includes Decision 486 of 2000 of the ACN (the Decision), which establishes the common intellectual property regime for all ACN Member Countries; Decree 3081 of 2005 of the Ministry of Commerce, Industry and Tourism; Resolutions 210 of 2001 and 33190 of 2007 of the Superintendence. These last provisions establish the procedures that shall be followed in Colombia for the granting of the protection.

§2. Subject Matter of Protection

485. A GI is a sign that is used to identify products that have a specific geographical origin. These indications can be divided into two kinds: appellations of origin and indications of origin. These two divisions differ from one another in several ways but mainly in the existing bond between the product and the geographic area. This division will be thoroughly analysed in the following paragraphs.

486. As set forth in Article 201 of the Decision, an appellation of origin is a GI used to identify a product originated therein. The appellation of origin consists of a name of a particular country, region or locality, or of any name that refers to a specific geographical area. This GI is intended to designate qualities, reputation or characteristics, which are exclusively or essentially attributable to the geographical area in which the product where manufactured, including both natural and human factors.

556. *See* Convention concerning Industrial Property with France (1901).
557. *See* Paris Convention for the Protection of Industrial Property (1883).
558. *See* General Inter-American Convention on Protection of Marks and Trade Names (1929).

487. Regarding indications of origin, Article 221 of the Decision establishes that they may be a name, an expression, an image, or a sign that indicates or evokes a particular country, region, locality, or place. These indications may be stamped in the product itself, used in advertising campaigns, or in any commercial documents concerning sale, exhibition, or offering of the product.[559] Indications of origin are applied mostly to finished products, regardless of the origin of their raw materials. Consequently, it is considered that indications of origin not necessarily specify the geographic area where the products are produced; they may just specify the place where they are assembled or the seat of the company that produces them.[560]

488. In sum, an appellation and an indication of origin have differences that refer to the form and to the essence. Regarding formal differences, while an appellation of origin consists solely of a name of a particular country, region or locality, an indication of origin may consist of names, expressions or images. For instance, an indication of origin may be a flag, a well-known building, as the Eiffel Tower, or just an expression, such as 'made in Colombia'. Regarding essential differences, it is possible to identify two types: as to the first kind, an appellation of origin is intended to designate qualities and a reputation exclusively or essentially attributable to a geographical area given its nature and human factors. In contrast, an indication of origin is intended to designate the place where the product is made or distributed, without a quality or a reputation underpinning. Therefore, they do not constitute a guarantee of quality to the consumer. As to the second, whereas an indication of origin does not grant an exclusive right, an appellation of origin does when certain conditions are fulfilled (for further details, refer to Section 5 regarding Scope of Exclusive Rights).

§3. Conditions of Protection

489. The conditions for protection vary, depending on whether it is an indication or an appellation of origin. Indications of origin are protected automatically against false geographic indications when it consists of a name, an expression, an image, or a sign that indicates or evokes a particular country, region, locality, or place. In turn, appellations of origin must fulfil two types of requirements: positive and negative,[561] as provided in the Decision. The positive requirements are:

(a) The geographical indication shall consist of a name that refers to a specific geographical area used to designate a product that has that specific origin.
(b) The product shall have some specific qualities, characteristics or reputation, which are exclusively or essentially attributable to the geographical area in which it is produced. This may include both natural and human factors.
(c) Regarding the application for the protection, the applicants shall have a legitimate interest.

559. *See* Art. 222 of the Decision.
560. *See* A.J. Quintero Clavijo, *Visión de las denominaciones de origen en Colombia*, 3 *Revist@ e-Mercatoria del Departamento de Derecho Comercial de la Universidad Externado de Colombia*, No. 1, 2004, 3.
561. *See* Art. 202 of the Decision.

The negative requirements are as follows:

(a) The geographical indication shall not consist of common or generic terms that distinguish the product concerned. Generic terms are those which are considered as such by persons with knowledge of the area concerned and by the general public.
(b) The geographical indication shall not be contrary to good manners or to public order.
(c) The geographical indication shall not mislead the public as to geographical source, nature, means of manufacture, or quality, reputation, or other characteristics of the products.

§4. Formalities and Procedure for Obtaining Protection

490. In this matter, it is also different the treatment given to indications of origin and to appellations of origin. Regarding indications of origin, it does not follow any formalities or procedures, since they are not subject of protection by means of registration before any authority. Nonetheless, an appellation of origin shall follow a detailed procedure for obtaining protection. First, an application must be filed before the Superintendence and a declaration of protection must be granted. Second, the authorization for its use must be requested. Each of these steps is explained in the following subsections.

I. The Application for the Declaration of Protection

491. The application for the declaration of protection of an appellation of origin should be filed in a written form before the Superintendence as a hard copy or using electronic systems such as SIPI[562] by a person with legitimate interest. The Superintendence has a term of thirty days to decide whether it complies or not with the requirements. According to Article 204 of the Decision and Resolution 57530 of 2012,[563] those requirements are the following:

(a) name, domicile, residence, and nationality of the applicant or applicants and proof of their legitimate interest; the legitimate interest can be proved by presenting articles of association, the number of manufacturers that are members of the association and a description of the activities relating to the product which is the subject of the appellation of origin. If the appellation of origin is requested by a municipal or provincial authority, a description of the impartial authorization that will be granted to the manufacturers and potential beneficiaries of the appellation of origin must be submitted as well;[564]
(b) the appellation of origin in respect of which the declaration is filed;

562. *See* Ch. 4 about Trademarks for more information about SIPI.
563. *See* Resolution 57530 by the Superintendence of Industry and Commerce, 28 Sep. 2012.
564. *Ibid.*

(c) the specific geographical area within which the production, extraction, or processing of the product to be identified by the appellation of origin takes place;
(d) the name of the products that are covered by the appellation of origin;
(e) a summary of the essential qualities, reputation, or other exclusive characteristics of the products that are designated by the appellation of origin;
(f) the payment receipt of the respective fee;
(g) the power of attorney, if applicable; and
(h) the certificate of existence and legal representation, if the applicant is a legal entity.

II. The Declaration of Protection

492. The declaration of protection shall be granted by the Superintendence ex officio or at the request of a party with a legitimate interest. Said person can be an individual or a legal entity directly engaged in the extraction, production, or processing of the products to be covered by the geographical indication. Moreover, a party with a legitimate interest may be an association of producers, or a state, departmental, provincial, or municipal authorities, provided that they are located in the place of origin of the appellation.[565]

493. By virtue of Article 218 of the Decision, the Superintendence shall recognize appellations of origin protected in another ACN Member Country or in a third country as long it is provided in an international Convention and when they have been already declared protected in their countries of origin. Producers, extractors, manufactures, craftsmen with a legitimate interest, or their respective public authorities may submit the application.[566] Colombia, for instance, has recognized PISCO (a spirit beverage) from Peru as an appellation of origin, by means of Resolution 1529 of 1999 of the Superintendence. Currently, the Superintendence has granted the following appellations of origin from other ACN Member Countries: *white Corn* from Peru and *Chulucanas* from Peru.[567]

III. Authorization for the Use of a Protected Appellation of Origin

494. Once the appellation of origin is protected, an authorization for its use shall be granted by the Superintendence or by a public or private institution that represents the producers that may be benefited by such appellation of origin.[568] Regarding the Superintendence, it shall grant or reject the authorization within a period of thirty days

565. *See* Art. 203 of the Decision.
566. *See* Arts 218 and 219 of the Decision.
567. *See* Technical Document, Superintendence of Industry and Commerce, 2015. Available at <<http://www.sic.gov.co/sites/default/files/files/Nuestra_Entidad/Publicaciones/Denominaciones_Origen_Marcas_Tradicionales%20%20.pdf>.
568. *See* Art. 208 of the Decision and Art. 19 Decree 3081 of 2005.

after the request is filed.[569] As for the private or public institution, the Superintendence's Resolution 57530 of 2012 establishes that legally recognized institutions, whatever their associative or legal form is, may file an application before the Superintendence for the delegation of the faculty to authorize the use of a protected appellation of origin. According to Article 7.2.2 of Resolution 57530, said application must comply with the following requirements:

(a) a description of its legitimate interest to apply for the delegation and its representation of the producers that may be benefited by such appellation of origin;
(b) a description of its financial and administrative capacity to grant authorizations to use a protected appellation of origin;
(c) a description of the information outlets with the names of the beneficiaries or those authorized to use the appellation of origin;
(d) a description of the rules to use the appellation of origin, as well as the compliance with the specific characteristics of the products. These rules must contain a description of the characteristics, requirements, duties and rights and penalties of the authorized producers in order to produce, package, process and market the product under the protected appellation of origin;
(e) a description of the mechanisms and entities in charge of assuring the qualities of the product. In this regard, these mechanisms must describe the mode of extraction, production or preparation processes and the packaging or labelling that guarantee the quality and origin of the products.

495. Pursuant to Article 7.3.1 of the Resolution, the application for the delegation of the faculty to authorize the use of a protected appellation of origin must be filed before the Superintendence accompanied with sufficient evidence that proves the fulfilment of the requirements previously established in items (b) and (c), as well as the payment of the official fees.

496. The Superintendence shall perform the formal exam of the application within the following thirty days counted from the filing date of the application and shall determine if it fulfils the formal requirements prescribed in Resolution 57530. If the requirements are not fulfilled, the Superintendence shall inform the applicant which requirements must be clarified and completed in a two-month term. Conversely, if the formal requirements are fulfilled, the Superintendence shall notify to the applicant the admissibility and must perform the substantial test within the following thirty working days counted from the day the applicant was notified. For purposes of this test, the director of the distinctive signs division of the Superintendence may carry out inspections and demand the expedition of technical concepts and documents, as well as the filing of the evidence needed to support the denial or acceptance of the delegation.

497. Article 207 of the Decision, establishes that the authorization for the use of a protected appellation of origin shall be requested by persons who:

(a) are directly engaged in the extraction, production, or processing of the products identified by the appellation of origin;

569. *See* Art. 7.3.1 Resolution 57530 by the Superintendence of Industry and Commerce, 28 Sep. 2012

(b) perform said activity within the particular geographical area specified in the declaration of protection.

498. Once the admissibility test is performed, the director of the distinctive signs division must arrange an on-site technical visit to receive statements from the community and request the necessary information in order to grant or deny the appellation of origin. This information will form part of the minutes of the visit meeting that must be signed by all the attendees.

499. Finally, the director of the distinctive signs division must take a Decision through a reasoned resolution, which will be published in the Intellectual Property Gazette. Within the following thirty working days of the publication, whoever has a legitimate interest can file a well-founded opposition to the declaration of protection.[570] The period to submit evidence is extendable for another thirty days, at the request of an interested party. When the opposition is received, the Superintendence shall notify the applicant so he/she can counter-argue. Consequently, during the following thirty days, the applicant will be able to contest the opposition. That period is also extendable for thirty days at the request of the applicant.

500. The Superintendence may declare either ex officio or at the request of an interested person, modify or terminate the protection of an appellation of origin through a resolution in the following cases:

(1) when the geographic conditions prescribed for the declaration of protection of the appellation of origin can no longer be verified in respect to the products;
(2) when the conditions and procedures of manufacture and extraction prescribed for the declaration of protection of the appellation of origin change;
(3) when the natural or human conditions regarding the quality of the product change.

501. The authorization to use a protected appellation of origin is granted for a period of ten years and this may be continually renewed for the same term. The authorization will lapse if it is not renewed after those ten years. Nevertheless, the user of the appellation of origin has a grace period of six additional months to file the application for renewal. The authorization shall also lapse if the user does not pay the respective fees

502. In addition, the Superintendence shall declare either ex officio or at the request of an interested person, the authorization null and void or cancelled. Regarding nullity, it shall be declared if the authorization was granted without fulfilling all requirements. As for the cancellation, it shall be declared when the misuse of the appellation of origin in the market has been proven.[571]

503. In Colombia, the protection of appellations of origin follows a complex procedure. The two-step procedure is burdensome and the fees prescribed for every step are excessive. Nevertheless, Colombia currently has twenty-seven products protected by appellations of origin becoming the second country in South America

570. *See* Art. 7.3.2 Resolution 57530 by the Superintendence of Industry and Commerce, 28 Sep. 2012.
571. *See* Arts 216 and 217 of the Decision.

with more appellations of origin after Brazil, Some examples are *Cholupa del Huila*,[572] *Cesteria en Rollo de Guacamayas*,[573] *Queso del Caquetá*,[574] *Arroz de la Meseta de Ibagué*,[575] and most recently Bocadillo Veleño.[576]

At this point the Case Café de Colombia must be mentioned, as it was the first appellation of origin granted in Colombia.

504. In Colombia, the local appellation of origin CAFE DE COLOMBIA has obtained protection by means of Resolution 4819 of 2005 of the Superintendence. The National Federation of Coffee Growers (*Federación Nacional de Cafeteros*) obtained the protection of appellation of origin for the coffee produced in Colombia. In its application, the Federation devoted its effort to establishing the exact geographical location of green coffee of the Arabic species that intended to protect. It also identified the characteristic components, mode of extraction, production or preparation processes, storage, and quality control of the coffee. In response to the application, the Superintendence recognized the character of 'appellation of origin' to the coffee produced in certain determined areas of Colombia complying with specific requirements related to aroma, flavour, consistency, and quality.

Another factor considered by the Superintendence when granting the protection, was the botanical origin of the species and the varieties of coffee produced, the cultural common practices that include selective harvesting and the transformation of the fruit through an adequate and profitable processing of the washing and drying stages.

The appellation CAFE DE COLOMBIA may only be used by those individuals or legal entities that can prove that the coffee offered comply with all the characteristics established in said Resolution 4819. The protection is also recognized by the European Union as a protected geographical indication (PGI). The PGI is a system of protection created by the European Union to promote and protect foods produced, processed or prepared in a specific country or region.[577]

§5. Scope of Exclusive Rights

505. Regarding indications of origin, the right granted to a producer provides protection against false geographic indications that mislead or cause confusion among the public. The misleading and confusion may refer to the origin, source, quality, or any other characteristics of the product. Any false geographic indication may affect consumers as well as producers of that geographic area. Therefore, the protection is effective by means of:

572. *See* Resolution 43536, 21 Dec. 2007 by Superintendence of Industry and Commerce.
573. *See* Resolution 30000, 19 Jul. 2009 by Superintendence of Industry and Commerce.
574. *See* Resolution 68463, 30 Nov. 2011 by Superintendence of Industry and Commerce.
575. *See* Resolution 76532, 4 Nov. 2016 by Superintendence of Industry and Commerce.
576. *See* Resolution 37563, 27 Jun. 2017 by Superintendence of Industry and Commerce.
577. *See* <eubusiness.com/Food/1190903521.74/view> (last visited 21 Nov. 2017).

(1) repression to unfaithful competition, for the use of indications or affirmations which may mislead the public with regard to the nature, method of manufacture, characteristics, usefulness, or quantity of the goods in question;[578]
(2) the prohibition to register as a trademark those signs that are likely to create confusion in business circles or the public, in particular as to the geographical origin, nature, manufacturing methods, characteristics, or qualities of the goods or services concerned, or their suitability for use;[579] and
(3) the regulation provided for consumer protection.[580]

506. Nevertheless, pursuant to Article 223 of the Decision, any person may label his/her name and domicile on the products traded, even if those products come from another country. The country or place where those products are manufactured or produced may be clearly stated, together with any other indication that may be needed to avoid mistaking their true origin.

507. Regarding appellations of origin, it is convenient to make a distinction between appellations of origin as such and protected appellations of origin. Even though, other appellations of origin are not protected as such by the Colombian competent authority, some of them are protected by means of international treaties, that is, Colombian-French Convention. For instance, although the Superintendence has not declared the protection of the appellation of origin 'Champagne', it cannot be registered as a trademark since it denotes a specific sparkling wine produced in the region Champagne of France. This was stated in Resolution 02662 of 1990 of the Superintendence as follows: 'in conformity with Article 8 of the Colombian-French Convention, the term "Champagne" cannot be registered as a trademark'.

508. Appellations of origin do not grant an exclusive right to a producer. Any other qualified producers depending on the geographical zone in which they are located, can also benefit from that geographical indication.[581] The use of the appellation of origin is reserved exclusively to producers, manufacturers, and craftsmen who have their production and manufacturing establishments in the geographic area identified or evoked by the appellation.[582] They may use the protected appellation of origin along with the expression APPELLATION OF ORIGIN. Nonetheless, they have to comply with other provisions for its duly use.

509. The declaration of protection impedes an appellation of origin to be considered as common or generic appellation.[583] Generic appellations differ from appellations of origin since they do not intend to identify products with its geographic origin; they intend to identify a type of product different from others of the same kind.

510. The right granted refers to a protection that impedes the use of such appellation of origin by other people who do not comply with the requirements. The

578. *See* Art. 22(2) TRIPS Agreement, 259(c) of the Decision, and Law 256 of 1996.
579. *See* Art. 135(i) of the Decision.
580. *See* Decree 3466 of 1982.
581. *See* A.J. Quintero Clavijo, 'Visión de las denominaciones de origen en Colombia', 3 *Revist@ e-Mercatoria del Departamento de Derecho Comercial de la Universidad Externado de Colombia*, No 1, 2004, 11.
582. *See* Art. 212 of the Decision.
583. *See* Art. 220 of the Decision.

use by unauthorized persons, even when such use is accompanied by indications of gender, type, or imitation, shall be considered as an infringement of the intellectual property right protected and as such, may be sanctioned.[584] This unauthorized use shall be likely to cause confusion among consumers.[585]

511. The Decision establishes a special protection for wines and spirits. Member Countries of the ACN shall prevent the use of a geographical indication identifying wines or spirits that do not come from the place indicated by the appellation of origin. This protection is applied even when the real origin of the product is also indicated, or when the appellation of origin is used accompanied by expressions such as 'kind', 'type', 'style', or 'imitation', among others.[586]

512. The protection granted for appellations of origin is effective by means of:

(1) repression to unfair competition that occur with the use of indications or affirmations which may mislead the public with regard to the nature, method of manufacture, characteristics, usefulness, or quantity of the goods in question;[587]
(2) prohibition of registering as a trademark those signs that reproduce or imitate appellations of origin;
(3) regulation provided for consumer protection; and
(4) nullity and cancellation of the authorization to use an appellation of origin.

§6. Overlapping and Relations to Other Intellectual Property laws

513. GIs and trademarks are slightly similar since they intend to indicate qualities, characteristics, and reputation of the product. Nevertheless, while GIs link the product to a geographic area and the characteristics related to that particular area, trademarks identify the product with its producer. From the Decision, it can be concluded that while GIs are intended to protect a public interest, trademarks protect a private interest.

Regarding similarities between trademarks and appellations of origin, we identify the following: First, both are protected for ten years and they may be renewed. Second, the remedies established to protect a trademark are the same to those set forth for an appellation of origin. Thus, Article 135 (i), (j), and (k) of the Decision, in accordance with Article 22(3) of TRIPS, establish that some signs may not be registered as trademarks when they:

(a) are liable to create confusion in business circles or the public, in particular as to the geographical origin, nature, manufacturing methods, characteristics, or qualities of the goods or services concerned, or their suitability for use;
(b) reproduce, imitate, or contain a protected appellation of origin. This sign shall be liable to create confusion or a mistaken association with the appellation in

584. *See* Arts 238, 241, 242, 243, 244, 245, 246, 247, 248, and 249 of the Decision.
585. *See* Art. 214 of the Decision.
586. *See* Arts 23(1) TRIPS Agreement, 215 of the Decision.
587. *See* Arts 22(2) TRIPS Agreement, 258 of the Decision, and Arts 10, 11, 14, and 15 of Law 256 of 1996.

relation to the goods themselves or different goods. In addition, it has to involve taking unfair advantage of the well-known character of that appellation among the public; and

(c) contain a protected appellation of origin for wines and spirits.[588]

§7. Infringements and Remedies

514. For a complete explanation on infringements, *see* Chapter 12.

588. *See* Art. 23(2) TRIPS Agreement.

Chapter 12. Infringements and Remedies

515. Decision 486 of the Andean Community (the Decision) establishes a general infringement regime applicable to all the industrial property rights regulated therein.[589] This implies that domestic legislation addressing infringement matters remains suspended;[590] and may only be applied provided that it regulates aspects that are not covered by Andean Law and that do not contradict its provisions.[591]

516. The Andean legislation: (i) sets up the regulation of actions for infringement of industrial property rights; (ii) outlines an unfair competition regime for acts which are contrary to honest commercial usage and practices; (iii) provides for the possibility to apply measures on the border; and (iv) mandates Member Countries to establish criminal procedures and sanctions against trademark infringers. Accordingly, in general terms, industrial property right holders are entitled to bring civil actions (actions for infringement of industrial property rights and unfair competition actions), administrative actions (measures on the border) and criminal actions, against whoever infringes their rights.

§1. Actions for Infringement of Industrial Property Rights

517. Pursuant to Article 238 of the Decision, the owner of an industrial property right is entitled to file infringement actions before the national competent authority, against whoever might be infringing said rights[592] or against whoever performs acts *evidencing imminence* of an infringement. The concept of *infringement* is obviously derived from the scope of the right subject matter of litigation, reason why it shall be analysed on a case-by-case basis. In general terms, the infringement of the right protected in Article 238 consists mainly of the violation to the right of exclusive exploitation.

518. As to the ownership of the procedural right to act before a given jurisdiction to defend an industrial property right, the Andean Court of Justice has stated that Article 238 recognizes the principle of correlation between the ownership of the substantial right and the right to defend it.[593] Therefore, the entitlement to file an infringement action rests on the head of the right holder of the industrial property right that can be either an individual or a legal entity, and may be transferred by an act *inter vivos* or *mortis causa.* Article 238 also states that, except as otherwise agreed, the

589. The infringement actions regarding copyrights are not contained in the Decision since this instrument only sets forth actions for industrial property rights. Actions for copyrights will be explained below.

590. *See* Andean Court of Justice, Proceeding No. 2-IP-98, 7 Apr. 1998, published in *Gaceta Oficial del Acuerdo de Cartagena*, No. 33, 26 Jul. 1998.

591. *See* Andean Court of Justice, Proceeding No. 10-IP-94, 17 Mar. 1995, published in *Gaceta Oficial del Acuerdo de Cartagena*, No. 177, 20 Apr. 1995.

592. *See* Art. 238 of the Decision.

593. *See* Andean Court of Justice, Proceeding No. 96-IP-2004, 22 Sep. 2004, published in *Gaceta Oficial del Acuerdo de Cartagena*, No. 1134, 3 Nov. 2004.

co-owner of an industrial property right may file an infringement action without the consent of the co-owner of the right.

519. Furthermore, Article 238 grants national competent authorities to initiate ex officio an infringement action against whoever violates an industrial property right when domestic legislation allows such possibility. However, Colombian legislation does not grant national authorities said faculty reason why it is not possible to initiate an infringement action ex officio.

520. In case of violation of an industrial property right, the right holder exercising the action may request one or several of the following measures:[594]

(1) cessation of all acts that constitute the infringement;
(2) compensation for damages;
(3) withdrawal from commercial channels of all products resulting from the infringement, including packaging, wrappings, labels, printed materials or advertising, together with the materials and implements, the predominant use of which has been the Commission of the infringement;
(4) prohibition against the importation or exportation of the products, or materials or implements referred to in the previous item;
(5) adjudication of the ownership of the products or materials or implements referred to in item (3), in which case the value of such goods shall be charged to the amount of compensation due for damages;
(6) adoption of the necessary measures to avoid continuation or repetition of the infringement, including destruction of the products or materials or implements referred to in item (c) or the temporary or definitive closure of the business belonging to the defendant or the accused; or
(7) publication of the guilty verdict and notification of interested parties at the infringer's expense.

521. Whenever the plaintiff requests indemnity for damages he/she shall indicate the amount of the damages suffered or, at least, the basis to fix this amount. Also, it is understood that damages will only be indemnified whenever there is a relation of causality between the damage and the act performed by the infringer.[595]The Decision provides guidance in the assessment of the amount of indemnity for damages. However, the use of these criteria is not mandatory, as the Decision does not establish an exhaustive *numerus clausus* regime. Also, Andean legislation does not expressly prohibit the use of more than one criterion to calculate damages in the same infringement action, giving the Judge the option to use his discretion to use more than one criterion in the same action.

522. The criteria established in the Decision to calculate the amount of indemnity for damages is the following:[596]

594. *See* Art. 241 of the Decision.
595. *See* Andean Court of Justice, Proceeding No. 96-IP-2004, 22 Sep. 2004, published in *Gaceta Oficial del Acuerdo de Cartagena*, No. 1134, 3 Nov. 2004.
596. *See* Art. 243 of the Decision.

(a) the consequential damage and lost profits suffered by the right holder as a result of the infringement;
(b) the amount of profit obtained by the infringer as a result of the acts of infringement; or
(c) based on the commercial value of the infringed right and such contractual licences as may have already been granted, the price the infringer would have paid for a contractual licence.

523. Regarding the first criterion, the Andean Court has established that consequential damages refer to the equity loss suffered by the owner as a direct consequence of the non-authorized exploitation of the industrial property right. The loss shall be calculated taking into account, mainly, the common value of the exploited right in the market. However, when the plaintiff also requests the adjudication of the products resulting from the infringement, as well as the means or materials that were used to commit it, the value of these goods will be deducted from the amount of the compensation.[597] In turn, the concept of *loss of profit* is understood as the benefits that the right holder would have obtained through the exploitation of his/her right in case the infringement would have not occurred. Consequently, the benefits to be considered are those obtained between the period when the infringement occurred and the payment of the compensation.[598]

524. Regarding the second criterion, there are no clear interpretations of the expression *benefits obtained by the infringer.* As the calculation of such portion as a direct consequence of the violation of the industrial property right is complex, Colombian judges have calculated this amount using their discretional, taking into account the evidence filed by the plaintiff and the opinion of the expert appointed for each case.

525. Finally, as to the last criterion, Andean case law has stated that apart from the price that the infringer would have paid for a contractual licence, the commercial value of the infringed right and that of the contractual licence which would have already been granted, the validity term of the industrial property right, the moment in which the infringement began to take place and the number and type of licences granted should also be taken into account.[599]

526. Actions for infringement of industrial property rights are subject to a two-year statute of limitations period, counted as from the date when the owner became aware of the infringement or in any event, to a five-year statute of limitations counted as from the time when the infringement occurred for the last time.[600]

527. In case of violation of an industrial property right, the plaintiff may request interim measures from the competent authority. The purpose of these measures is to stop the infringement, avoid its consequences, obtain or maintain evidence, or ensure the effectiveness of the action or the indemnity for damages.[601] By allowing the right

597. *See* Art. 243e of the Decision.
598. *See* Andean Court of Justice, Proceeding No. 96-IP-2004, 22 Sep. 2004, published in *Gaceta Oficial del Acuerdo de Cartagena*, No. 1134, 3 Nov. 2004.
599. *See* Andean Court of Justice, Proceeding No. 96-IP-2004, 22 Sep. 2004, published in *Gaceta Oficial del Acuerdo de Cartagena*, No. 1134, 3 Nov. 2004.
600. *See* Art. 244 of the Decision.
601. *See* Art. 245 of the Decision.

holder to request interim measures, the Decision recognizes the existing risk that between the period in which the lawsuit is filed and the time in which the final Decision is issued. This because the damage caused by the infringement could compromise the effectiveness of the judicial protection.[602]

The plaintiff in an infringement action proceeding may request, among others, the following interim measures:

(a) immediate cessation of all acts constituting the alleged infringement;
(b) withdrawal from commercial channels of all products resulting from the alleged infringement, including packaging, wrappings, labels, printed material or advertising, or other materials, together with the materials and implements the predominant use of which has been the Commission of the infringement;
(c) suspension of the importation or exportation of the goods or materials or implements referred to under the previous paragraph;
(d) establishment by the alleged infringer of an adequate guarantee; and
(e) temporary closure of the business belonging to the defendant or accused, if necessary, to avoid continuation or repetition of the alleged infringement.

528. As it is the case with Article 246,[603] the list of possible injunction measures that may be requested is not exhaustive as the plaintiff may request the measures that he/she deems appropriate.

529. Interim measures may be requested prior to initiating the judicial action, simultaneously therewith, or subsequently to its initiation.[604] In Colombian litigation, whenever such measure is requested and executed prior to initiating the judicial action for infringement, the plaintiff shall initiate the judicial action within the ten days following the execution of the measure. If this does not occur, the interim measure shall not have any effects.[605] Whenever the measure is executed without the intervention of the defendant, such process shall be served upon the affected party, immediately after the execution. Once the defendant is served upon, he/she will have the opportunity to file reconsideration and appeal remedies against this Decision.[606]

530. The competent Judge may only decree a preventive injunction measure when whoever requests it accredits his/her entitlement to act, the existence of the right infringed and submits evidence that may allow to reasonably assume the commission of the infringement or its imminence.[607] This rule imposes upon the plaintiff the burden to file evidence allowing the judge to consider as real and probable the existence of the right (*fumus boni iuris*), and to recognize the existence of the risk to which the effectiveness of the final Decision could be exposed due to its delay (*periculum in*

602. COMOGLIO, Luigi Paolo, *Lezioni sul Processo Civile, seconda edizione, Il Mulino*, 1998, Bologna-Italia, 365 ss. Cited by Andean Court of Justice, Proceeding No. 96-IP-2004, 22 September, published in *Gaceta Oficial del Acuerdo de Cartagena*, No. 1134, 3 Nov. 2004.
603. *See* Art. 246 of the Decision.
604. *See* Art. 248 of the Decision.
605. *Ibid.*
606. *Ibid.*
607. *See* Art. 247 of the Decision.

mora).[608] Hence, the execution of a preventive injunction measure does not require certainty as to the existence of the infringement, but just the existence of the probability of it, reason why the judge cannot decide the case in an anticipated manner.

531. Prior to ordering an interim measure, the judge in charge has the discretionary power to require from whoever requested the measure a bond to guarantee possible damages that may be caused to the defendant with the measure.[609]

532. For the purpose of infringement actions, the *national competent authority* is the administrative or judicial entity that, established by the internal legislation, is entitled with the authority to decide this type of actions. The Colombian General Procedural Code has provided the competence to decide actions for infringement of industrial property rights, in the first instance, to civil circuit judges.[610]

This regulation also provides the Superintendence of Commerce and the National Direction of Copyright with judicial powers, in an attempt to provide specialized justice in matters that are highly technical. Under this rule, the jurisdictional powers are exercised by these administrative authorities without excluding the jurisdiction granted by law to civil circuit judges as judicial authorities regarding intellectual property cases. Therefore, in a case of a violation of industrial property rights, the plaintiff can choose between filing before the civil circuit judge as the legally competent judicial authority or before the Superintendence of Industry and Commerce as the administrative authority authorized by law to exercise jurisdictional powers in this matter.[611]

§2. Specific Actions Regarding Patents and Utility Models

533. The general infringement regime is also applicable to patent infringement proceedings. However, the Decision establishes some specific rules applicable to this type of proceedings, which obey to the nature of the right subject matter of debate.

534. First, the Decision states that the owner of a patent is entitled to exercise judicial actions for damages concerning the unauthorized use of the invention or the utility model during the period comprised between the date when it acquires the character of public and the relevant file may be inspected, and the date in which the patent is granted. In this cases, the indemnity shall only proceed with respect to the subject matter covered by the granted patent and will be calculated based on the effective exploitation of the right performed by the defendant during the mentioned period.

535. Additionally, the Decision provides that in those cases were an infringement of a patent whose purpose is a process for obtaining a product is alleged, the defendant bears the burden of proving that the process that has been utilized for obtaining the product is different from the process protected by the patent whose infringement is

608. *See* Andean Court of Justice, Proceeding No 96-IP-2004, 22 September, published in *Gaceta Oficial del Acuerdo de Cartagena*, No. 1134, 3 Nov. 2004.
609. *See* Art. 247 of the Decision.
610. *See* Art. 20 Colombian General Procedural Code (Law 1564 of 2012).
611. *See* Art. 24 Colombian General Procedural Code (Law 1564 of 2012).

alleged. This represents a shift in the burden of proof that regularly rests upon the party that alleges the infringement.

536. The Decision presumes that, unless otherwise is proved, every identical products produced without the consent of the patent has been obtained through the patented process when:

(a) the product obtained through the patented process is novel; or
(b) there exists a substantial likelihood that the identical product shall have been manufactured through the process, and the owner of the patent may not be able to establish through reasonable efforts which has been the process effectively utilized.

537. During the submission of evidence to the contrary, the legitimate interest of the defendant or the denounced party is taken into account concerning protection to his/her entrepreneurial secrets.

I. Criminal Actions

538. As mentioned before, Andean legislation mandates Member Countries to establish criminal procedures and sanctions against industrial property infringers. In this sense, pursuant to Article 306 of Colombian Criminal Code (Law 599 of 2000), whoever unlawfully uses trade names, emblems, trademarks, patents, utility models, industrial designs, or appropriates plant breeder's rights, which are legally protected or confusingly similar to the ones protected, incurs in prison from four to eight years and a fine from 26.66 to 1,500 minimum monthly wages (approx. USD 7,626 to USD 429,000).[612] In the same penalty incurs whoever finances, provides, distributes, markets, commercializes, transports, acquires for commercial purposes, products or plants produced, bred or distributed in those circumstances.

Regarding the compensation payable due to trademark infringement, it can be subject to a pre-established compensation system or the general rules to set compensatory damages, depending on the choice made by the plaintiff.[613] If the plaintiff files the claim opting for the pre-established compensation system, he/she will not have to prove the amount of damages caused by the infringement, as established in Article 243 of the Andean Decision 486. The amount of the pre-established compensation shall be the equivalent of 3 to 100 minimum monthly wages (approx. USD 735 to USD 24,468), for each trademark infringement. Additionally, when the trademark infringed is a well-known trademark, this amount may be increased up to 200 minimum monthly wages (approx. USD 48,936).[614]

612. Calculated on 20 Nov. 2017 using <xe.com/ucc/> COP 3,015.33= USD 1.
613. *See* Art. 3 of Law 1648 of 2013.
614. *See* Art. 2 of the Decree 2264 of 2014.

§3. COPYRIGHTS

539. Colombian legislation contemplates different ways to protect copyrights, which can be summarized in civil and criminal actions for infringement of copyright provisions. Law 23 of 1982 provides for oral proceedings for conflicts referring to copyright, pursuant to Articles 242 and subsequent of said law.

I. Civil Actions

540. Civil judges, through action brought before the general jurisdiction, can offer an alternative to obtain economic compensation for unauthorized use of a copyrighted work or for breach of Contract Law.

For the effective protection of their rights, authors can initiate a preventive injunction process, which is contemplated in Article 244 of Law 23. According to this provision, 'the author, the publisher, the artist, the producer of sound recordings, the broadcasting organization, their successors and assignees, and whoever may act on their behalf, may request from a judge a preventive injunction measure, ordering the seizure of: (i) the entire work, production, edition and copies; (ii) the revenues from the sale and rental of such works, productions, editions or copies; and (iii) the revenues from the sale or rental of spectacles such as drama works, films, musical works and other analogous works'.

For this action to proceed, Article 246 provides that the person requesting the measure affirms that a lawsuit has been or will be filed against whoever was allegedly infringing copyright provisions. Also, in the terms of Article 245 of Law 23, the persons mentioned in Article 244 can request a judge to issue an order to interrupt and suspend the performance, execution, and exhibition of a theatrical or musical work, a film, and any other similar works, which are to be performed, executed or exhibited without authorization.

In order to calculate the monetary indemnification for damages for infringement of copyright, the judges were given the following criteria in Article 243 of the Decision:

(a) the actual harm and the loss of revenue suffered by the rights-owner as a result of the infringement;
(b) the amount of profit earned by the infringer as a result of the infringing acts; and
(c) the price that the infringer would have paid for a contractual license, due regard being had to the market value of the rights infringed and to contractual licences that have already been granted.

II. Criminal Actions

541. Title VIII of the Colombian Criminal Code (Law 599 of 2000) lists the crimes against copyrights. Specifically, Articles 270–272 indicate the criminal punishments for infringement of copyright provisions. Criminal actions for copyright infringements are to be brought before the National Unit in charge of Copyrights and

Unlawful Access to or Provision of Telecommunication Services of the Office of the Prosecutor General.

Selected Bibliography

Books

Chaparro, F. et al., *Manual sobre la Propiedad Intelectual de Productos Derivados de la Actividad Académica en Universidades y Centros de Investigación.* Bogotá: Universidad Nacional de Colombia, 1997.

Escobar, M. and J.D. Martínez, J.D., *Análisis de las diferencias existentes entre la utilidad y la aplicación industrial como requisito de patentabilidad.* Bogota: Pontificia Universidad Javeriana, 2006.

Idrovo Cubides, J.M., *Principios Básicos de las Inversiones, Seis Países de América Latina.* 1st ed. Bogotá-Colombia: Legis, 2005.

Metke Méndez, R. *Lecciones de Propiedad Industrial.* 1st ed., Medellín-Colombia: Editorial Diké, 2001.

Pico Mantilla, G., *Derecho Andino.* Ecuador: Tribunal de Justicia del Acuerdo de Cartagena, 1989.

Rengifo García, E., *Propiedad Intelectual: El Moderno Derecho de Autor.* Bogotá: Universidad Externado de Colombia, 1996.

S. Rodríguez, S., *La era digital y las excepciones y limitaciones al derecho de autor.* Bogotá: Universidad Externado de Colombia, 2004.

Superintendencia de Industria y Comercio, *Manual del Inventor.* Bogotá: Superintendencia de Industria y Comercio, 2007.

Multiple authors, Derecho de Patentes, Universidad Externado de Colombia, Bogotá, 2017.

Journals

Antequera, R., 'El comercio electrónico, puesta a disposición de contenidos y transmisiones digitales', *Revista de Derecho Privado*, No. 26 (August 2001).

Madrid, L.A., 'La salud pública y la discusión de propiedad intelectual en el TLC Colombia-Estados Unidos', *Centro de Documentación TLC Colombia*, Sergio Arboleda University. In: <usergioarboleda.edu.co/tlc/tlc_salud.htm>.

Miceli, C., 'Quietly Tying Down Gulliver. The Software Patent Fairy Tale', *Revista de Derecho Informático*, No. 098 (September 2006).

Wilson Rafael Ríos Ruiz, Propiedad Intelectual respecto de los Circuitos Integrados (Chips), in Revista dela Propiedad Intelectual No 2, Universidad Externado de Colombia 2001, at < http://revistas.uexternado.edu.co/index.php/propin/article/view/1197/1135>

Internet Resources

<www.dane.gov.co>

<www.comunidadandina.org>

<www.proexport.com.co>

<www.wipo.int>

<www.sayco.org>

<www.acinpro.org.co>

<www.wto.org>

<www.sic.gov.co>

<www.nic.co>

Table of Cases

Colombian Case Law

Constitutional Court, judgment C-334 of 1993.

Constitutional Court, judgment C-533 of 1993.

Constitutional Court, judgment C-040 of 1994.

Constitutional Court, judgment SU-056 of 1995.

Constitutional Court, judgment C-276 of 1996.

Constitutional Court, judgment C-226 of 199.

Constitutional Court, judgment C-282 of 1997.

Constitutional Court, judgment C-155 of 1998.

Constitutional Court, judgment C-1490 of 2000.

Constitutional Court, judgment C-053 of 2001.

Supreme Court of Justice, judgment of 23 April 1987.

Supreme Court of Justice, judgment of 1 September 1988.

Supreme Court of Justice, *Louis Vuitton S.A. v. Natalio Isaac Lustgarten Coldman*, 8 February 2002.

Centre of Arbitration and Conciliation of the Chamber of Commerce of Bogotá, *Colombia Ltda. v. Informatica y Gestion SA*, 17 October 2006.

Council of State, *Ebel S.A. v. Superintendence of Industry and Commerce*, 22 April 1995.

Council of State, *Thomas Greg & Sons de Colombia S.A. v. Superintendence of Industry and Commerce*, 30 September 1999.

Council of State, *Ecogel v. Superintendence of Industry and Commerce*, 7 April 2000.

Council of State, *Harrods Limited v. Superintendence of Industry and Commerce*, 22 October 2001.

Council of State, *Laura Ashley Manufacturing B.V. v. Superintendence of Industry and Commerce*, 15 November 2002.

Council of State, *Fenolicos Colombianos Ltda. v. Superintendence of Industry and Commerce*, 13 March 2003.

Council of State, *Compañia Nacional de Chocolates S.A. v. Superintendence of Industry and Commerce*, 17 July 2003.

Council of State, *Canal Societe Anomyme v. Superintendence of Industry and Commerce*, 5 October 2003.

Council of State, *Fenolicos Colombianos Ltda. v. Superintendence of Industry and Commerce*, 13 March 2003.

Council of State, *Alpina Productos Almineticios S.A. v. Superintendence of Industry and Commerce*, 4 July 2003.

Council of State, *Kraft Foods Inc. v. Hershey Foods Corp.*, 19 February 2004.

Council of State, *Allergan. Inc. v. Superintendence of Industry and Commerce*, 1 July 2004.

Council of State, *Warner-Lambert Co. v. Nobel Farmaceutica S.A.*, 21 July 2004.

Council of State, *Corn Products International Inc. v. Superintendence of Industry and Commerce*, 17 February 2005.

Council of State, *Salomon S.A. v. Superintendence of Industry and Commerce*, 24 February 2005.

Council of State, *Rhone-Poulenc Agro v. Superintendence of Industry and Commerce*, 3 March 2005.

Council of State, *Parke, Davis & Co. Limited v. Superintendence of Industry and Commerce*, 2 March 2005.

Council of State, *Sociedad J.P. Morgan Chase & Co. v. Superintendence of Industry and Commerce*, 17 March 2005.

Council of State, *Conavi Banco Comercial y de Ahorro S.A. v. Superintendence of Industry and Commerce*, 14 April 2005.

Council of State, *Golden Brown International Limited v. Superintendence of Industry and Commerce*, 14 April 2005.

Council of State, *Alpha Shoes S.A. v. Superintendence of Industry and Commerce*, 16 June 2005.

Council of State, *Gaseosas Posada Tobón S.A. v. Superintendence of Industry and Commerce*, 4 August 2005.

Council of State, *Societé des Produits Nestlé S.A. v. Superintendence of Industry and Commerce*, 4 August 2005.

Council of State, *Santander Investment Bank Limited v. Superintendence of Industry and Commerce*, 11 August 2005

Council of State, *Henkel Kommanditgesellshaft auf Aktien v. Superintendence of Industry and Commerce*, 9 March 2006.

Council of State, *Gaseosas Posada Tobón S.A. v. Superintendence of Industry and Commerce*, 8 June 2006.

Table of Cases

Council of State, *Industrias Dormiluna Ltda. v. Superintendence of Industry and Commerce*, 27 July 2006.

Council of State, *Sodimac Colombia S.A. v. Superintendence of Industry and Commerce*, 24 August 2006.

Council of State, *Supertex Medical S.A. v. Superintendence of Industry and Commerce*, 20 October 2006.

Andean Court of Justice

Andean Court of Justice, Proceeding No. 1-IP-87, 3 December 1987, published in *Gaceta Oficial del Acuerdo de Cartagena*, No. 28, 15 February 1988.

Andean Court of Justice, Proceeding No. 4-IP-88, 9 December 1988, published in *Gaceta Oficial del Acuerdo de Cartagena*, No. 39, 24 January 1989.

Andean Court of Justice, Proceeding No. 2-IP-89, 19 October 1989, published in *Gaceta Oficial del Acuerdo de Cartagena*, No. 49, 10 November 1989.

Andean Court of Justice, Proceeding No. 6-IP-89 of 6 November 1989, published in *Gaceta Oficial del Acuerdo de Cartagena*, No. 50, 17 November 1989.

Andean Court of Justice, Proceeding No. 3-IP-95, 7 August 1995, published in *Gaceta Oficial del Acuerdo de Cartagena*, No. 189, 10 September 1995.

Andean Court of Justice, Proceeding No. 4-IP-94, 7 August 1995, published in *Gaceta Oficial del Acuerdo de Cartagena*, No. 189, 15 September 1995.

Andean Court of Justice, Proceeding No. 7-IP-95, 7 August 1995, published in *Gaceta Oficial del Acuerdo de Cartagena*, No. 189, 10 September 1995

Andean Court of Justice, Proceeding No. 7-IP-95, 7 August 1995, published in *Gaceta Oficial del Acuerdo de Cartagena*, No. 199, 26 January 1996.

Andean Court of Justice, Proceeding No. 8-IP-95, 30 August 1996, published in *Gaceta Oficial del Acuerdo de Cartagena*, No. 231, 17 October 1996.

Andean Court of Justice, Proceeding No. 4-IP-95, 15 December 1996, published in *Gaceta Oficial del Acuerdo de Cartagena*, No. 253, 7 March 1997.

Andean Court of Justice, Proceeding No. 33-IP-1995, 15 November 1996, published in *Gaceta Oficial del Acuerdo de Cartagena*, No. 257, 14 April 1997.

Andean Court of Justice, Proceeding No. 30-IP-96, 12 September 1997, published in *Gaceta Oficial del Acuerdo de Cartagena*, No. 299, 17 October 1997.

Andean Court of Justice, Proceeding No. 15-IP-97, 21 November 1997, published in *Gaceta Oficial del Acuerdo de Cartagena*, No. 314, 18 December 1997.

Andean Court of Justice, Proceeding No. 31-IP-96, 3 December 1997, published in *Gaceta Oficial del Acuerdo de Cartagena*, No. 318, 26 January 1998.

Andean Court of Justice, Proceeding 11-IP-1995, 7 April 1998, published in *Gaceta Oficial del Acuerdo de Cartagena*, No. 349, 19 June 1998.

Andean Court of Justice, Proceeding No. 04-IP-97, 20 January 1997, published in *Gaceta Oficial del Acuerdo de Cartagena*, No. 354, 13 July 1998.

Andean Court of Justice, Proceeding No. 9-IP-97, 4 February 1998, published in *Gaceta Oficial del Acuerdo de Cartagena*, No. 336, 27 April 1998.

Andean Court of Justice, Proceeding No. 30-IP-97, 8 May 1998, published in *Gaceta Oficial del Acuerdo de Cartagena*, No. 355, 14 July 1998.

Andean Court of Justice, Proceeding No. 4-IP-98, 17 August 1998, published in *Gaceta Oficial del Acuerdo de Cartagena*, No. 375, 7 October 1998.

Andean Court of Justice, Proceeding No. 23-IP-98, 25 September 1998, published in *Gaceta Oficial del Acuerdo de Cartagena*, No. 379, 27 October 1998.

Andean Court of Justice, Proceeding No. 7-IP-97, 7 July 1998, published in *Gaceta Oficial del Acuerdo de Cartagena*, No. 412, 26 February 1999.

Andean Court of Justice, Proceeding No. 35-IP-98, 30 October 1998, published in *Gaceta Oficial del Acuerdo de Cartagena*, No. 422, 30 March 1999.

Andean Court of Justice, Proceeding No. 26-IP-99, 23 July 1999, published in *Gaceta Oficial del Acuerdo de Cartagena*, No. 475, 1 September 1999.

Andean Court of Justice, Proceeding No. 36-IP-99, 8 October 1999, published in *Gaceta Oficial del Acuerdo de Cartagena*, No. 504, 9 November 1999.

Andean Court of Justice, Proceeding No. 12-IP-97, 7 July 2000, published in *Gaceta Oficial del Acuerdo de Cartagena*, No. 588, 2 August 2000.

Andean Court of Justice, Proceeding No. 21-IP-2000, 21 October 2000, published in *Gaceta Oficial del Acuerdo de Cartagena*, No. 631, 10 January 2001.

Andean Court of Justice, Proceeding No. 105-IP-2000, 21 March 2001, published in *Gaceta Oficial del Acuerdo de Cartagena*, No. 660, 10 April 2001.

Andean Court of Justice, Proceeding No. 84-IP-2000, 21 March 2001, published in *Gaceta Oficial del Acuerdo de Cartagena*, No. 677, 13 June 2001.

Andean Court of Justice, Proceeding 43-IP-2001, 24 August 2001, published in *Gaceta Oficial del Acuerdo de Cartagena*, No. 716, 18 September 2001.

Andean Court of Justice, Proceeding No. 58-IP-2001, 19 September 2001, published in *Gaceta Oficial del Acuerdo de Cartagena*, No. 724, 16 October 2001.

Andean Court of Justice, Proceeding No. 55-IP-2001, 22 November 2001, published in *Gaceta Oficial del Acuerdo de Cartagena*, No. 741, 6 December 2001.

Andean Court of Justice, Proceeding No. 60-IP-2001, 16 November 2001, published in *Gaceta Oficial del Acuerdo de Cartagena*, No. 750, 15 January 2002.

Andean Court of Justice, Proceeding No. 63-IP-2002, 28 August 2002, published in *Gaceta Oficial del Acuerdo de Cartagena*, No. 837, 20 September 2002.

Andean Court of Justice, Proceeding No. 65-IP-2001, 17 October 2001, published in *Gaceta Oficial del Acuerdo de Cartagena*, No. 836, 18 September 2002.

Andean Court of Justice, Proceeding 89-AI-2000, 11 September 2002, published in *Gaceta Oficial del Acuerdo de Cartagena*, No. 838, 22 September 2002.

Table of Cases

Andean Court of Justice, Proceeding No. 43-IP-2000, 16 October 2002, published in *Gaceta Oficial del Acuerdo de Cartagena*, No. 870, 9 December 2002.

Andean Court of Justice, Proceeding No. 82-IP-2002, 4 December 2002, published in *Gaceta Oficial del Acuerdo de Cartagena*, No. 891, 29 January 2003.

Andean Court of Justice, Proceeding No. 97-IP-2002, 5 February 2003, published in *Gaceta Oficial del Acuerdo de Cartagena*, No. 912, 25 March 2003.

Andean Court of Justice, Proceeding No. 16-IP-2003, 1 March 2003, published in *Gaceta Oficial del Acuerdo de Cartagena*, No. 916, 2 April 2003.

Andean Court of Justice, Proceeding 60-IP-2003, 16 July 2003, published in *Gaceta Oficial del Acuerdo de Cartagena*, No. 967, 18 August 2003.

Andean Court of Justice, Proceeding No. 07-IP-2004, 17 March 2004, published in *Gaceta Oficial del Acuerdo de Cartagena*, No. 1057, 21 April 2004.

Andean Court of Justice, Proceeding No. 12-IP-2004, 14 April 2004, published in *Gaceta Oficial del Acuerdo de Cartagena*, No. 1072, 28 May 2004.

Andean Court of Justice, Proceeding No. 67-IP-2004, 30 June 2004, published in *Gaceta Oficial del Acuerdo de Cartagena*, No. 1102, 6 August 2004.

Andean Court of Justice, Proceeding No. 43-IP-2004, 14 July 2004, published in *Gaceta Oficial del Acuerdo de Cartagena*, No. 1109, 26 August 2004

Andean Court of Justice, Proceeding No. 55-IP-2004, 14 July 2004, published in *Gaceta Oficial del Acuerdo de Cartagena*, No. 1110, 27 August 2004.

Andean Court of Justice, Proceeding No. 194-IP-2005, 25 November 2005, published in *Gaceta Oficial del Acuerdo de Cartagena*, No. 1297, 16 February 2006.

Andean Court of Justice, Proceeding No. 159-IP-2005, 30 November 2005, published in *Gaceta Oficial del Acuerdo de Cartagena*, No. 1297, 16 February 2006.

Resolutions

Superintendence of Industry and Commerce, Resolution 1526, 25 October 1993.

Superintendence of Industry and Commerce, Resolution No. 2314, 28 October 1996.

Superintendence of Industry and Commerce, Resolution 11067, 29 May 2000.

Superintendence of Industry and Commerce, Resolution 07167, 28 February 2002.

Superintendence of Industry and Commerce, Resolution 011956, 17 May 2005.

Superintendence of Industry and Commerce, Resolution 8269, 31 March 2006.

Superintendence of Industry and Commerce, Resolution 26260, 6 October 2006.

Legal Opinions

National Direction of Copyright, Legal Opinion (Concepto) No. 97003008, 25 June 1997.

National Direction of Copyright, Circular No. 1, 9 October 2001.

National Direction of Copyright, Legal Opinion (Concepto) on the Plagiarism of a Literary Work, 9 June 2003.

National Direction of Copyright, Legal Opinion (Concepto) on the Generalities of Copyright of 13 August 2003.

National Direction of Copyright, Circular No. 10, 5 December 2003.

National Direction of Copyright, Legal Opinion (Concepto) No. 1-2004-21716 on the implementation of Article 20 of Law 23 of 1982, 22 December 2004.

National Direction of Copyright, Legal Opinion (Concepto) No. 1-2005-14246 on the Transfer of Economic Rights, 18 July 2005.

National Direction of Copyright, Legal Opinion (Concepto) No. 1-2005-21288 on Works Made for Hire, 13 October 2005.

National Direction of Copyright, Legal opinion (Concepto) No. 1-2005-23251, 21 November 2005.

Superintendence of Industry and Commerce, Legal Opinion (Concepto) No. 00068772, 19 October 2000.

Superintendence of Industry and Commerce, Legal Opinion (Concepto) No. 0108164, 16 November 2001.

Superintendence of Industry and Commerce, Unique Circular, August 2001.

Superintendence of Industry and Commerce, Legal Opinion (Concepto) No. 02038289, 26 June 2002.

Superintendence of Industry and Commerce, Legal Opinion (Concepto) No. 02043592, 30 July 2002.

Superintendence of Industry and Commerce, Legal Opinion (Concepto) No. 03005202, 28 February 2003.

Superintendence of Industry and Commerce, Legal Opinion (Concepto) No. 03087905, 17 December 2003.

Superintendence of Industry and Commerce, Legal Opinion (Concepto) No. 03093878, 30 December 2003.

Superintendence of Industry and Commerce, Memorandum No. 04127967, 22 December 2004.

Superintendence of Industry and Commerce, Legal Opinion (Concepto) No. 04121719, 17 January 2005.

Table of Cases

Superintendence of Industry and Commerce, Legal Opinion (Concepto) No. 05014398, 5 April 2005.

Others

European Patent Office, T 385/86 (OJ EPO 8/1988. 308).

European Patent Office, T 290/86 (OJ 1992. 412).

Federación Nacional de Cafeteros de Colombia & República de Colombia v. Colombian Coffee Shop S.A. Edgar Muñoz Camacho, Mastercafe SL, WIPO, Arbitration and Mediation Centre. Case No. D2004-0677, 21 October 2004.

Franklin Pierce Law Center in Cooperation with the World Intellectual Property Organization (WIPO), Ninth Comprehensive PCT Seminar, Concord, New Hampshire, 27–28 April 2007, 2.

International Bureau of WIPO, *Manual for the Examination of Invention Patent Applications in the Industrial Property Offices in the Andean Community Countries* (Secretariat-General of the Andean Community, WIPO, European Patent Office, Quito-Ecuador, 2004).

The International Standard Book Number System: ISBN's Users Manual, International Edition. 5th edn. Berlin, 2005.

United Nations Education, Scientific and Cultural Organization-World Intellectual Property Organization, Second Committee of Governmental Experts, Geneva, 1982.

WTO Dispute Settlement Body, Panel Report, United States – Measures Affecting the Cross-Border Supply of Gambling and Betting Services.

Index

The numbers here refer to paragraph numbers.

Index

Made in United States
North Haven, CT
04 November 2026

21730351R00124